Editorial Director   Arthur Hettich
Editor   Nora O'Leary
Art Director   Joseph Taveroni
Special Books Editor
Marie T. Walsh

Associate Editors
Sandra Stern, Susan Kiely Tierney
Karen Laurence
Copy   Marjorie Magidson
Workroom   Carolyn Silberg
Art Associate   Walter Schwartz
Assistant Editor   Ceri E. Hadda
Assistant To The Editor
Anita Counsman

CREATIVE CRAFTS

Created by Family Circle Magazine and published 1978 by Arno Press Inc., a subsidiary of The New York Times Company.
Copyright © 1977 by The Family Circle, Inc. All rights reserved. Protected under Berne and other international copyright con-
ventions. Title and Trademark FAMILY CIRCLE registered U.S. Patent and Trademark Office, Canada, Great Britain,
Australia, New Zealand, Japan and other countries. Marca Registrada. This volume may not be reproduced in whole or in part
in any form without written permission from the publisher. Printed in U.S.A. Library of Congress Catalog Card Number
78-59202. ISBN 0-405-11408-7.

CONTENTS

4 Needlewear
7 Scrapbasket Patchwork
8 The Warm-ups
9 Corn Husk Dolls: Plain & Fancy
11 Vested Interest
13 Beachcomber's Basic Knit
15 Layers: Warm/Warmer/Warmest
16 Jewel-Less Jewelry To Make
19 Cold Weather Classic
20 For All Seasons
25 Great Ideas

26 Indian Adaptations

32 From Amish Tradition

48 Turn Any Box Into a Treasure

34 Foolproof Knitting to Measure

38 Victorian Needlepoint

40 White on White on White
44 Stitchery: An Artistic Triumph
46 Wear Your Works of Art
50 14-Karat Knitting
52 From Russia With Love

56 Portrait of Two Dresses
58 Sew A Mix & Match Wardrobe
60 Weather Report
62 Picture Perfect Frames
64 Black Forest Smocks To Sew

66 The Rainbow Division

Special Instructions:
10 How-to Knit
14 Pattern Backviews
122 How-to Crochet
75 How to Enlarge and Reduce Designs
80 Body Measurements
89 Yardage Chart
92 Basic Needlepoint
93 Basic Embroidery
128 Buyer's Guide

NEELEWEAR

Nancy Dent, not content with creating needlepoint for throw pillows, found her niche with works of art to wear. Needlepoint is worked with tapestry yarn, to fit coat or jacket pattern of your choice. Nancy calls the sleeveless jacket (lower left) "Murmur"—it is a subtly shaded patchwork. The full length coat, entitled "Carte Blanche," is an exuberant display of pattern-on-pattern needlepoint. These abstractions are proudly presented for your inspiration. You can duplicate the "Siamese Kitty" design (upper left) in a basic pattern of your choice… cat's eye chart is on page 76.

These coats are the result of imagination, color sense, and the confidence to try something new. Nancy Dent tells us that the "Carte Blanche" masterpiece (above) was only her fourth try at needlepoint! Why not try YOUR luck.

RICHARD BLINKOFF

Make yourself happy by knitting this authentic Guatemalan vest in the lively colors favored by native craftspeople. From two 45″ widths of red cotton fabric by Jacques, Ltd., you can sew a cheerful skirt and a muslin peasant blouse. Ballet shoes, Capezio. Vest instructions on page 127.

KNIT HAPPY COLORS

GOLF CLASSICS

RON COLBY

Just to prove that knitters can be good sports too, three championship sweater designs are dedicated to men who spend a lot of time on the course, from women who sometimes wish they didn't.

SCRAPBASKET PATCHWORK

Calico fabric scraps come into their own, forming traditional patchwork patterns on these three bags. Easy-to-make shoulder bag has braided strap. Fringe trim adds interest to triangle patch design, and strap adjusts in length. Granny square patch carpetbag holds knitting or needlepoint. Flower stripe borders the edge. To order Granny Handles, see coupon, page 120. Instructions and diagram see page 75.

THE WARM UPS

Warm the winter away in these wrong-side-out jackets. We've turned the cuddly pile fabric inside for greatest warmth. Felt Central Shippee appliqués brighten the white underwear-knit side of the fabric.

Strawberries dance over this sleeveless vest. Worn over a turtleneck and pants, it is an ideal cold chaser. Below, the full anti-freeze treatment: hooded coat is decorated with stylized tulips. Both jackets, Simplicity 7688. Malden Mills pile fabric. Turn to page 77.

While a corn husk doll will never forget its humble roots, it can enjoy fashion as much as city folk. Ellen Egan's corn husk ladies wear skirts and pinafores made from scraps. Bits of lace and ribbon add fashion details. Party-favor baskets and tiny dried flowers are sized for corn husk hands. To make dolls, turn to page 77.

CORN HUSK DOLLS: PLAIN AND FANCY

SUSAN WOOD

IRISH DUO

It takes a bit of Irish inspiration to texture a bag and hat with such nice nubby stitches. The bag is a straight piece of popcorn and cable stitch knitting, folded in half, then mounted on wooden rods. The flipped brim hat is done in rounds of single crochet. Both are made with Bernat yarn in natural white. See instructions, page 24.

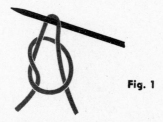

KNITTING ABBREVIATIONS AND SYMBOLS

Knitting directions are always written in standard abbreviations. They look mysterious at first, but you'll soon know them. **beg** — beginning; **bet** — between; **bl** — block; **ch** — chain; **CC** — contrasting color; **dec(s)** — decrease(s); **dp** — double-pointed; **"** or **in(s)** — inch(es); **incl** — inclusive; **inc(s)** — increase(s); **k** — knit; **lp(s)** — loop(s); **MC** — main color; **oz(s)** — ounce(s); **psso** — pass slipped stitch over last stitch worked; **pat(s)** — pattern(s); **p** — purl; **rem** — remaining; **rpt** — repeat; **rnd(s)** — round(s); **sc** — single crochet; **sk** — skip; **sl** — slip; **sl st** — slip stitch; **sp(s)** — space(s); **st(s)** — stitch(es); **st st** — stockinette stitch; **tog** — together; **yo** — yarn over; **pc** — popcorn st.

* (**asterisk**) — directions immediately following * are to be repeated the specified number of times indicated, in addition to the first time — i.e., "repeat from * 3 times more means 4 times in all.

( ) **parentheses** — directions should be worked as often as specified — i.e., (k 1, k 2 tog, k 3) 5 times, means to work what is in ( ) 5 times in all.

THE BASIC STITCHES

Get out your needles and yarn and slowly read your way through this special section — practicing the basic stitches illustrated here as you go along. Once you know them you're ready to start knitting.
CASTING ON: This puts the first row of stitches on the needle. Measure off about two yards of yarn, (or about an inch for each stitch you are going to cast on). Make a slip knot at this point by making a medium size loop of yarn; then pull another small loop through it. Place the slip knot on one needle and pull one end gently to tighten (FIG. 1).

Fig. 1

• Hold needle in right hand. Hold both strands of yarn in the palm of your left

VESTED INTEREST

Autumn-hued tweeds combine with off-white in a crocheted vest that makes an important addition to your wardrobe. Laura Demme's vest, with shell-stitch edging, is constructed to follow the lines of the body. Bernat yarn. Instructions, see page 78.

CLOSE-UP SHOT BY RENE VELEZ INSET SHOT BY JOHN STEMBER

hand securely but not rigidly. **Slide your left thumb and forefinger between the two strands** and spread these two fingers out so that you have formed a triangle of yarn. Your left thumb should hold the free end of yarn, your forefinger the yarn from the ball, while the needle in your right hand holds the first stitch (FIG. 2).

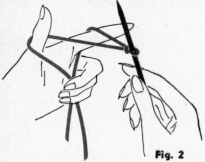

Fig. 2

You are now in position to cast on. See ABBREVIATIONS for explanation of asterisk (*).

• * Bring the needle in your right hand toward you; slip the tip of the needle under the front strand of the loop on left thumb (FIG. 3).

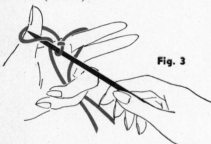

Fig. 3

• Now, with the needle, catch the strand of yarn that is on your left forefinger (FIG. 4).

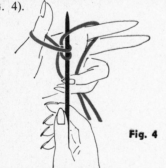

Fig. 4

• Draw it through thumb loop to form a stitch on needle (FIG. 5).

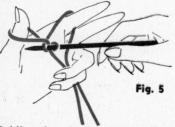

Fig. 5

• Holding the stitch on the needle with the right index finger, slip loop off left thumb (FIG. 6). Tighten up the stitch on the needle by pulling the freed strand back with left thumb, bringing the yarn back into position for casting on more stitches (FIG. 2 again).

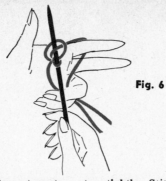

Fig. 6

• **Do not cast on too tightly.** Stitches should slide easily on the needle. Repeat from * until you have cast on the number of stitches specified in your instructions.

KNIT STITCH: (k): Hold the needle with the cast-on stitches in your left hand (FIG. 7).

Fig. 7

• Pick up the other needle in your right hand. With yarn from ball in **back** of the work, insert the tip of right-hand needle from **left to right** through front loop of first stitch on left-hand needle (FIG. 8).

Fig. 8

• Holding both needles in this position with left hand, wrap the yarn over your little finger, under your two middle fingers and over the forefingers of your right hand. Hold the yarn firmly, but loosely enough so that it will slide through your fingers as you knit. Return right-hand needle to right hand.

• With right forefinger, pass the yarn under (from right to left) and then over (from left to right) the tip of the right-hand needle, forming a loop on needle (FIG. 9).

Fig. 9

• Now draw this loop through the stitch on left-hand needle (FIG. 10).

Fig. 10

• Slip original stitch off the left-hand

needle, leaving new stitch on right-hand needle (FIG. 11).

Fig. 11

Keep stitches loose enough so that you can slide them along the needles, but firm enough so they do not slide when you don't want them to. Continue until you have knitted all the stitches from the left-hand needle onto the right-hand needle.

• To start the next row, pass needle with stitches on it to the left hand, reversing it, so that it now becomes the left-hand needle.

PURL STITCH: (p): Purling is the reverse of knitting. Again, keep the stitches loose enough to slide, but firm enough to work with. To purl, hold the needle with the stitches in your left hand, with the yarn in **front** of your work. Insert the tip of the right-hand needle from **right to left** through the front loop of the first stitch on left-hand needle (FIG. 12).

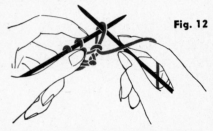

Fig. 12

• With your right hand holding the yarn in the same manner as to knit, but in **front** of the needles, pass the yarn over the tip of right-hand needle, then under it, forming loop on needle (FIG. 13).

Fig. 13

• Holding the yarn firmly, so that it won't slip off, draw this loop through the stitch on left-hand needle (FIG. 14).

Fig. 14

• Slip original stitch off the left-hand needle, leaving new stitch on the right-hand needle (FIG. 15).

Fig. 15

(continued on page 73)

Meredith Gladstone's no-frills sweater is as refreshingly natural as sand and water. The seams of the knitted turtleneck are chain-stitched together, and we've paired the sweater with a flowered skirt. Liberty of London fabric. Coats & Clark yarn. See page 79.

BEACHCOMBER'S BASIC KNIT

PATTERN BACKVIEWS

All yardage for Size 10, with or without nap. Please note special instructions where specified. (Prices are in U.S. currency.)

SIMPLICITY 7688 — page 10. Child's Coat. Children's sizes 3-6; $1.25. Size 4 requires 1¼ yds. of 58/60" fabric. See instructions, page 85 for variation and appliqué.

SIMPLICITY 7936 — page 36. Misses' Coat. Misses' sizes 6-14; $1.75. Our coat was made from a Pendleton blanket, measuring 64" x 80". See instructions, page 96.

BUTTERICK 5137 — page 41. Misses' Vest. Misses' sizes 8-16; $1.50. Requires ¾ yd. of 58/60" fabric. For all felt vests, see instructions, page 103.

BUTTERICK 4526 — page 48. Misses' Pants. Misses' sizes 8-16; $1.50. Requires 1⅝ yds. of 58/60" fabric.

SIMPLICITY 7625 — page 51. Misses' Skirt (view 2). Misses' sizes 10-20; $1.25. Requires 1⅝ yds. of 58/60" fabric.

McCALL'S 5477 — page 53. Misses' Vest. Misses' size 6-16; $1.75. Requires 1⅛ yds. of 44/45" fabric. See instructions, page 110.

McCALL'S 5136 — page 54. Misses' Top. Misses' sizes Petite, Small, Medium and Large; $1.50. Small requires 1¼ yds. of 44/45" fabric. See instructions, page 111.

TO ORDER McCALL'S 5136 — State size, send check or money order to: McCall's Pattern Co., FC '77, McCall Road, Manhattan, Kansas 66502.

BUTTERICK 4916 — page 55. Misses' Dress. Misses' sizes Petite, Small, Medium and Large; $1.50. Small requires 2¾ yds. of 45" fabric. See instructions, page 112.

TO ORDER BUTTERICK 4916 — State size, send check or money order plus 25¢ postage & handling for each pattern ordered to: Butterick Fashion Marketing, FCC 7-77, P.O. Box 1861, Altoona, Pa. 16603.

SIMPLICITY 7372 — page 55. Misses' Jumper. Misses' size 8-16; $1.50. Requires 2½ yds. of 44/45" fabric. See instructions, page 112.

SIMPLICITY 6573 — page 59. Misses' Skirt (view 3). Misses' sizes 8-16; $1.00. Requires 2¼ yds. of 58/60" fabric.

McCALL'S 5663 — page 60. Misses' Blouse (view B, for our Russian Costume). Misses' sizes Petite, Small, Medium and Large; $1.75. Requires 2½ yds. of 44/45" fabric. See instructions, page 116 for blouse trims and skirt.

VOGUE 9871 — page 64. Misses' Dress & Vest. Misses' sizes 6-14; $3.50. Requires 3⅝ yds. of 44/45" fabric for the dress; and 1 yd. of 54" fabric for the vest.

VOGUE 1738 — page 65. Misses' Top & Skirt. Misses' sizes 8-16; $7.50. Requires 4 yds. of 44/45" fabric for both.

VOGUE 9858 — pages 66-67. Misses' Suit & Blouse and Long Skirt. Misses' sizes 8-16; $4.50. Misses' suit requires 3 yds. of 54" fabric; long skirt 2½ yds. of 44/45" fabric; and blouse with scarf 2⅛ yds. of 44/45" fabric.

SIMPLICITY 7376 — page 67. Misses' Vest. Misses' sizes 6-16; $1.50. Requires 1¼ yds. of 36" fabric.

BUTTERICK 4067 — page 67. Misses' Skirt. Misses' waist sizes 24-30; $1.25. Size 25 waist requires 2 yds. of 36" fabric.

SIMPLICITY 7467 — page 67. Misses' Top. Misses' sizes Petite, Small, Medium and Large; $1.50. Small requires 2½ yds. of 44/45" fabric.

VOGUE 9588 — page 68. Misses' Poncho (view B). Misses' sizes Small, Medium and Large; $3.00. Small requires 2¾ yds. of 43" fabric. To make the poncho reversible, cut the pattern again in a contrasting fabric, eliminating pocket pieces. (The reverse side forms the pocket facing.) Be sure to reverse collar so that it will fold over its matching side.

FOLKWEAR 108 — pages 72-73. Black Forest Smock sized for Men & Women; $3.00. Average men's shirt requires 2¾ yds. of 44/45" fabric. Average women's dress requires 3⅝ yds. of 44/45" fabric.

FOLKWEAR 110 — pages 72-73. Little Kittel sizes 4-6-8-10 in one package; $3.00. Boys' shirt size 4 requires 1⅜ yd. of 44/45" fabric. Girls' dress size 4 requires 1¾ yards of 44/45" fabric.

To order Folkwear patterns: Send check or money order (add 75¢ for postage & handling per order) to: FOLKWEAR, P.O. Box 98, Forestville, California 95436. (California residents, add 6% Sales Tax.)

SIMPLICITY 7629 — page 76. Toddler's Pants. Toddlers' sizes 1-4. $1.50. Size 2 requires ¾ yd. of 58/60" fabric. See instructions, page 124 for applique.

SIMPLICITY 7815 — page 76. Children's Pants with Detachable Bib. Children's sizes 3-6; $1.25. Size 4 requires 1 yd. of 58/60" fabric. See instructions, page 124 for appliqué.

BUTTERICK 4930 — page 79. Children's Jumper. Children's sizes 2-6X; $1.25. Size 4 requires 1 yd. of 44/45" fabric. See instructions, page 131 for appliqué.

McCALL'S 5668 — page 79. Children's and Girls' Skirt with Detachable Bib. Children's sizes 4-6; girls' sizes 7-12; $1.25. Size 4 requires 1 yd. of 44/45" fabric. See instructions, page 131 for appliqué.

For pattern information: Butterick or Vogue write: Butterick Fashion Marketing, 161 Sixth Avenue, New York, N.Y. 10013; McCall's 230 Park Avenue, New York, N.Y. 10017; Simplicity Pattern Co., Inc. 200 Madison Avenue, New York, N.Y. 10016.

JOHN STEMBER

When the daily forecast calls for cool, crisp weather, ward off the winds with layered sweaters and a blanket cape. Earth-toned turtleneck pullover is knit from softest alpaca yarn by Plymouth. Knitted fisherman's vest adds extra warmth. Bucilla yarn. Both by Carol Golden. Our dramatic cape lets you sweep through chilly days untouched by the cold. It is made from a wool Icelandic blanket, and has a high-collared drawstring closing. Instructions for sweaters and cape, turn to page 79.

Diamonds may be a girl's best friend, but these jewel-less neckpieces are the sign of a creative individualist. (1) Wendy Palitz wrapped shiny floss and silver yarn into a glittering pendant. (2) Tiny felt purses keep mad money close to the heart.

1 2

3 4

RON COLBY

JEWEL-LESS JEWELRY TO MAKE

(3) Heavy DMC pearl cotton is twisted and knotted to form chokers and a tassel necklace. (4) Two tiny puffed Heart and Butterfly pendants of fabric scraps, twisted pearl cotton. Instructions, page 89. (2), (3) and (4) designed by Sandy Paisley and Teri Leve.

CHAIN LINK PULLOVER

(page 6)

Directions are given for size Small (30½-32½). Changes for sizes Medium (34-36) and Large (38-40) are in parentheses.
MATERIALS: Reynolds Lopi: 5(6,7) skeins #51 Natural White (A); 2(2,3) skeins each #53A Light Brown (B) and #52 Dark Brown (C); circular needles No.9 and No.10½, 29″ length; straight needles, 1 pair each of No.9 and No.10½ OR ANY SIZE NEEDLES WHICH WILL OBTAIN THE STITCH GAUGE BELOW: two stitch holders; 1 set double-pointed needles, No.9.
GAUGE: On No. 10½ needle - 7 sts = 2″; 4 rows = 1″.
MEASUREMENTS:

Sizes:	Small	Medium	Large
	(3 0 ½ - 32½)	(34-36)	(38-40)
Bust:	34½″	38½″	41″
Width across sleeve at upper arm:	13¼″	14″	15½″

DIRECTIONS — BODY: Start at lower edge of back and front combined with No.9 circular needle and A, cast on 112(126,134) sts. Place a marker on needle to indicate end of rnd; being careful not to twist sts, join, Sl marker on every rnd. Work in rnds of k 1, p 1 ribbing for 5″. **Next Rnd:** K around, increasing 8(10,10) sts evenly spaced around — 120 (136,144) sts.
Note: Do not use bobbins for color changes on pattern, wind B and C into small balls. When changing colors,lock strands on wrong side by picking up new color from under dropped color to prevent making holes in work. Carry colors loosely across wrong side. Cut and attach colors as needed. Darn in ends on wrong side when done.
PATTERN: Change to No.10½ circular needle. Pat is worked in rnds of st st (k each rnd). **Rnd 1: Following repeat only** on first row of Chart (8 sts), work rep to end of rnd. Starting with next row, continue to follow Chart in same way to end of top row. Rpt 12 rows of Chart for pat until total length is 18(18½-19)″ or desired length to underarm, end last rnd 3(4,5) sts before marker.
To Divide Stitches: Keeping continuity of pat throughout, bind off 6 (8,10) sts loosely for underarm, work until there are 54(60,62) sts from bound-off sts; place these sts just made on a st holder for front; bind off next 6 (8,10) sts loosely for other underarm, complete rnd in pat; place on another st holder for back.
SLEEVES: With No.9 straight needles and A, cast on 26(28,30) sts. Work in rows in k 1, p 1 ribbing for 3½″ increasing 8(8,10) sts evenly spaced on last row — 34(36,40) sts. Change to No.10½ straight needles and work pat as follows:
Row 1 (right side): Starting and ending at arrow indicating size being made and working pat rpt across, k across follow-

CHAIN LINK PULLOVER

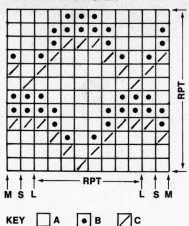

KEY ☐ A ⊡ B ◲ C

ing first row on Chart from right to left.
Row 2: Starting and ending at arrow indicating size being made and working pat rpt across, p across, following second row on Chart from left to right. Continuing in rows of st st (k 1 row, p 1 row), follow Chart back and forth as for first 2 rows from third row to end of top row. Keeping continuity of pat, and working inc sts in pat, work in rows of st st, increasing one st at each end of next row and every 5th row thereafter 7(8,8) times in all — 48(52,56) sts. Continue in pat until total length is about 16½(17,17½)″ or desired length to underarm, but ending with same pat row as on body to underarm.
Underarm Shaping: Keeping continuity of pat, bind off 3(4,5) sts at beg of next 2 rows. Place rem 42(44,46) sts on a contrasting double strand of yarn.
YOKE: With right side of each section facing, place sts on No.10½ circular needle in the following order: One sleeve, place a marker on needle; front, place a marker on needle; other sleeve, place a marker on needle; back, place a marker on needle — 192(208,216) sts. Sl markers on every rnd.
Raglan Shaping — Rnd 1: From right side, keeping continuity of pat over each section, *k 2 tog, work in pat to within 2 sts before next marker, sl 1, k 1, p s s o; rpt from * 3 more times — 8 decs made. **Rnd 2:** Keeping continuity of pat over each section, k around. Rpt last 2 rnds alternately 14(16,17) more times — 72 sts.
Turtleneck: Change to No.9 d p needles and with A, work in rnds of k 1, p 1 ribbing for 7″. Bind off loosely in ribbing.
FINISHING: Sew sleeve seam. Sew bound-off sts of sleeves at underarms to bound-off sts of body. Steam lightly on wrong side.

ICELANDIC PULLOVER

(page 6)

Directions are given for size Small (38-40). Changes for sizes Medium (42-44) and Large (46-48) are in parentheses.

MATERIALS: Reynolds Lopi: 6(7,8) skeins #7356 Heather Grey (A), 1 skein each Natural White (B), #7353A Natural Brown (C) and #7352 Natural Black (D); circular needles, No.7 and No.10½, 29″ length OR ANY SIZE NEEDLE WHICH WILL OBTAIN THE STITCH GAUGE BELOW; double-pointed needles, 1 set each No.7 and No.10½; 2 large stitch holders.
GAUGE: On No.10½ needle - 3 sts = 1″; 4 rnds = 1″.
MEASUREMENTS:

Sizes:	Small (38-40)	Medium (42-44)	Large (46-48)
Chest:	42″	46″	50″
Width across sleeve at upper arm:	14¾″	16″	16½″

DIRECTIONS — BODY: Start at lower edge of back and front combined with B and No.7 circular needle, cast on loosely 116(128,140) sts. Place a marker on needle to indicate end of rnd. Being careful not to twist sts, join. Sl marker on every rnd. Work in k 1, p 1 ribbing for 2″. **Next Rnd:** Knitting around, inc one st in every 11th(12th,0) st, 4(2,0) times; then in every 12th(13th,14th) st, 6(8,10) times — 126(138,150) sts. Change to No. 10½ circular needle and k 1 rnd.
Notes: Do not use bobbins for color changes; wind pat colors into small balls. When changing colors lock strands on wrong side by picking up new color from under dropped color to prevent making holes in work. Carry colors not in use loosely across wrong side of work. Cut and attach colors as needed. Darn in all ends on wrong side when knitting has been completed. Pat is worked in rnds of st st (k each rnd).
Bottom Border — Rnd 1: Attach C. **Following Chart 1,** start at arrow on Rnd 1 and working in st st, work rpt to end of rnd. Continue to follow Chart 1 in same way from next rnd to top of Chart. Break off B and C. With A, work in st st until total length is 16″ or 1″ less than desired length to underarm.
To Divide Stitches — Next Rnd: Bind off 7(9,10) sts for underarm, k until there are 56(60,65) sts on right-hand point of needle; place these sts on a st holder for front; bind off 7(9,10) sts for other underarm, complete rnd; place these 56(60,65) sts on a separate st holder for back.
SLEEVES: Start at cuff edge with B and No.7 d p needles, cast on 28(30,32) sts; divide sts onto 3 d p needles. Mark end of rnds as before. Being careful not to twist sts, join. Work in k 1, p 1 ribbing for 2½(3,3)″. **Next Rnd:** K around, increasing 8(6,10) sts evenly spaced around — 36(36,42) sts. Change to No.10½ d p needles. Work border same as Bottom Border of Body. With A, working in st st (k each rnd) inc one st at beg and end of next rnd and every 10th(8th,10th) rnd thereafter 4(6,4) times in all — 44(48,50) sts. Continue to work even in st st until total length is 16½(17,17½)″ or 1″ less than desired length to underarm. **Next**

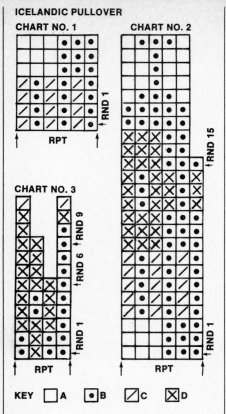

ICELANDIC PULLOVER

CHART NO. 1 **CHART NO. 2**

CHART NO. 3

KEY ☐ A • B ╱ C ☒ D

Rnd: K around to within 3(4,5) sts before end of rnd; bind off loosely next 7(9,10) sts for underarm. Place rem 37(39,40) sts on a contrasting double strand of yarn. Work other sleeve in same way.

YOKE: With right side of each piece facing, place on No.10½ circular needle sts in the following order: front, one sleeve, back and other sleeve — 186(198,210) sts. Place a marker at end of rnd and sl this marker in every rnd. With A, join and k 1(1,2) rnds.

Yoke Pattern (see Note): Following Chart 2, start at arrow on Rnd 1 and work rpt to end of rnd. Continue to follow Chart 2 in this manner to end of Rnd 14. **Rnd 15:** Follow Rnd 15 on Chart 2, working first 2 sts of each rpt tog for a dec as indicated, making 31(33,35) decs around — 155(165,175) sts. Follow Chart 2 to end of top rnd. **Next Rnd:** With B only, (k 3,k 2 tog) 31(33,35) times — 124(132,140) sts. **Next Rnd:** With B, k around. When sts no longer fit on circular needle, change to No.10½ d p needles. Following Chart 3, start at arrow on Rnd 1 and work to end of Rnd 5. Follow Rnd 6 on Chart 3, making a dec on each rpt as indicated — 93(99,105) sts. Continue to follow Chart 3 to end of top row, making dec on each rpt on Rnd 9, as indicated — 62(66,70) sts. **Next Rnd:** With B only, k around, decreasing 2(4,4) sts evenly spaced around.

Neckband: With B and No.7 d p needles, work in k 1, p 1 ribbing around for 3". Bind off loosely in ribbing.

FINISHING: Sew bound-off underarm sts tog. Fold neckband in half to wrong side and sew in place,

ARAN ISLES PULLOVER

(page 6)

Directions are given for size Small (38-40). Changes for sizes Medium (42-44) and Large (46-48) are in parentheses.

MATERIALS: Reynolds Fisherman Yarn (2 oz. skeins): 13(14,15) skeins; knitting needles, 1 pair each No.7 and No.10½ OR ANY SIZE NEEDLES WHICH WILL OBTAIN THE STITCH GAUGE BELOW; 1 set double-pointed needles, No.9.

GAUGE: Reverse st st - 7 sts = 2"; 5 rows = 1". 21 sts of pat = 5½".

MEASUREMENTS:

Sizes:	Small (38-40)	Medium (42-44)	Large (46-48)
Chest:	40"	44"	48"
Width across back or front at underarms:	20"	22"	24"
Width across sleeve at upper arm:	16"	17"	17½"

DIRECTIONS — PATTERN STITCH: Multiple of 21 sts, plus 10 (16,3) sts. **Row 1 (right side):** P 1(4,8) *in next st (k loosely in front and in back) 3 times (6 sts made in one st), then with left-hand needle sl each of the first 5 sts over last st made — popcorn made; p 1, from front of work k in 2nd st on left-hand needle but do not sl st off needle, k first st and drop both sts off left-hand needle — right across st made; k in back of 2nd st on left-hand needle, do not sl st off needle, k in back of first st and drop both sts off left-hand needle — left cross st made; p 1, make popcorn in next st, p 4, sl next 3 sts on a d p needle and hold in back of work, k next 2 sts, from d p needle p 1, k 2; p 4; rpt from * 2 more times; make popcorn in next st, p 1, right cross st, left cross st, p 1, popcorn in next st, p 1(4,8).* **Row 2:** K 1(4,8), *p 1, k 1, p 4, k 1, p 1, k 4, p 5, k 4; rpt from * 2 more times; p 1, k 1, p 4, k 1, p 1, k 1(4,8). **Row 3:** P 1(4,8), *k 1, p 1, right cross st, left cross st, p 1, k 1, p 3, sl next st on d p needle and hold in back of work, k next 2 sts, k st from d p needle, p 1, sl next 2 sts on d p needle and hold in front, k next st, k 2 from d p needle, p 3; rpt from * 2 more times; k 1, p 1, right cross st, left cross st, p 1, k 1, p 1(4,8). **Row 4:** K 1(4,8), *p 1, k 1, p 4, k 1, p 1, k 3, p 2, k 1, p 1, k 1, p 2, k 3; rpt from * 2 more times; p 1, k 1, p 4, k 1, p 1, k 1(4,8). **Row 5:** P 1(4,8), *popcorn in next st, p 1, right cross st, left cross st, p 1, popcorn, p 2, sl next st on d p needle and hold in back of work, k next 2 sts, p st from d p needle, k 1, p 1, k 1, sl next 2 sts on d p needle and hold in front, p next st, k 2 from d p needle, p 2; rpt from * 2 more times; popcorn, p 1, right cross st, left cross st, p 1, popcorn, p 1(4,8). **Row 6:** K 1(4,8), * p 1, k 1, p 4, k 1, p 1, k 2, p 3, k 1, p 1, k 1, p 3, k 2; rpt from * 2 more times; p 1, k 1, p 4, k 1, p 1, k 1(4,8). **Row 7:**

P 1(4,8), *k 1, p 1, right cross st, left cross st, p 1, k 1, p 1, sl next st on d p needle and hold in back, k next 2 sts, k st from d p needle, p 1, (k 1, p 1) twice; sl next 2 sts on d p needle and hold in front, k next st, k 2 from d p needle, p 1; rpt from * 2 more times; k 1, p 1, right cross st, left cross st, p 1, k 1, p 1(4,8). **Row 8:** K 1(4,8), *p 1, k 1, p 4, k 1, p 1, k 1, p 2, (k 1, p 1) 3 times; k 1, p 2, k 1; rpt from * 2 more times; p 1, k 1, p 4, k 1, p 1, k 1(4,8). **Row 9:** P 1(4,8), *popcorn, p 1, right cross st, left cross st, p 1, popcorn, sl next st on d p needle and hold in back, k next 2 sts, p st from d p needle, (k 1, p 1) 3 times; k 1, sl next 2 sts on d p needle and hold in front, p next st, k 2 from d p needle; rpt from * 2 more times; popcorn, p 1, right cross st, left cross st, p 1, popcorn, p 1(4,8). **Row 10:** K 1(4,8), p 1, *(k 1, p 4) twice; (k 1, p 1) 3 times; k 1, p 4; rpt from * 2 more times; k 1, p 4, k 1, p 1, k 1(4,8). **Row 11:** P 1(4,8), *k 1, p 1, right cross st, left cross st, p 1, k 3, (p 1, k 1) 4 times; p 1, k 2; rpt from * 2 more times; k 1, p 1, right cross st, left cross st, p 1, k 1, p 1 (4,8). **Row 12:** Rpt Row 10. **Row 13:** P 1(4,8), *popcorn, p 1, right cross st, left cross st, p 1, popcorn, sl next 2 sts on d p needle and hold in front, p next st, k 2 from d p needle, (k 1, p 1) 3 times; k 1, sl next st on d p needle and hold in back, k next 2 sts, p st from d p needle; rpt from * 2 more times; popcorn, p 1, right cross st, left cross st, p 1, popcorn, p 1(4,8). **Row 14:** Rpt Row 8. **Row 15:** P 1(4,8), *k 1, p 1, right cross st, left cross st, p 1, k 1, p 1, sl next 2 sts in d p needle and hold in front, p next st, k 2 from d p needle, (p 1, k 1) twice; p 1, sl next st on d p needle and hold in back, k 2, p st from d p needle, p 1; rpt from * 2 more times; k 1, p 1, right cross st, left cross st, p 1, k 1, p 1(4,8). **Row 16:** Rpt Row 6. **Row 17:** P 1(4,8), *popcorn, p 1, right cross st, left cross st, p 1, popcorn, p2, sl next 2 sts on d p needle and hold in front, p next st, k 2 from d p needle, k 1, p 1, k 1, sl next st on d p needle and hold in back, k next 2 sts, p st from d p needle, p 2; rpt from * 2 more times; popcorn, p 1, right cross st, left cross st, p 1, popcorn, p 1(4,8). **Row 18:** Rpt Row 4. **Row 19:** P 1(4,8), *k 1, p 1, right cross st, left cross st, p 1, k 1, p 3, sl next 2 sts on d p needle and hold in front, p next st, k 2 from d p needle, p 1, sl next st on d p needle and hold in back, k next 2 sts, p st from d p needle, p 3; rpt from * 2 more times; k 1, p 1, right cross st, left cross st, p 1, k 1, p 1(4,8). **Row 20:** Rpt Row 2. Rpt these 20 rows (Rows 1 through 20) for pat.

BACK: Start at lower edge with No. 7 needles, cast on 73(79,87) sts. **Row 1:** P 1, *k 1, p 1; rpt from * across. **Row 2:** K 1, *p 1, k 1; rpt from * across. Rpt these 2 rows alternately for ribbing until length is 2(2½,2½)" from beg. Change to No. 10½ needles and work in pat until

(continued on page 24)

COLD WEATHER CLASSIC

The shoulder-to-shoulder motif of this knitted sweater says "Fair Isle," the Scottish home of classic patterned knitting. This crew-neck pullover and hat, in winter white with rust and teal, take naturally to the great outdoors. Bucilla yarn. For instructions, see page 83.

These two waist-length sweaters share a fashion secret: made of cotton, they span the seasons! The crocheted pair are great for summer (worn with madras pleated skirts) or worn over blouses and pants for winter. Opposite: No shrinking violet, this sweater of muted lilac is a standout combination of double crochet and popcorn stitches. This page: Sophisticated styling makes this V-neck sweater something special. Both by Kathy Sorkin. Lily yarn. Earl-Glo fabric. Photographed in New Orleans by Anthony Edgeworth. See page 84.

FOR ALL SEASONS

21

JACKET PLAY

The new way to bundle up for winter is in chic layers of texture and color. Two zip-front jackets are teamed with a mad mix of warm-ups for head, hands and legs. This page: A ribby knit snuggles up close to your body, made of tweed yarn by Reynolds. Crocheted leg huggers and cap, with color turned on full blast, are by Jacqueline Jewett for Coats & Clark. Mittens and scarf, La Tienda. All instructions, page 24.

Try the Irish way with knitting, as interpreted by Beattie Bodenstein for Bucilla.

Rib scarf and tie-on hat find their match.

An Irish cap and scarf are winter naturals.

ARAN ISLES PULLOVER

total length is 15(16,16½)", end with a wrong-side row.

Note: In shaping, popcorn and cross sts will be discontinued at each end of rows. Keep continuity of remainder of pat as much as possible.

Armhole Shaping: Keeping continuity of pat throughout, bind off 4(4,5) sts at beg of next 2 rows. Dec one st at each end every other row 4(6,7) times — 57(59,63) sts. Work even until length is 9(9½,10)" from first row of armhole shaping end with a wrong-side row.

Shoulder Shaping: Keeping in pat, bind off 6 sts at beg of next 6(6,4) rows. Bind off 0(0,8) sts at beg of following 0(0,2) rows. Place rem 21(23,23) sts on a st holder for back of neck while working Front.

FRONT: Work same as for Back until length is about 7(7½,8)" above first row of armhole shaping, if possible ending with Row 1 of pat.

Neck Shaping: Keeping continuity of pat, work over first 21(21,23) sts. Place rem sts on another st holder. Working over sts on needle only, dec one st at neck edge every other row 3 times. Work even over 18(18,20) sts until length of armhole is same as on Back, end at armhole edge.

Shoulder Shaping—Row 1: At armhole edge, bind off 6 sts; complete row. **Row 2:** Work even. Rep last 2 rows. Bind off rem 6(6,8) sts. Leaving center 15(17,17) sts on front holder, sl rem 21(21,23) sts on a No.10½ needle; attach yarn at neck edge and work to correspond with opposite side, reversing shaping.

SLEEVES: With No.7 needles, cast on 37(39,41) sts. Work ribbing same as for Back for 3(3½,3½)". Change to No. 10½ needles. Now work in pat as follows: **Row 1(right side)**; P 8(9,10), make left cross st over next 2 sts, p 1, popcorn in next st, p 4, sl next 3 sts on d p needle and hold in back of work, k next 2 sts, from d p needle p 1, k 2; p 4, popcorn in next st, p 1, right cross st, p 8(9,10). **Row 2:** K 8(9,10), p 2, k 1, p 1, k 4, p 5, k 4, p 1, k 1, p 2, k 8(9,10). Working center 21 sts in pat as established and all sts on each side in reverse st st (p on right side, k on wrong side), inc one st at each end on next row and every 6th row thereafter 10(11,12) times in all — 57(61, 65) sts. Keeping center 21 sts in pat throughout, work even until total length is 19(19½, 20)" or desired length to underarm, end with a wrong-side row.

Top Shaping: Bind off 4(4,5) sts at beg of next 2 rows. Dec one st at each end every other row until 21(23,23) sts rem; then every row until 11 sts rem. Bind off.

FINISHING: Pin finished pieces to measurements specified on page 98 on a padded surface; cover with a damp cloth and allow to air dry; do not press. Sew side, shoulder and sleeve seams. Sew in sleeves.

Turtleneck: With right side facing and d p needles, k sts from back holder, pick up and k 18 sts along side edge of neck, k sts from front holder, pick up and k 18 sts along other side edge of neck — 72(76,76) sts. Divide sts on 3 d p needles, join. Work in k 1, p 1 rnds of ribbing for 6". Bind off loosely in ribbing. Steam seam lightly. When dry, fold over to form turtleneck.

IRISH DUO HAT AND BAG

(page 10)

BAG

MATERIALS: Bernat Blarney-Spun (2 oz. balls): 8 balls; knitting needles, 1 pair No. 10½ OR ANY SIZE NEEDLES WHICH WILL OBTAIN THE STITCH GAUGE BELOW: 1 cable stitch needle; 1 pair 12" dowels with knobs for handles; ½ yd. fabric for lining; 1 yd. braid trim.

GAUGE: 5 sts = 2 inches

DIRECTIONS: Note: Yarn is used double throughout.

PANEL: Make 2. Using yarn double, cast on 62 sts. **Row 1:** K 1, p 1 across row. **Row 2:** P 1, k 1 across row. Rpt these 2 rows of seed st for border until piece measures 3", ending with Row 2. Now working in pattern st, work as follows: **Row 1:** P 3, sl 1 as if to p, k 1, inc 1 st in next st, psso 2 sts (twist 2), p 2, sl next 2 sts onto cable needle and hold in *front* of work, k 2, k 2 sts from cable needle (Cable 4), p 16, sl next 2 sts onto cable needle and hold in *back* of work, k next 2 sts, k 2 sts from cable needle, sl next 2 sts onto cable needle and hold in *front* of work, k next 2 sts, k 2 sts from cable needle (Cable 8), p 16, cable 4, p 2, twist 2, p 3. **Row 2:** K 3, p 2, k 2, p 4, k 2, (k, p, k in next st, p 3 tog) 3 times, k 2, p 8, k 2, (k, p, k in next st, p 3 tog) 3 times, k 2, p 4, k 2, p 2, k 3. **Row 3:** P 3, twist 2, p 2, k 4, p 16, k 8, p 16, k 4, p 2, twist 2, p 3. **Row 4:** K 3, p 2, k 2, p 4, k 2, (p 3 tog, k, p, k in next st) 3 times, k 2, p 8, k 2, (p 3 tog, k, p, k in next st) 3 times, k 2, p 4, k 2, p 2, k 3. **Row 5:** P 3, twist 2, p 2, k 4, p 16, k 8, p 16, k 4, p 2, twist 2, p 3. **Row 6:** K 3, p 2, k 2, p 4, k 2, (k, p, k in next st, p 3 tog) 3 times, k 2, p 8, k 2, (k, p, k in next st, p 3 tog) 3 times, k 2, p 4, k 2, p 2, k 3. **Row 7:** P 3, twist 2, p 2, cable 4, p 16, cable 8, p 16, cable 4, p 2, twist 2, p 3. **Row 8:** K 3, p 2, k 2, p 4, k 2, (p 3 tog, k, p, k in next st) 3 times, k 2, p 8, k 2, (p 3 tog, k, p, k in next st) 3 times, k 2, p 4, k 2, p 2, k 3. Rpt Rows 3 through 8 of pattern st 5 times more. P 1 row. Bind off.

STRAP: Make 2. Using yarn double, cast on 6 sts. **Row 1:** K 1, p 1 across row. **Row 2:** P 1, k 1 across row. Repeat these 2 rows of seed st until piece measures 25 inches. Bind off.

FINISHING: With wrong sides touching and starting 5 inches from seed edge, sew panels tog. Sew lining in place. Fold seed st border in half and leaving ends open, sew in place. Sew straps in place. Sew braid around opening. Insert dowels, after removing knobs, then replace knobs.

HAT

MATERIALS: Bernat Blarney-Spun (2 oz. balls): 3 balls; crochet hooks, one Size J, one Size K OR ANY SIZE HOOKS WHICH WILL OBTAIN THE STITCH GAUGE BELOW.

GAUGE: 9 sts = 4" on Size K.

DIRECTIONS: Note: Yarn is used double throughout. Using larger hook, ch 17 sts. **Rnd 1:** 2 s c in 2nd st of ch, 1 s c in each of next 14 sts, 3 s c in next st, working along other side of ch, 1 s c in each of next 15 sts, 3 s c in next st. Put a marker in work to mark beg of rnds and carry marker up. **Rnd 2:** 1 s c in each of next 16 sts, 3 s c in next st, 1 s c in each of next 17 sts, 3 s c in next st, 1 s c in next st. **Rnd 3:** 1 s c in each of next 18 sts, 3 s c in next st, 1 s c in each of next 19 sts, 3 s c in next st. **Rnd 4:** 1 s c in each of next 20 sts, 3 s c in next st, 1 s c in each of next 21 sts, 3 s c in next st - 48 sts. **Rnd 5:** Work even in s c. Rpt Rnd 5 five times more. On the next rnd, remove marker and work even in s c to last 4 sts, put a marker in work to mark beg of rnds and carry marker up. Change to smaller hook and work even in s c for 3 rnds.

BRIM: Change to larger hook. 2 s c (inc st) in first st, * 1 s c in each of next 11 sts, inc 1 st in next st, rpt from * twice more, ending 1 s c in each of next 11 sts — 52 sts. Work 1 rnd even in s c. On the next rnd, inc 1 st in first st, 1 s c in each of next 25 sts, inc 1 st in next st, 1 s c in each of next 25 sts - 54 sts. Work 1 rnd even in s c. On the next rnd, inc 1 st in first st, * 1 s c in each of next 13 sts, inc 1 st in next st, 1 s c in each of next 12 sts *, inc 1 st in next st, repeat between *'s once — 58 sts. Work 2 rnds even in s c. On the next rnd, inc 1 st in first st, 1 s c in each of next 28 sts, inc 1 st in next st, 1 s c in each of next 29 sts. Work 1 rnd even in s c on 60 sts. Fasten off.

TWEED JACKET WITH SCARF AND HAT

(page 22)

Directions for jacket are given for size Small (34-36). **Changes for sizes Medium (38-40), Large (42-44) and Extra Large (46-48) are in parentheses.** Directions for hat are given for size Small. Changes for sizes Medium and Large are in parentheses.

(continued on page 122)

We've packed this issue with new and innovative ideas,
and we invite you to choose from our
creative harvest: Knit-to-measure sweaters, rainbow kid
stuff, peasant fashions and exciting crafts!

GREAT IDEAS

Try your hand at decorating boxes or making colorful felt
vests. Sew yourself a versatile suit wardrobe
or make needlepoint picture frames! Our bountiful collection begins with an Indian-inspired portfolio.

An authentic headdress tops a blanket poncho. Photographed in
Monument Valley. To make needlepoint necklace, see page 85.

INDIAN PORTFOLIO PHOTOGRAPHS BY ANTHONY EDGEWORTH

INDIAN ADAPTATIONS

As patterns in woven Indian beadwork are determined by counting, they can be easily adapted to needle-point canvas as designer Margot Johnson has done with the belt and neckpiece shown here. The shape of the needlepoint stitches duplicates the appearance of bead-work. Yarn, Columbia-Minerva. Instructions, page 85.

RENÉ VELEZ

Two American classics: traditional beadwork and modern tee shirt. Wright's readymade neckline trim has been re-embroidered with Bucilla Glossilla and Sheru beads. Headband, from collection of Margot Johnson.

Kathy Sorkin has combined the colors of a desert rainbow with Indian design in a quick-to-crochet vest. Bernat yarn. Instructions, see page 87.

More Indian-inspired appliqué. Wright's squashblossom neckline trim is embellished with DMC cotton floss and Sheru beads. Shirts by Collage. Belt buckle and bracelet, Goulding's Trading Post. Instructions, see page 87.

Geometric elements of early Indian weavings are evident in the patterning of this coat, made from a Pendleton blanket. Coat, Simplicity 7936. Cutting layout, page 88. Belt details, page 26.

A Southwestern sense of color prevails in a raglan sleeve, hooded jacket by Marianne Ake. Tassels add extra detail. Reynolds yarn. See page 88.

A simple Navajo hogan provides perfect background for the basic shapings of Jacqueline Jewett's garter-stitched sweaters. His is easy knitting; an ideal project for beginners. Hers has shoulder buttons and matching hat. Bernat yarn. Turn to page 90.

Jacqueline Jewett's cro-
cheted tabard, with decorative whip-stitched edging, is a
triumphant mix of color and pattern. It laces on the sides and
is a fine topper for layered dressing, as we've shown here.
Coats & Clark yarn. For instructions, see page 90.

FROM AMISH TRADITION

The no-nonsense symmetry of Amish quilt patterns finds new dimension on pillows, wall hangings and vests. Instructions, see page 95.

The sparse lines and bold colors of the Amish patterns are ideal for contemporary interpretations. Segments of the geometric designs opposite create strong, visual patterns on the versatile, wear-with-everything vests. Butterick 5137. For cutting layout, turn to page 95.

Our versions of 19th century Amish quilt patterns have the sophistication of modern graphics. Margot Johnson has dramatically rendered three "plain folk" designs in felt. Simplicity of shapes allows pillow strips to be glued in place. All felt fabric, Central Shippee, Inc.

RICHARD BLINKOFF

Creative people are always seeking new ways to exercise their skills. With great excitement, we present our fail-safe method of knitting to measure. Establish your gauge, knit to the dimensions given—and you can't go wrong. Family Circle's first knit-to-measure sweaters, created especially for this issue, are a treat for beginners. Be your own designer, varying colors and stitches. Here, four great versions of one basic T-shape.

FOOLPROOF KNITTING TO MEASURE

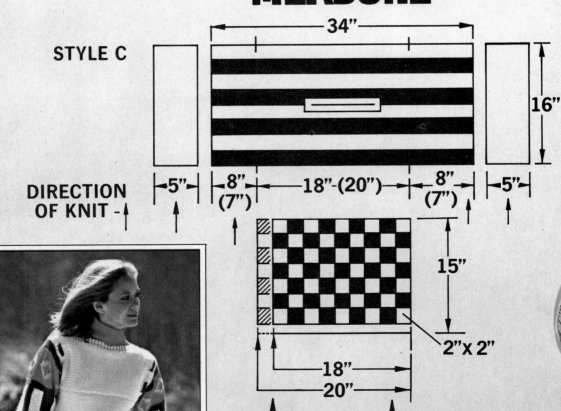

STYLE C

34"

16"

DIRECTION OF KNIT →

5" 8" (7") 18"-(20") 8" (7") 5"

15"

2" x 2"

18"
20"

This page: Stockinette and garter stitches combine to make a sensational patterned-sleeve sweater. Yarn, Columbia-Minerva. Opposite: A dynamic checkerboard pattern on short-sleeve T-sweater. Brunswick yarn. Inset: Bold stripes of a great new yarn. Sweater has drawstrings at wrists and waist. Reynolds yarn. See page 96.

JOHN STEMBER

Our garter-stitch cover sweater, also knit to measure, is a veritable kaleidoscope of color. Variegated scarf, wrapped as you wish, is an easy-knitting extra. Paternayan yarn.

Turn to page 97.

The versatility of needlepoint is often
overlooked. Opposite, are some suggestions
for showing this super design to its
best advantage.

VICTORIAN NEEDLEPOINT

Based upon a Victorian design,
our needlepoint bouquet presents a double
challenge. The first lies in the intricate
shading of leaves and flowers. The second is
in choosing one of the countless ways
the canvas may be used! Designed by
Margot Johnson for Columbia-Minerva. To
order kit, see coupon page 112.

RENE VELEZ

Renew worn-out chairs with needlepoint backs and seat covers.

Needlepoint tops an antique table— or a modern one.

Display your work proudly in a subject-enhancing frame.

Needlepoint needn't be a stay-at-home. Here it brightens the well-traveled tote bag.

The throw pillow: needlepoint's home companion—and a decorating asset in any room in the house.

DRAWINGS BY JULIA NOONAN

Off-white is on target as this year's important neutral. The clean, crisp look of this sweater is the result of simple lines—and natural yarn. Garter-stitched pullover has front pocket, side vents and matching hat. Designed by Meredith Gladstone. Yarn, Columbia-Minerva. Paired with white flannel pants, Butterick 4526. To make sweater and hat, see page 98.

WHITE ON WHITE ON

Designer Marianne Ake paints the town white with three special sweaters. Below, pull-over is a glorious example of horizontal cable knit. Matching hat. Bernat yarn.

Marianne's cardigan is an experiment in texture. The crocheted, loop-stitch body contrasts beautifully with the garter-stitch sleeves. Sweater hooks in front. Bernat yarn.

A snappy popcorn stitch cardigan has a drawstring waist and knitted hat to match. A one-of-a-kind challenge for experienced knitters. Tahki yarn. Skirt, Simplicity 7625. Instructions, all sweaters, see page 99.

WHIT

ANTHONY EDGEWORTH

STITCHERY: AN ARTISTIC TRIUMPH

Using varied techniques, Laura Demme has created an artistic masterpiece—to wear! From trapunto and embroidery, she has fashioned a scene normally confined to painter's canvas. As a timesaver, the body of the vest is cut from sweater-knit fabric, or an old sweater. For vest, we suggest McCall's 5477. The details are applied with crewel yarn and cotton floss. The fullylined vest has a crocheted shellstitch edging. Laura calls her visual poem "New Hampshire Spring." Instructions, page 102.

It is high time that needlepoint takes the big step into the fashion limelight! Designer Daria McGuire, using needlepoint as fabric, has created three magnificent examples of artwork to wear. Duplicate Daria's art gallery florals or design your own. Wear your needlepoint proudly— a masterpiece deserves to be seen! DMC yarn. See page 103.

WEAR YOUR WORK OF ART

This page: Taking color cues from Mother Nature, Daria has surrounded a group of flowers with varied bargello patterns. A dazzling interplay of texture covers the entire front of a square-necked tabard. McCall's 5136.

Above: Art-nouveau inspired tulips dominate the needle-point bib of a square-necked jumper. Flame stitch bargello background offers dramatic contrast. Jumper, Simplicity pattern 7372.

Below: Needlepoint pocket is the beautiful focal point of a shoulder-tie dress, Butterick 4916. Worked in subtly muted shades, the bargello butterfly and floral motifs have a lyrical feeling.

TURN ANY BOX

These inventively decorated boxes tell a Cinderella story. Once plain, they now sport frills that are easily applied. Gold spray paint and doilies turn an oval candy box into a jewel case. Any hatbox, covered with a special fabric, becomes a showpiece. Kids' crayons rest in a cigar box, covered with storybook illustrations. A tea tin, with drawer-pull knob, becomes a bright yellow bank. On larger boxes, use wallpaper; on smaller ones, fabric scraps, odd pieces of lace, gold trim—and your imagination. For easy guidelines, see page 104.

INTO A TREASURE

14-KARAT KNITTING

RICHARD BLINKOFF PHOTOGRAPHED AT LE MANGEOIRE RESTAURANT

Light up the night in sweaters that sparkle! With the magic of the Midas touch, our cardigans have gone from sporty to sophisticated, proving that comfort can be a part of dressing up. Above: Diamonds of silver and gold sequins are knitted into V-neck cardigan by Monna Weinman. Bernat yarn.

A slinky ribbed cardigan slips over a matching strapless tube, designed by Viola Sylbert. Metallic gold yarn is a lustrous trim. Necklace by Les Bernard. Long white flannel skirt, Simplicity 6573. Yarn, Columbia-Minerva. Instructions, all sweaters, see page 105.

Costume courtesy of "The Glory of Russian Costume" exhibit at the Costume Institute of the Metropolitan Museum of Art (inset photo), on loan from the Soviet Union.

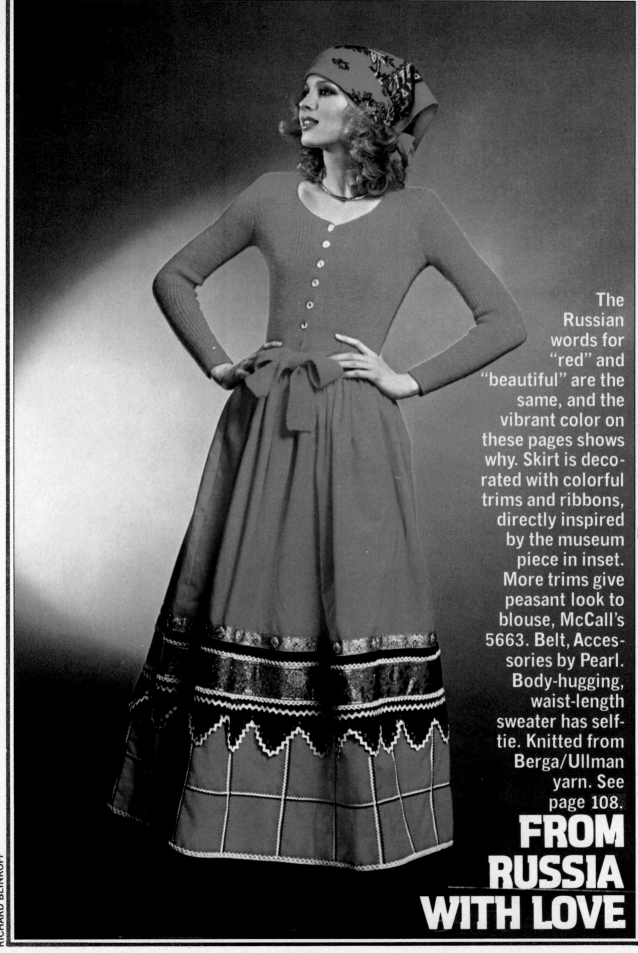

The Russian words for "red" and "beautiful" are the same, and the vibrant color on these pages shows why. Skirt is decorated with colorful trims and ribbons, directly inspired by the museum piece in inset. More trims give peasant look to blouse, McCall's 5663. Belt, Accessories by Pearl. Body-hugging, waist-length sweater has self-tie. Knitted from Berga/Ullman yarn. See page 108.

FROM RUSSIA WITH LOVE

More present-day peasants. Above, Meredith Gladstone has adapted the patterns of Provence onto a needlepoint vest. We've paired it with Meredith's Russian-red cowl neck sweater. The soft knit has drawstring satin ribbons on the sleeves. Both, Columbia-Minerva yarn. For instructions for vest and sweater, see page 111.

← The near-Eastern sparkle of Jean Simpson's embroidered mirrors stands out dramatically against this vest of black felt, paired with red skirt. Vest, Butterick 5137. Central Shippee felt. Bucilla floss. To order mirrors, see coupon on page 112.

This beautiful peasant can go anywhere—to an art gallery, to dinner, to the theatre. Its soft, fluid styling takes you through the busiest of days, and the wool challis fabric takes you from season to season. Mohair vest completes the look. Vogue 9871; Mohair by Franetta; Liberty of London challis.

This two-piece dress in Liberty of London floral wool challis has the fashion savvy so identified with its designer, Yves St. Laurent. Combining impeccable style with great comfort, it is a versatile asset to your wardrobe. Blouse and skirt are braid bound, both can be worn separately. Vogue 1738.

PORTRAIT OF TWO DRESSES

SEW
A
MIX
& MATCH
WARDROBE

1

2

5

We all dream of the perfect capsule wardrobe. It's easy to plan one when you sew. (1) Begin with a two-piece wool suit and striped cotton satin blouse in Arthur Zeiler fabrics, Vogue 9858. Add a long skirt to match, a velveteen vest and skirt (Stylecrest) and a crepe de chine overblouse. (2) The crepe blouse (Simplicity 7467) with the long skirt. (3) Vest (Simplicity 7376) and matching skirt (Butterick 4067). Challis scarf, Accessory Street. (4) Velveteen skirt and suit jacket, Echo scarf. (5) Suit blouse, long skirt as a dinner dress. Belt, Accessories by Pearl. (6) Blouse, long skirt, with velveteen vest.

4

3

6

Completely reversible poncho allows you to keep your sunny side out, whatever the weather. Rainproof slicker reverses to show plaid wool. Vogue 9588. Slicker fabric, Waldon Textiles. Plaid Harris tweed, Arthur Zeiler.

WEATHER

Let the cold winds blow! You'll be warm in a super wool poncho made from a fringed Pendleton motor robe. A decorative blanket stitch finishes the cut edges. Instructions for making poncho, see page 110.

REPORT

PICTURE
PERFECT
FRAMES

RENÉ VELEZ

Show off favorite photographs by framing them with needlepoint. Sara Gutierrez's designs will enhance any photo as well as the room decor. The key to easy framing is Columbia-Minerva's FashionEase plastic canvas which needs no blocking. Canvas simply slips into dime-store box frames. See page 116.

Mama, Papa and the kinder can find loose-fitting comfort in these Black Forest Smocks. The smocks are sewn from Folkwear Patterns. Order form page 14.

BLACK FOREST SMOCKS TO SEW

One pattern adjusts to fit men or women, another for boys or girls. With exception of embroidery on woman's version, detailing is the same on all smocks. Sleeves fit into side panels with gussets and are pleated at wrists. Man's smock is worn as over-shirt. Concord fabric. Lord Jeff sweater. Boy's smock, Dan River gingham.

RICHARD BLINKOFF

The smocks are based on the overgarment worn by cart drivers of the Black Forest. Neckbands, shoulder strips, and wrist bands may be sewn in contrasting fabric or embroidered with chainstitches as shown. Girl's fabric, Cohama. Baskets, Manila Bay Corporation.

THE RAINBOW DIVISION

The world of children is filled with vivid imagination and bright color. This portfolio of things to make for kids includes a charming fairy tale quilt, appliquéd sewing and rainbow-hued clothes to knit and crochet.

RENÉ VELEZ

Sleepyheads can snuggle under this quilt and dream sweetly of the adventures of Red Riding Hood, Cinderella and Rapunzel. The nine ''chapters'' in this tribute to the bedtime story also include Pinocchio, the Ugly Duckling, and the Princess and the Pea. Designer Frederica Siegelbaum's choice of fabrics enhances the picture-book squares which do double duty as a wall hanging. Turn to page 112.

This trio proudly shows its true stripes by wearing paintbox colors. Left to right: Ann flaunts bold bands of color on a crocheted jumper by Dorothy Ganie, Coats & Clark yarn. John and Lisa wear Meredith Gladstone's garter-stitched sweaters. His hat and cardigan, Columbia-Minerva. Her boat-neck pullover, Lion Brand yarn. Instructions, page 113.

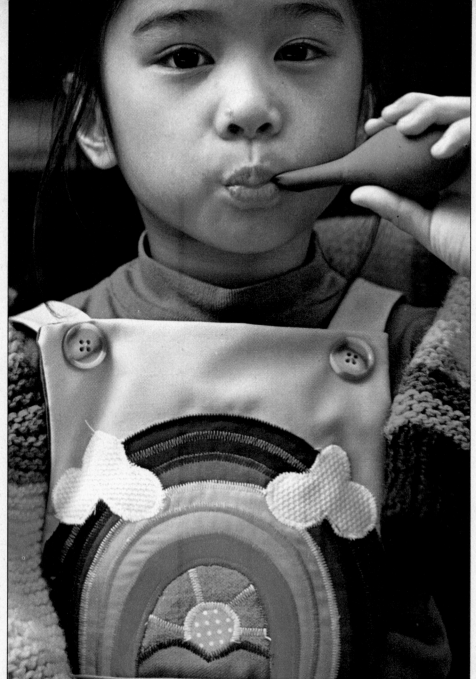

margaret Grace's
rainbow appliqué
(left) puts a little sunshine
on bib of khaki overalls,
Simplicity 7815. Fabric,
Earl-Glo. Knitted cardigan
puts rainbow 'round her
shoulders. Appliqué
pattern, see page 124.
Sweater instruction,
page 115.

animal crackers form
a zoo parade around
pant legs and kimono
jacket. Appliqué,
Margaret Grace. Pants,
Simplicity 7629. Earl-Glo
poplin. Jacket diagram
and appliqué pattern, turn
to page 115.

opposite page: Sweat-
shirt sweater with
grown-up fashion savvy.
Meredith Gladstone's
garter-stitch knit has front
pocket and boat neck.
Columbia-Minerva yarn.
See page 115.

the littlest rainbows
are seen coming
and going on a crocheted
jumper and jacket,
designed by Jane
Pappidas. Stripes circle
hem and sleeves, and
rainbow motifs decorate
jacket back and jumper
bib. Coats & Clark yarn.
Instructions, see
page 116.

meredith Gladstone's crayon-bright colors (left) make this patchwork knit the pride of the playground. Yarn by Lion Brand. Instructions, see page 116.

a rainbow variation by Susan Toplitz (above, left). This knitted cardigan has crocheted edging from hood to hem for added detail. Yarn, Coats & Clark. Instructions, see page 118.

susan Toplitz adds an embroidery sampler to a classic knitted pullover (above, right). Yarn, Coats & Clark. A turkey trots across the front of a jumper, Butterick 4930. Appliqué by Margaret Grace. See diagrams and instructions, page 119.

green thumb seamstresses can appliqué a vegetable garden on the skirt, sun and clouds appear on bib of jumper. McCall's 5668. Appliqué by Margaret Grace. Diagrams and instructions, see page 119.

This most unusual sweater is knitted on the bias. The gradation of six heathery shades from Berga/Ullman creates a mood akin to nature. The design, by Helen Maris, has a boat neckline and picot trim. The scarf is seamed into a soft tube. Turn to page 121.

(Continued from page 12)

SLIP STITCH (sl st): Insert the tip of the right-hand needle into the next stitch on left-hand needle, as if to purl, unless otherwise directed. Slip this stitch off the left-hand needle onto the right, **without working it** (FIG. 16.)

Fig. 16

BINDING OFF: This makes a finished edge and locks the stitches securely in place. Knit (or purl) two stitches. Then, with the tip of the left-hand needle, lift the first of these two stitches over the second stitch and drop it off the tip of the right-hand needle (FIG. 17).

Fig. 17

One stitch remains on the right-hand needle and one stitch has been bound off. * Knit (or purl) the next stitch; lift the first stitch over the last stitch and off the tip of the needle. Again, one stitch remains on the right-hand needle and another stitch had been bound off. Repeat from * until the required number of stitches has been bound off.

• Remember that you work **two** stitches to bind off one stitch. If, for example, the directions read, "k 6, bind off the next 4 sts, k 6 . . ." you must knit six stitches, then knit **two more** stitches before starting to bind off. Bind off four times. After the four stitches have been bound off, count the last stitch remaining on the right-hand needle as the first stitch of the next six stitches. When binding off, always knit the knitted stitches and purl the purled stitches.

• Be careful not to bind off too tightly or too loosely. The tension should be the same as the rest of the knitting.

• To end off the last stitch on the bound-off edge, if you are ending this piece of work here, cut yarn leaving a six-inch end; pass the cut end through the remaining loop on the right-hand needle and pull snugly (FIG. 18).

Fig. 18

SHAPING TECHNIQUES

Now that you know the basics, all that's left to learn are a few techniques which will help shape whatever it is you are making.

Increasing (inc): This means adding stitches in a given area to shape your work. There are several ways to increase.

1. To increase by knitting twice into the same stitch: Knit the stitch in the usual way through the front loop (FIG. 19), but

Fig. 19

before dropping the stitch from the left-hand needle, knit **another** stitch on the same loop by placing the needle into the **back** of the stitch (FIG. 20).

Fig. 20

Slip the original stitch off your left-hand needle. You have made two stitches from one stitch.

2. To increase by knitting between stitches: Insert tip of the right-hand needle under the strand of yarn **between** the stitch you've just worked and the following stitch; slip it onto tip of the left-hand needle (FIG. 21).

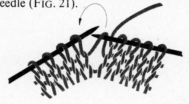

Fig. 21

Now knit into the back of this new loop (FIG. 22).

Fig. 22

3. To increase by "yarn-over" (yo): Pass the yarn over the right-hand needle after finishing one stitch and before starting the next stitch, **making an extra stitch (arrow in Fig. 23). If you are knitting,** bring the yarn under the needle to the back. **If you are purling,** wind the yarn around the needle once. On the next row, work all yarn-overs as stitches.

Fig. 23

Decreasing: (dec): This means reducing the number of stitches in a given area to shape your work. Two methods for decreasing are:

1. To decrease by knitting (FIG. 24 or **purling** (FIG . 25) **two stitches together:**

Fig. 24

Fig. 25

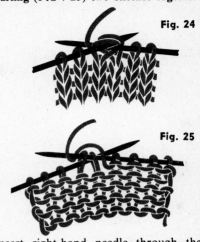

Insert right-hand needle through the loops of two stitches on left-hand needle at the same time; complete stitch. This is written k 2 tog, or p 2 tog.

• If you work through the **front** loops of the stitches in the usual way, your decreasing stitch will slant to the right. If you work through the **back** loops of the stitches, your decreasing stitch will slant to the left.

2. Slip 1 stitch, knit 1 and psso: Insert right-hand needle through the stitch on the left-hand needle, but instead of working it, just slip it off onto the right-hand needle (go back to FIG. 16). Work the next stitch in the usual way. With the tip of the left-hand needle, lift the slipped stitch over the last stitch worked and off the tip of the right-hand needle (FIG. 26).

Fig. 26

Your decreasing stitch will slant to the left. This is written sl 1, k 1, psso.

Pass Slipped Stitch Over (psso): Slip one stitch from the left-hand needle to the right-hand needle and, being careful to keep it in position, work the next stitch. Then, with the tip of the left-hand needle, lift the slipped stitch over the last stitch and off the tip of the needle (FIG. 26 again).

ATTACHING YARN When you end one ball of yarn or wish to change colors: Begin at the start of row and tie new yarn with previous yarn, making a secure joining. Continue to knit or purl.

(Continued from page 28)
CHAIN STITCH (CH)

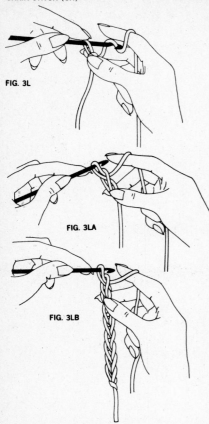

FIG. 3L

FIG. 3LA

FIG. 3LB

forget to make a ch 1 turning chain at the end before turning your work. Keep practicing until your rows are perfect.

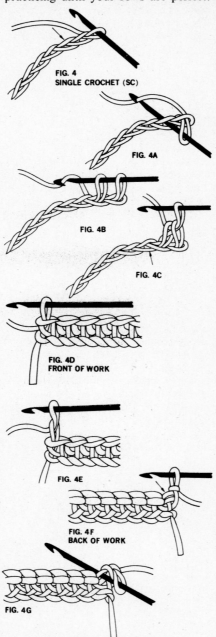

FIG. 4
SINGLE CROCHET (SC)

FIG. 4A

FIG. 4B

FIG. 4C

FIG. 4D
FRONT OF WORK

FIG. 4E

FIG. 4F
BACK OF WORK

FIG. 4G

For Left-handed Crocheters
From here on we won't be showing hands — just the hook and stitches. Left-handed crocheters can use all the following right-handed illustrations by simply turning the magazine upside down and placing a mirror (with backstand) so that it reflects the left-handed version.

Chain Stitch (ch): Follow the Steps in FIG. 3. As you make the chain stitch loops, the yarn should slide easily between your index and middle fingers. Make about 15 loops. If they are all the same size, you have maintained even tension. If uneven, rip them out by pulling on the long end of the yarn. Practice making chains and ripping out until you have a perfect chain.

Single Crochet (sc): Follow the Steps in FIG. 4. To practice, make a 20 loop chain (this means 20 loops in addition to the slip knot). Turn the chain, as shown, and insert the hook in the second chain from the hook (*see arrow*) to make the first sc stitch. Yarn over (yo); for second stitch see next arrow. Repeat to end of chain. Because you started in the second chain from the hook, you end up with only 19 sc. To add the 20th stitch, chain one (called a turning chain) and pull the yarn through. Now turn your work around (the "back" is now facing you) and start the second row of sc in the first stitch of the previous row (at the arrow). Make sure your hook goes under both of the strands at the top of the stitch. Don't

Ending Off: Follow Steps in FIG. 5. To finish off your crochet, cut off all but 6″ of yarn and end off as shown. (To "break off and fasten," follow the same procedure.)

FIG. 5

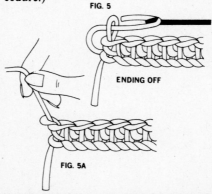

ENDING OFF

FIG. 5A

Double Crochet (dc): Follow the Steps in FIG. 6. To practice, ch 20, then make a

row of 20 sc. Now, instead of a ch 1, you will make a ch 3. Turn your work, yo and insert the hook in the second stitch of the previous row (*at the arrow*), going under both strands at the top of the stitch. Pull the yarn through. You now have three loops on the hook. Yo and pull through the first two, then yo and pull through the remaining two — one double crochet (dc) made. Continue across row, making a dc in each stitch

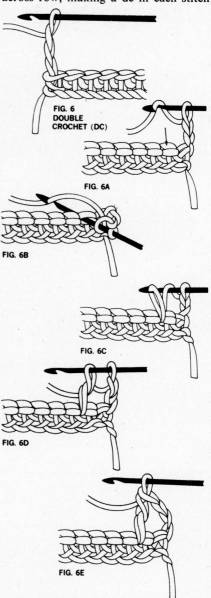

FIG. 6
DOUBLE
CROCHET (DC)

FIG. 6A

FIG. 6B

FIG. 6C

FIG. 6D

FIG. 6E

(st) across. Dc in the top of the turning chain (*see arrow in* FIG. 7). Ch 3. Turn work. Dc in second stitch in the previous row and continue as before.

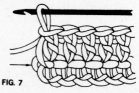

FIG. 7

Note: You may also start a row of dc on a base chain (omitting the sc row). In this case, insert hook in fourth chain from hook, instead of second (*see* FIG. 8).

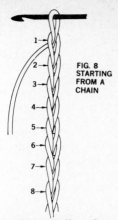

FIG. 8
STARTING
FROM A
CHAIN

Slip Stitch (sl st): Follow Steps in FIG. 11. This is a utility stitch you will use for joining, shaping and ending off. After you chain and turn, *do not yo.* Just insert the hook into the *first* stitch of the previous row (*see* FIG. 8), and pull the yarn through the stitch then right through the loop on the hook — sl st made.

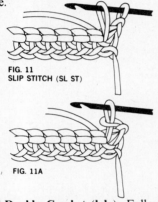

FIG. 11
SLIP STITCH (SL ST)

FIG. 11A

Half Double Crochet (hdc): Follow the Steps in FIG. 12. To practice, make a chain and a row of sc. Ch 2 and turn; yo. Insert hook in second stitch, as shown; yo and pull through to make three loops on hook. Yo and pull the yarn through *all* three loops at the same time — hdc made. This stitch is used primarily as a transitional stitch from an sc to a dc. Try it and see — starting with sc's then an hdc and then dc's.

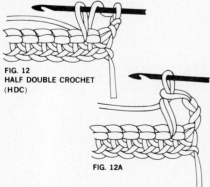

FIG. 12
HALF DOUBLE CROCHET
(HDC)

FIG. 12A

The Techniques of Crocheting: Now that you have practiced and made sample squares of all the basic stitches, you are ready to learn about adding and subtracting stitches to change the length of a row whenever it's called for. This is achieved by increasing (inc) and decreas-

ing (dec).

To increase (inc) — Just make two stitches in the same stitch in the previous row (*see arrow in* FIG. 13). The technique is the same for any kind of stitch.

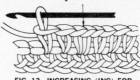

FIG. 13 INCREASING (INC) FOR
SINGLE CROCHET

To decrease (dec) for single crochet (sc) — Yo and pull the yarn through two stitches to make three loops on hook (*see Steps in* FIG. 14). Pull yarn through all loops at once — dec made. Continue in regular stitches.

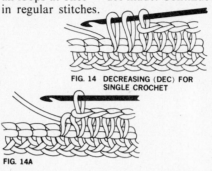

FIG. 14 DECREASING (DEC) FOR
SINGLE CROCHET

FIG. 14A

To decrease for double crochet — In a dc row make the next stitch and stop when

you have two loops on the hook. Now yo and make a dc in the next stitch. At the point where you have three loops on the hook, pull yarn through all loops at the same time. Finish the row with regular dc.

Abbreviations for Crochet: The box that follows is a crochet abbreviations listing, with definitions of the terms given. To help you become accustomed to them, we have repeated these abbreviations throughout our stitch instructions.

CROCHET ABBREVIATIONS

beg — begin, beginning; **ch** — chain; **dc** — double crochet; **dec** — decrease, **dtr** — double treble crochet; **hdc** — half double crochet; **in(s)** or **"** — inch(es); **inc** — increase; **oz(s)** — ounce(s) **pat** — pattern; **pc** — picot; **rem** — remaining; **rnd** — round; **rpt** — repeat; **sc** — single crochet; **skn(s)** — skein(s) **sk** — skip; **sl st** — slip stitch; **sp** — space; **st(s)** — stitch(es); **tog** — together; **tr** — triple crochet; **work even** — continue without further increase of decrease; **yo** — yarn over; ***** — repeat whatever follows * as many times as indicated; **( )** — do what is in parentheses as many times as indicated.

HOW TO ENLARGE AND REDUCE DESIGNS
METHOD 1
If the design is not already marked off in squares, make a tracing of it. Then mark the tracing off in squares; for a small design, make squares ¼"; for larger designs, use ½", 1" or 2" squares. Decide the size of your reduction or enlargement; on another sheet of tracing paper; mark off the same number of squares that are on the design or original tracing. Remember that to make your design six times larger than the original design, each new square must be six times larger than the original. Carefully copy the outline from your original tracing to the new one, square by square.

Use dressmaker's carbon and a tracing wheel to transfer the design to the material you're decorating.

METHOD 2
First, take the original design and make a tracing. Then determine the finished size you want and draw another outline. To accurately proportion the new design, first draw diagonal lines through both outlines. Second, draw one horizontal and one vertical line at the center where the two diagonal lines meet. In each quarter of the original design and outline, complete the other diagonal lines; then divide the quarters with horizontal and vertical lines where the diagonals intersect. Follow Method 1 to copy design from original tracing.

There are several shortcuts you can take when enlarging or reducing a design:
1. A wire screen, placed over the original design makes squaring off easier.
2. Transfer the original design to clear,

acetate graph paper.
3. Use Printing Technology Institute's "Craft Plan"™. It's a light, transparent, 100% nylon fabric printed in a grid of dots.

THREE ALL-PURPOSE TOTES

(page 6)

TO MAKE CRAZYWORK PATCH FABRIC: Loosely arrange patches, right side up, over muslin foundation, recutting and overlapping as desired for "crazy" shapes. Overlapped edges are left raw. Uppermost edges must be turned in. Pin from center outwards. Slipstitch through all layers. At outside edges, trim patches to match size and shape of foundation piece required below and baste along seamline. Embroidery stitches may be worked over the crazywork seams, if desired.

PATCHWORK FRINGED TOTE
MATERIALS: Ecru cotton fringe, 1⅛ yds.; one set wooden handles (see coupon, page 120); 44"-wide brown print for patches, ¼ yd.; 44"-wide muslin for patches and lining, ⅜ yd.; striped fabric, ⅜ yd.

DIRECTIONS—PATTERN: Draw a 3" square on thin cardboard. Draw diagonal line connecting two opposite corners. Cut on line for triangle pattern.

CUTTING: Cut 48 brown and 48 muslin triangles; from striped fabric, cut five strips 4"x12½" and one handle 3"x50", piecing if necessary.

SEWING: ¼″ *seam allowance.* Seam triangles on long edges to make squares. Seam six squares to make a row. Make eight rows in all. Seam two rows together at the long edges, to make four double rows. Alternate the single strips with the four double patchwork rows. Pin and stitch. Lay this piece over muslin, right sides together. Stitch ¼″ from edges around three sides and four corners. Turn right side out. Slipstitch opening. Turn under each end and stitch, to make 1¾″ casings. Fold bag in half crosswise, wrong sides together and, starting at bottom, edgestitch each side to middle of top patched row. Topstitch fringe at sides and bottom of bag. Fold fabric handle in half lengthwise, right sides together. Stitch long sides. Turn. Slipstitch ends. Slide wooden handles through casing. Slip fabric through slots and tie in a bow.

PATCHWORK TOTE WITH BRAIDED HANDLE

MATERIALS: One calico back and two pieces of ticking, each 11″ square; two 4″x44″ strips each of blue, yellow and lavender calico; scraps of blue, yellow, lavender and aqua calico to cut patches and borders.

DIRECTIONS—CUTTING: Cut four lavender and one blue patch, each 2¼″ square. Make a triangle pattern of the dimensions illustrated. Trace four aqua triangles. Cut them ¼″ *outside* the drawn lines. Fold triangle pattern in half to get pattern for corner patches. Trace four times on aqua and cut ¼″ *outside* drawn lines. Cut two yellow borders 5½″x1¾″ and two 8″x1¾″. Cut two lavender borders 8″x2″ and two 11″x2″.

SEWING: ¼″ *seam allowance.*
Patch Panel: Seam two large aqua triangles to opposite sides of two lavender squares. Seam two lavender squares to opposite sides of the blue square. Seam 3 rows of squares together, with blue square at center. Seam small triangle to each lavender patch, making a 5½″ square.
Borders: Seam short yellow border to opposite sides of patch panel. Seam long yellow border to remaining sides, to make 8″ square. Seam short lavender borders, then long ones, in the same way, to make 11″ square. Press. Seam front to back, right sides together, at side and bottom edges. Seam two pieces of ticking the same way. Turn bag right side out. Drop ticking inside. Turn under ¼″ at top edges, pin together and edgestitch.
Handles: Sew each two 44″ strips of matching color together at short ends to make one strip. Fold in half lengthwise, turn in raw edges and edgestitch. Braid the three strips and sew together securely 3″ from ends. Cut two 1″x2″ strips of lavender. Turn

in long edges and wrap around handle at ends of braiding. Whipstitch to top of bag at side seams, over handle with braid "tassel" extending.

BORDER PRINT TOTE *(with wooden handles)*

MATERIALS: Thirty assorted patches, each 2¼″ square; 3¼″-wide border, 1¼ yds.; ½ yd. muslin for lining; 15″x14″ calico for bag back; wooden handles (see page 120).

DIRECTIONS: ¼″ *seam allowance.* Sew six rows of five patches each. Seam rows to each other to make bag

front panel. To make bag front, sew border to one short and two long sides of panel, mitering corners. Seam front to back at lower edge. Cut muslin lining to match. Lay bag over muslin, right sides together. Stitch ¼″ from edges around three sides and four corners. Turn right side out. Slipstitch opening. Fold bag in half crosswise, right sides together. Stitch sides for 9″ from the bottom. Turn bag right side out. Fold under top edges about 1½″, through slot in handles. Turn in raw edges and slipstitch.

SIAMESE KITTY (AS SHOWN ON PAGE 4)

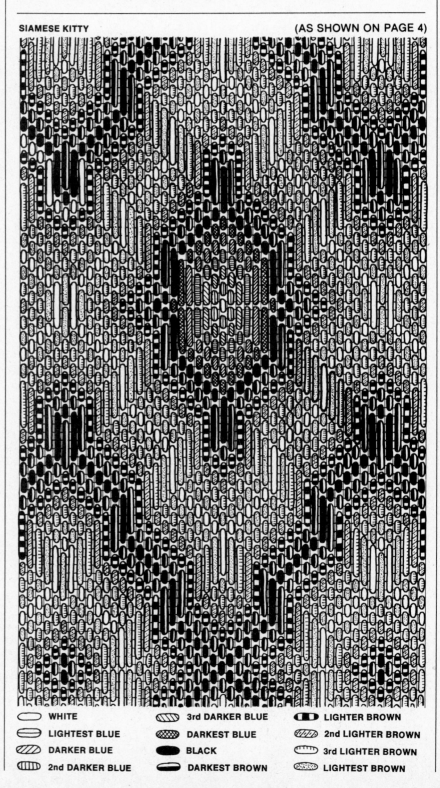

⬭ WHITE	◖▨ 3rd DARKER BLUE	◖■ LIGHTER BROWN
⬭ LIGHTEST BLUE	▨ DARKEST BLUE	▨ 2nd LIGHTER BROWN
▨ DARKER BLUE	⬤ BLACK	▨ 3rd LIGHTER BROWN
▥ 2nd DARKER BLUE	⬬ DARKEST BROWN	▨ LIGHTEST BROWN

STRAWBERRY VEST

(page 8)

MATERIALS: Simplicity pattern #7688—Jacket length, using pattern pieces C and E *only;* Malden Off White pile fabric (#1018), in yardage as pattern requires; sharp scissors; Central Shippee Mead Felt: ⅛ yd. Fire Red (#200); ⅛ yd. Kelly Green (#288); ⅛ yd. Fuchsia (#215); ⅛ yd. Moss (#286) (see Buyer's Guide, page 136); single-edged razor blade or mat knife; straight pins; thread to match; white thread.

(**Note:** When cutting pattern pieces, allow 1″ beyond the seam allowance at the hem of the vest to fold over for a furry self-trim. We used this fabric pile-side in.)

DIRECTIONS: Cut two pieces of pile fabric 16″ long and 2½″ wide for sleeve binding. Cut one piece of pile fabric 13″ long and 2½″ wide for neck binding. Using a single-edged razor blade or a mat knife, carefully cut the felt fabric. Cut two strips of Kelly Green felt 17″ long and 2¼″ wide for front bindings. Cut one strip of Kelly Green felt 36″ long and 1¼″ wide for trim at hemline of vest. Enlarge strawberry and hull designs in diagram, following directions on page 83. Cut out 6 Fire Red strawberries, 8 Fuchsia strawberries and 14 Moss hulls. Pin strawberries in place on unsewn pattern pieces and appliqué in place with matching thread. Use a wide, fine zig-zag setting. The seeds are done with a fine narrow setting in white thread. Trim pile away ¼″ from backing on all seam edges on the vest, as well as on the neck and armhole pieces. Join side and shoulder seams. Zig-zag the 36″ x 1¼″ piece of Kelly Green felt 2½″ from the bottom edge of the vest. Fold the 17″ x 2¼″ Kelly Green strips around both sides of the front closing and zig-zag in place. Fold the pile binding strips around armholes and neckline. Pin and zig-zag in place, using a wide loose zig-zag setting and red thread. Fold up the hem 1″, pile-side out, and zig-zag in place with red thread.

TULIP COAT

(page 10)

MATERIALS: Simplicity pattern #7688, using pattern pieces G, K, E, F and C only (we suggest buying the pattern a size larger to allow for the bulk of the pile inasmuch as we used the pile on the inside. Adjust arm length accordingly); Malden Off White (#1018) fabric, in yardage as pattern requires; Central Shippee's Mead Felt: ⅜ yd. each of Fire Red (#200) and Kelly Green (#288), ⅛ yd. each of Fuchsia (#215) and Moss

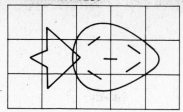

1 SQ. = 1 IN.

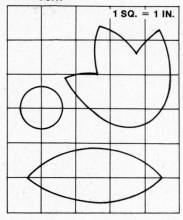

(#286) (see Buyer's Guide, page 136); white fabric for pockets; sharp scissors; straight pins; pinking shears; thread to match fabrics.

(**Note:** When cutting pattern pieces, allow 1″ beyond the seam allowance to fold over for furry self-trim.)

DIRECTIONS: Following directions on page 83, enlarge and cut out shapes as follows: Make approximately 10 tulips from Fire Red, 14 leaves from Kelly Green and 9 dots from Fuchsia. From Moss, cut ½″-wide soft "S" shapes, in lengths from 9″ to 12″, to make 7 stems. Arrange the tulips, stems, leaves and dots on the unsewn pattern pieces. Pin and appliqué in place with wide zig-zag stitch. Mark and sew white pockets in place. Make felt binding: Cut 1¼″ strips of Fire Red and ⅜″ strips of Kelly Green with pinking shears to go around cuffs, hems, hoods and two front closings. Carefully trim away the pile ¼″ at hems and cuffs so that you can easily topstitch the red and green binding flat. Topstitch on the green with matching thread, using wide zig-zag stitch. After trimming pile from seam allowance, join all seams. For hood, trim pile and join center seam. Fold over flat to one side and topstitch down on the flat side of the fabric. Then fold back hems of hood, trim pile and sew in place with red and green felt trim. On buttonhole side, use red and green felt trim, backed with a facing of red felt to "sandwich" the pile fabric. Allow for an overlap of ¼″. For vertical buttonholes, straight stitch twice around a rectangle 1″ long and ⅛″ wide. Slash with razor blade. Add the hood last. Whipstitch seam flat.

CORN HUSK DOLLS

(page 9)

MATERIALS: Dry corn husks, from 2-3 ears of corn for each large doll (sun-dried until all green is gone); thin string; flexible wire; white glue; scissors; corn silk; waterproof marking pens in vivid colors.

(**Note:** Bleach dark spots out.)

DIRECTIONS: To use husks, dampen until flexible, then wipe excess water off thoroughly. Separate and arrange husks by widths and lengths. (**Note:** Only dampen enough husks to use for each step. If husks dry before using, dampen again. They must be flexible to work with, otherwise they will crack and break.) Take six or seven 1″-wide, 7″-long strips; tie in center tightly (diagram #1). Pull top strips down like a banana peel over bottom half (diagram #2). Tie 1″ down from the top. This is the foundation of the head (diagram #3). Repeat procedure again, making another bundle as before. Pull down top leaves. Place first bundle under second (diagram #4) and tie as before. This is the full head section. It will look like diagram #3. Cover neck string with thin strip of husk, tying in a knot at back of neck. Trim ends (see head section diagram #7). Cut flexible wire to desired length, e.g. a 10″ doll needs 8″-9″ wire for arms (diagram #5). Roll wire inside several layers of husks (diagram #5). Tie at center and each end with string. Cover string at ends with thin strips of corn husk (diagram #6). Knot. Trim long ends. Divide husk below neck in half. Center arms (diagram #6) between husks (diagram #7). Tie with string criss-cross below neck and across chest. This will hold arms in place (diagram #8). Cover with two strips of husk in a criss-cross fashion to cover string. Tie at waist (diagram #9). Skirt is formed by placing husks along waist. Tie in place with string, a few at a time, layering until skirt is as full as desired (diagram #10). Save the best clean husks for the last outside layer. Tie tightly with string. Trim husk ends at waist. Finally, tie waist with husk covering string (diagram #11). While doll is still flexible, bend arms toward front of doll. Doll will take at least 24 hours to dry thoroughly. When dry, glue corn silk on head in desired style, a little at a time. To decorate doll, use waterproof marking pens. (**Note:** Colors will not be as vivid on husks.) Cut front husk of skirt to form apron, then decorate. Cut side and back top husk layer to form tunic, then decorate. For head scarves, use flexible husks; tie on. Let dry in place, then decorate. The dolls in the photo are plain corn husk dolls which we

CORN HUSK DOLLS

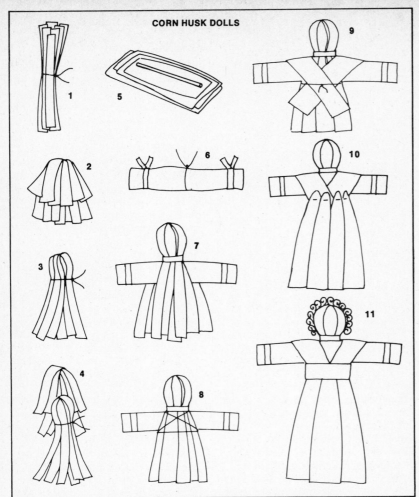

decorated with yarn wigs, lace-trimmed aprons from your scrap bag, scarves, shawls and hats. Some carry tiny baskets filled with small bits of lace, yarns and buttons. Some hold dried or artificial bouquets in their arms. Marking pens or acrylic paints can be used to make designs on an occasional skirt or sleeve. Some of the skirts are gathered at the waist, attached to narrow ribbon and tied in place. **To make a yarn wig:** Loop a fine yarn loosely around your fingers, about 25 or 30 times. Lay the yarn down flat, mark the center with chalk, and sew back and forth two or three times on a sewing machine. Center the stitch line at the part line of the doll's head, and glue in place with white glue. When the glue is dry, braid and trim, or simply trim as is.

STRIPED VEST

(page 11)

Directions are given for size Small (8-10). Changes for sizes Medium (12-14) and Large (16-18) are in parentheses.

MATERIALS: Bernat Blarney Spun (2 oz. balls): 3(4,4) balls # 7907 Hazelmist (A), 3(4,4) balls # 7959 White (B), 1 ball each of # 7955 Copper (C) and # 7998 Abbey (D); and Bernat Catkin

Yarn: 1(2,2) balls of # 6018 Chestnut (E); crochet hook, Size D OR ANY SIZE HOOK WHICH WILL OBTAIN THE STITCH GAUGE BELOW.

GAUGE: 4 hdc = 1″; 5 rows = 2″.

MEASUREMENTS:

Sizes:	Small (8-10)	Medium (12-14)	Large (16-18)
Bust (including border):	32″	35″	39″
Width across back at underarms:	16½″	18″	20″
Width across each front at underarm (including border):	7¾″	8½″	9½″

(**Note:** Back and Fronts are worked all in one piece, starting and ending at center front. Pattern is worked entirely from right side. Break off and fasten at end of each row. Always work over loose ends of previous row at beg and end of each row to keep work neat).

DIRECTIONS—LEFT FRONT: Starting at Left Front edge with A, ch 72(74,76). **Row 1:** Hdc in 3rd ch from hook, hdc in each ch across—70(72,74) hdc (do not count chain at beg of row as one st). Cut yarn and fasten. **Row 2:** Do not turn; attach B to top of chain at beg of last row, with B ch 2, leaving top 2 loops of hdc free (this forms a ridge on right side of

work) *make 2 hdc in back loop of first hdc*—**inc made at lower edge;** leaving top loops free as before, work 1 hdc in back loop of each hdc across to within last 2 sts, *yarn over hook, draw up a loop in back loop of each of last 2 sts, yarn over hook and draw through all 4 loops on hook*—**dec made at shoulder edge.** Cut yarn and fasten. *Hereafter, leaving top loops free, work in back loop only of each hdc throughout.* Break off and fasten at end of each row and do not turn. **Row 3:** Attach A to top of ch-2 at beg of row, working as directed, make 2 hdc in first hdc, hdc in each st across to end of row—71(73,75) hdc (do not count ch-2 as one st). Rpt last 2 rows (Rows 2 and 3) 1(2,2) more times—72(75,77) hdc.

Left Armhole Shaping—Row 1: Attach B to top of ch-2 at beg of last row, ch 2, 2 hdc in first hdc, hdc in each of next 45 hdc, dec over next 2 sts; do not work over rem sts—48 sts on all sizes. **Row 2:** Attach A to top of ch-2, ch 2, hdc in each hdc to within last 2 sts on last row, dec over rem 2 sts. **Row 3:** Using B, work same as last row. **Rows 4 and 5:** Rpt last 2 rows—44 hdc. Continuing to alternate A and B rows for stripe pat, work even (making hdc in each hdc) for 8(8,12) rows. There are 13(13,17) rows in all on armhole. Keeping continuity of stripe pat, inc one st at end of each of next 4 rows—48 hdc. At end of last row, do not cut yarn; ch 24(27,29) for other edge of armhole. Cut yarn and fasten.

BACK—Row 1: Attach A to top of ch-2, ch 2, hdc in each hdc and in each ch across—72(75,77) hdc. For Left Shoulder, keeping in stripe pat, inc one st at end of every other row 2(3,3) times—74(78,80) hdc, ending with A row.

Neck Shaping—Row 1: Work in stripe pat to within last 4 sts; do not work over last 4 sts. **Rows 2 and 3:** Keeping in pat, dec one st at end of each row—68(72,74) hdc. Work even in pat over these sts for 10(10,12) more rows. Inc one st at end of each of next 2 rows. At end of last row, ch 4. Cut yarn and fasten. **Next Row:** Work hdc in each hdc and in each ch across—74(78,80) hdc. For Right Shoulder, (work 1 row even; dec one st at end of next row) 2(3,3) times—72(75,77) hdc.

Right Armhole Shaping: Work same as for Left Armhole Shaping until the ch 24(27,29) at end of last row has been made.

RIGHT FRONT—Row 1: Keeping in pat, attach next color to top of ch-2, ch 2, hdc in each hdc and in each ch st across—72(75,77) hdc. **Row 2:** Attach next color to top of ch-2, ch 2, dec over first 2 hdc, hdc in each hdc to last hdc, 2 hdc in last hdc. **Row 3:**

Attach next color, ch 2, dec over first 2 hdc, hdc in each hdc to end of row. Rpt last 2 rows 1(2,2) more times—70(72,74) hdc—right front edge.

Underarm Edge: With right side facing, attach matching color to end of B row at beg of underarm edge, place A along underarm edge, * with B, working over A, sc over end of B row, *draw up a loop over end of same row, drop B, pick up A and draw a loop through the 2 loops on hook—color change made;* with A, working over B, make 2 sc over end of next A row, changing to B in last sc; rpt from * across underarm edge. Cut both colors and fasten. Work across other underarm edge in same manner.

EDGING: With right side facing, attach E to center of any underarm edge, ch 2, hdc evenly along entire outer edge of vest, making 3 hdc in same st at each corner, and being very careful to keep work flat (dec 2 or 3 sts across underarm edges, if necessary, to keep edges flat).

FINISHING: Pin vest to measurements on a padded surface; cover with a damp cloth and allow to dry; do not press. Fold fronts over back and sew shoulder seams.

BORDER—Rnd 1: With right side facing, attach C to back loop of hdc at center back of neck, ch 2, working in back loop only as before, hdc in each hdc along outer edge of vest, increasing 3 or 4 hdc evenly spaced along lower curved edge of each front (be sure to have a number of hdc divisible by 6). Join with sl st in top of ch-2. Cut yarn and fasten. **Rnd 2:** Attach D to same st used for joining, * sc in back loop of next hdc, sk next 2 sts, 7 dc in back loop of next hdc, sk next 2 sts; rpt from * around. Join with sl st to first sc. Cut yarn and fasten.

Armhole Border—Rnd 1: Starting at center of underarm, attach C to back loop of hdc, ch 2, hdc in each st around, decreasing one st at each inner corner. Join with sl st to top of ch-2. Cut yarn and fasten. **Next Row:** Sk underarm sts, attach D to back loop of first st after inner corner, sc in same st, * sk 2 sts, 7 dc in back loop of next hdc, sk next 2 sts, 1 sc in back loop of next hdc; rpt from * across to within underarm sts. Cut yarn and fasten. Finish other armhole in same manner.

NATURAL TURTLENECK SWEATER

(page 13)

Directions are given for size Small (8-10). Changes for sizes Medium (12-14) and Large (16-18) are in parentheses.

MATERIALS: Coats & Clark's Red Heart "Fabulend" Knitting Worsted 4 Ply (4 oz. skeins): 5(6,7) skeins of desired color; crochet hook; knitting needles, 1 pair No. 8 OR ANY SIZE NEEDLES WHICH WILL OBTAIN THE STITCH GAUGE BELOW.

GAUGE: 9 sts = 2″; 8 rows (4 ridges) = 1″.

MEASUREMENTS:

	Small	Medium	Large
Sizes:	(8-10)	(12-14)	(16-18)
Bust:	33″	36″	40″
Width across back at underarms:	16½″	18″	20″
Width across sleeve at upper arm:	11¼″	12″	13″

DIRECTIONS—BACK: Starting at lower edge, cast on 74(80,90) sts. Work in k 1, p 1 ribbing for 3½″. Now work in garter st (k each row) until total length is 17(17½,18)″ from beg, or desired length to shoulder. Bind off all sts.

FRONT: Work same as Back.

SLEEVES: Starting at lower edge, cast on 48(50,52) sts. Work in k 1, p 1 ribbing for 3½″. **Next Row:** K across, inc 2(4,6) sts evenly spaced across row — 50(54,58) sts. Work even in garter st until length is 18(18½,19)″ above ribbing, or desired length to shoulder.

COLLAR: Cast on 78(80,82) sts. Work even in garter st until total length is 5(5½,6)″. Bind off.

FINISHING: Pin each piece to measurements on a padded surface, cover with a damp cloth and allow to dry; do not press. (**Note:** Pieces are crocheted together, using sl sts.) To join, first baste (or pin) sections together as directed; with crochet hook, working through both thicknesses of joining edges, sl st evenly across each seam. Starting at side edges, baste 4(4½,5½)″ shoulder seams, leaving center sections of top edges open for neck. Fold sleeves in half lengthwise to find center at top edge, match top end of fold of each sleeve with end of shoulder seam; baste top edges of sleeves along 6(6½,7)″ of side edges of back and front, adjusting to fit. Baste side and sleeve seams. With crochet hook, sl st evenly across each seam, keep work flat. Sl st short edges of collar together. With collar seam at center back, sl st one long edge of collar to neck edge, adjusting to fit. Fold collar in half to right side.

FISHERMAN VEST

(page 15)

"FOR EXPERIENCED KNITTERS ONLY"

Directions are given for size Small (8-10). Changes for sizes Medium (12-14) and Large (16-18) are in parentheses.

MATERIALS: Bucilla "Shamrock" color natural 4 ply (2 oz. balls): 12(13,15) balls; Size I crochet hook; DP needle; knitting needles, 1 pair No. 8 OR ANY SIZE NEEDLES WHICH WILL OBTAIN THE STITCH GAUGE BELOW.

GAUGE: Seed st — 4 sts = 1″; 7 rows = 1″

MEASUREMENTS:

	Small	Medium	Large
Sizes:	(8-10)	(12-14)	(16-18)
Bust:	32″	36″	40″
Width across back at underarm:	16″	18″	20″
Width across each front at underarm:	8¼″	9¼″	10¼″

DIRECTIONS—PATTERN STITCH: Row 1: K 1, p 1 for 8(12,16) sts, p 1, k 1, p 4, k 1, p 1, (k 2, p 2) twice k 1, (p 2, k 2) twice p 1, k 1, p 4, k 1, p 1, k 1, p 1, k 1, p 1, k 1, p 1, k 1, p 4, k 1, p 1 (k 2, p 2) twice k 1, (p 2, k 2) twice p 1, k 1, p 4, k 1, p 1 [k 1, p 1 for 8(12,16) sts]. **Row 2:** [p 1, k 1 for 8(12,16) sts] K loosely in front, in back, in front, in back, in front, in back of next st. Then slide first 5 loops over last loop just made (popcorn st). P 1, sl next st to DP needle and *hold in front*, k 1 then k 1 from DP needle, sl next st to DP needle and *hold in back* k 1, then k 1 from DP needle (wave st I) p 1, popcorn st in next st. P 2, k 2, p 2 sl next 3 sts to DP needle and *hold in back*, k 2, sl purl st from DP back to left-hand needle and purl it, then k 2 from DP needle p 2, k 2, p 2 (4-rib braid) popcorn, p 1, wave st I in next 4 sts, p 1, popcorn, p 1, k 1, p 1, k 1, p 1, popcorn, p 1, wave st I, p 1, popcorn, p 1, 4-rib braid, popcorn, p 1, wave st I, p 1, popcorn [p 1, k 1, for 8(12,16) sts]. **Row 3:** [K 1, p 1 for 8(12,16) sts] (seed stitch) p 1, k 1, p 4, k 1, p 1, (k 2, p 2) twice, k 1, (p 2, k 2) twice, p 1, k 1, p 4, k 1, p 1, k 1, p 1, k 1, p 1, k 1, p 1, k 1, p 4, k 1, p 1, (k 2, p 2) twice k 1, (p 2, k 2) twice p 1, k 1, p 4, k 1, p 1, seed st over 8(12,16) sts. **Row 4:** Seed st over 8(12,16) sts, k 1, p 1, sl next st to DP needle and *hold in back*, k 1, then k 1 from DP needle sl next st to DP needle and *hold in front* k 1, then k 1 from DP needle (wave st II) p 1, k 1, p 2, sl 2 sts to DP needle and *hold in front*, p 1 then k 2 from DP needle (*front cross*-FC) sl 1 st to DP needle and *hold in back*, k 2 then p 1 from DP needle (back cross-BC) p 1, FC, BC, p 2 k 1, p 1, wave st II. P 1, k 1, p 1, k 1, p 1, k 1, p 1, wave st II, p 1, k 1, p 2, FC, BC, p 1, FC, BC, p 2, k 1, p 1, wave st II, p 1, k 1, seed st. **Row 5:** Seed st, p 1, k 1, p 4, k 1, p 1 (k 3, p 4) twice k 3, p 1, k 1, p 4, k 1, p 1, k 1, p 1, k 1, p 1, k 1, p 1, k 1, p 1, k 1, p 4, k 1, p 1 (k 3, p 4) twice

k 3, p 1, k 1, p 4, k 1, p 1, seed st.
Row 6: Seed st, popcorn, p 1, wave st 1, p 1, popcorn (*p 3, sl next 2 sts to DP needle and *hold in back* k 2, then k 2 from DP needle, p 3, sl next 2 sts to DP needle and *hold in front,* k 2, then k 2 from DP needle p 3) popcorn, p 1, wave st 1, p 1, popcorn, p 1, k 1, p 1, k 1, p 1, popcorn p 1, wave st 1, p 1, popcorn, repeat from * to end of parenthesis, popcorn, p 1, wave st 1, p 1, popcorn, seed st.
Row 7: Repeat Row 5. **Row 8:** Seed st, k 1, p 1, wave st II, p 1, k 1, p 2, BC, FC, p 1, BC, FC, p 2, k 1, p 1, wave st II, p 1, k 1, p 1, k 1, p 1, k 1, p 1, k 1, p 1, wave st II, p 1, k 1, p 2, BC, FC, p 1, BC, FC, p 2, k 1, p 1, wave st II, p 1, k 1, seed st. **Row 9:** Repeat row 1. **Row 10:** Seed st, popcorn, p 1, wave st I, p 1, popcorn, p 2, k 2, p 2, slip the next 3 sts to DP needle and *hold in front* k 2, then slip the purl st from DP needle back to left-hand needle and purl it, then k 2 from DP needle, p 2, k 2, p 2, popcorn, p 1, wave st I, p 1, popcorn, p 1, k 1, p 1, k 1, p 1, popcorn, p 1 wave st I, p 1, popcorn, p 2, k 2, p 2, slip the next 3 sts to DP needle back to left-hand needle and purl it, then k 2 from DP needle, p 2, k 2, p 2, popcorn, p 1, wave st I, p 1, popcorn seed st. **Rows 11 thru 16:** Repeat Rows 3 through 8. Repeat these 16 rows throughout.
BACK: With No. 8 needles, cast on 87(95,103) sts. Work in pattern for 15(15,16)".
ARMHOLES: Bind off 4(5,6) sts at beg of next 2 rows. Dec 1 st each end every other row 3(4,5) times. Work even until armhole is 7(7½,8)".
Neckline Shaping: Work 15(16,18) sts and slip on holder. Bind off center 43(45,45) sts. Work rem sts— 15(16,18).
Shoulder Shaping: At armhole edge, bind off 5(5,6) sts every other row 2

times; then 5(6,6) sts once. Shape other side to correspond.
LEFT FRONT: Cast on 46(50,54) sts, work in pattern as for back, ending at center front edge with 5 rib sts. Keeping continuity of 5 rib sts for front border, work even for 15(15,16)" to armhole. Bind off 4(5,6) sts at armhole, dec 1 st at same edge every other row 3(4,5) times. Work even until armhole is 6½(6½,7)".
Neckline Shaping: At front edge, bind off 21(22,22) sts. Work 1 row even. Bind off 1 st at neck edge every other row 3 times.
Shoulder Shaping: At armhole edge, bind off 5(5,6) sts every other row 2 times. Bind off rem sts.
RIGHT FRONT: Work to correspond to left front, reversing pattern and shaping.
FINISHING: Sew side and shoulder seams; with right side facing, using crochet hook Size I, start at right lower corner, attach strand and ch 2, sk next st, sc in next 2 sts, *ch 2 (picot st) skip next st, sc in next 2 sts; rpt from * to end of front edge. 3 sc in last st (corner), sc across entire neck edge to left front edge, 3 sc in corner st, continue picot edging down entire left front edge. Break off and fasten. Picots serve as button loops, using popcorn sts opposite as buttons.

ALPACA STRIPED TURTLENECK

(page 15)

Directions are given for size small (8-10). Changes for size Medium (12-14) are in parentheses.
MATERIALS: Plymouth "Indiecita" Alpaca Yarn, 3 Ply (50 gr. balls): 4 sks #100 Ecru (A); 3 skns each of #206 Light Brown (B), #301 Medium Brown (C), #306 Dark Brown (D), #403 Charcoal (E), #402 Dark Grey (F), #401 Light Grey (G); knitting

needles, No. 6 OR ANY SIZE NEEDLES WHICH WILL OBTAIN THE STITCH GAUGE BELOW; dp needles; circular needles, #5.
GAUGE: On No. 6 needles—15 sts = 2"; 8 rows = 1"
MEASUREMENTS:

	Small	Medium
Sizes:	(8-10)	(12-14)
Bust:	32"	36"
Width across back or front at under-arms:	12"	14"
Width across sleeve at upper arm:	9½"	10½"

(**Note:** Use 2 strands together throughout.)
DIRECTIONS—BACK: Work k 1, p 1 ribbing for entire sweater. With 2 strands of A and using No. 6 needles, cast on 110 (122) sts, work 15 rows. Drop 1 strand of A and join 1 strand B, work 15 rows. Drop A and join 1 strand B, work 8 rows. Drop 1 strand B and join 1 strand C, work 15 rows. Drop B and join C, work 8 rows. Drop 1 strand of C and join 1 strand D, work 15 rows. Drop C and join 1 strand of D, work 8 rows. Drop 1 strand D and join 1 strand E, work 15 rows. Drop D and join E, work 8 rows. Drop 1 strand E and join 1 strand F, work 10 rows.
Armhole: Bind off 6 sts at beg of the next 2 rows. Keeping stripes of 8 rows solid and 15 rows mixed shades, continue to dec 1 st at each edge every other row 3 (4) times—92 (102) sts. After 15 rows of stripe, drop 1 strand E and join 1 strand F, work 8 rows. Drop 1 strand F and join 1 strand G, work 15 rows. Drop F and join 1 strand G, work 8 rows. Drop 1 strand G and join 1 strand A, work 15 rows. Drop G and join 1 strand A, work 8 rows.
Shoulders: Bind off 7 (8) sts at beg of next 6 (8) rows, then 8 (10) sts at beg of next 2 rows. Place 34 (38) sts on a st holder.
FRONT: Work as Back until 8th row of G/A stripe. Work over 33 (37) sts. Place rem sts on a holder. Working only on sts on needle, dec 1 st at neck edge every other row until 29 (32) sts are left. Work evenly until armhole equals that on Back. End at armhole.
Shoulders: Bind off 7 (8) sts at beg of next 3 rows at armhole edge only. From armhole edge, bind off rem sts. Leave center 26 (28) sts on holder and put rem 33 (37) sts on needle. Attach 1 strand each of G and A at neck edge and reverse shaping to correspond with other side.
SLEEVES: With 2 strands of A, cast on 50 (54) sts. Work in k 1, p 1 ribbing for 25 rows. Keeping pattern of ribbing, inc 1 st at each end of row. Drop 1 strand A; join 1 strand B. Continuing with striping pattern, inc 1 st each

---

HOW TO TAKE BODY MEASUREMENTS: It's easy to determine the correct size for any crocheted or knitted garment. First, make sure the person you're measuring is wearing the usual undergarments. For all women's and girls' sizes, measure at the fullest part of natural waistline, hips and bust. We've made allowances for ease to insure a proper fit. If you have to make adjustments between the measurements and size differential, do it during the blocking and finishing. Determine men's sizes by loosely holding the tape around the fullest part of the chest.

STANDARD BODY MEASUREMENTS:

All measurements in inches.

JUNIORS

Size	7	9	11	13	15
Bust	31	32	33½	35	37
Waist	22½	23½	24½	26	28
Hip	33	34	35½	37	39

TEENS

Size	7/8	9/10	11/12	13/14
Bust	29	30½	32	33½
Waist	23	24	25	26
Hip	32	33½	35	36½

MISSES

Size	8	10	12	14	16	18
Bust	31½	32½	34	36	38	40
Waist	23	24	25½	27	29	31
Hip	33½	34½	36	38	40	42

WOMEN

Size	38	40	42	44	46	48
Bust	42	44	46	48	50	52
Waist	34	36	38	40½	43	45½
Hip	44	46	48	50	52	54

MEN

Size	34	36	38	40	42	44
Chest	34	36	38	40	42	44
Waist	30	32	34	36	38	40

end of row every 7th row until 80(88) sts. Work even until 10th row of E/F stripe. Bind off 6 sts at beg of next 2 rows, keeping striping as on body of sweater. Dec 1 st at each end every other row 12 (15) times. Then dec 1 st each row 6 times. Bind off 3 sts at beg of next 6 rows. Bind off rem sts.

COWL: Sew shoulder seams together. With right sides facing and 2 strands of A, using dp needles, pick up and k 110 (116) sts around neck, picking up sts from holders. Divide sts on 3 needles and mark end of each rnd. Work in ribbing for 3 rows. Drop 1 strand A and join 1 strand B. Work 3 rows, inc 1 st in each p st. Work k 1, p 2 ribbing throughout for 3 rows. Drop A and join 1 strand B, work 3 rows. Drop 1 strand B and join 1 strand C, work 7 rows. Drop B and join 1 strand C, work 3 rows. Drop 1 strand C and join 1 strand D, work 7 rows. Drop C and join 1 strand D, work 3 rows. Drop 1 strand D and join 1 strand E, work 7 rows. Drop D and join 1 strand E, work 5 rows. Drop 1 strand E and join 1 strand F, work 10 rows. Drop E and join 1 strand F, work 8 rows. Drop 1 strand F and join 1 strand G, work 10 rows. Drop F and join 1 strand G, work 8 rows. Drop 1 strand G and join 1 strand A, work 5 rows. Drop G and join 1 strand A, work 2 rows. Bind off loosely in ribbing.

FINISHING: Sew side and sleeve seams. Set in sleeves. Do not block.

ICELANDIC WOOLEN BLANKET CAPE

(page 15)

MATERIALS: Icelandic Fashion Corp. blanket, 60"x80" (see Buyer's Guide); 2-ply yarn (2 oz. balls): 2 balls beige, 1 ball white; metal crochet hook.

DIRECTIONS: Fold one 60" end back 23", pin in place about 5" down from fold. Sew across blanket through both layers 4" and 5" down from folded edge to make casing. Make 7" fringe: Cut white and beige yarn in 15" lengths. Using metal crochet hook, pull 2 strands, one of each color, through blanket ½" in from edge - ½" apart. Braid 9 strands of beige yarn together to make cord 80" long. Pull through casing. Make tassels at both ends.

TURQUOISE NECKLACE

(page 17)

MATERIALS: 12 feet Wright's turquoise tubular cording; Forklorico "El Molino" Embroidery Floss: approximately 15 feet each of green, raspberry, lavender, yellow and light blue; 1 ball (20 grams) Bucilla's Spotlight; needle; button or bead (chosen after you've completed the necklace so you'll know what size will fit best).

DIRECTIONS: (**Note:** Refer to photographs to follow color pattern.) Thread needle with green embroidery floss; tie knot at other end. Sew to end of cord and begin wrapping around cord until 1" of cord is covered (see figure #1). Then begin to leave ¼" space between wraps; every 4 or 5 wraps, fasten floss to cord (see figure #2). Wrap 8" more of cord in this way. Using raspberry, wrap 8 times around cord, covering cord completely; end raspberry. Using silver yarn, wrap 5 times, leaving ¼" space between wraps; change to raspberry, wrap 8 times around cord, covering cord. Change to lt. blue, wrap 6 times;

FIG. 1 BASIC WRAP TECHNIQUE

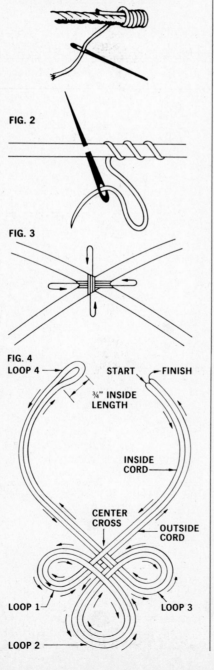

FIG. 2

FIG. 3

FIG. 4
LOOP 4
START   FINISH
¾" INSIDE LENGTH
INSIDE CORD
CENTER CROSS
OUTSIDE CORD
LOOP 1   LOOP 3
LOOP 2

change to yellow, wrap 16 times; change to lt. blue, wrap 6 times. Change to lavender, wrap 8 times. Using green, wrap 10 times around cord, leaving ¼" space between wraps. Change to raspberry, wrap 8 times. Bend cord into a loop (loop #1 in figure #4), running unwrapped cord over wrapped cord at point where yellow floss changes to lt. blue. Using lt. blue, wrap 6 times (see figure #3) to attach two pieces of cord together. Wrap 12 more times. Change to raspberry, wrap 8 times; change to lt. blue, wrap 8 times. Change to lavender, wrap 16 times; change to lt. blue, wrap 8 times. Using silver yarn, wrap 5 times, leaving ¼" space between wraps; change to raspberry, wrap 6 times. Using green, wrap 8 times, leaving ¼" space between wraps; change to raspberry, wrap 6 times. Using silver yarn, wrap 5 times, leaving ¼" space between wraps; change to lt. blue, wrap 8 times. Change to lavender, wrap 8 times. Bend cord to form loop #2 (see figure #4), running unwrapped cord under wrapped cord at point where raspberry thread changes to lavender. Using lt. blue, wrap 6 times (see figure #3) to attach two pieces of cord together. Change to raspberry, wrap 8 times; change to lt. blue, wrap 12 times; change to raspberry, wrap 8 times. Using green, wrap 10 times, leaving ¼" space between wraps; change to lavender, wrap 8 times. Bend cord to form loop #3 (see figure #4), running unwrapped cord under wrapped cord at point where lt. blue changes to raspberry. Using lt. blue, wrap 6 times (see figure #3). Using yellow, wrap 16 times. Attach at center cross (see figure #4) by running unwrapped cord under wrapped cord at point where lt. blue changes to yellow. Using lt. blue, wrap 6 times (see figure #3). Change to raspberry, wrap 8 times; using silver yarn, wrap 5 times, leaving ¼" space between wraps; change to raspberry, wrap 8 times. Using green, wrap approximately 10" of cord, leaving ¼" space between wraps. Bend to form loop #3 (see figure #4) so that the inside length of loop is approximately ¾". Continue to wrap outside cord with green, leaving ¼" spaces; with each wrap, stitch two pieces of cord together by running needle under surface of inside cord. (**Note:** Continue to stitch outside cord to inside cord every ¼" or so for remainder of directions unless otherwise instructed). When you reach point on inside cord where green changes to raspberry, change to lavender, wrap 8 times. Using lt. blue, wrap 5 times, leaving ¼" space between wraps. Change to lavender, wrap 8 times; change to lt. blue, wrap and stitch to inside cord until you reached point on inside cord where lavender changes to green. Change to green and wrap 10 times, leaving space between wraps so that green stripes on outside cord line up with those on inside cord. Using lt. blue, wrap 5 times, stitching to inside cord, then continue to wrap without stitching, running cord underneath where loop #3 meets at center (see figure #4). Continue to wrap and stitch to inside cord (see figure #4). At point on inside cord where lt. blue changes to lavender, change to yellow and wrap 16 times. Using lt. blue, wrap 5 times so lt. blue stripes line up with silver stripes. Change to lavender, wrap 8 times. Using lt. blue, wrap 8 times, leaving ¼" space between wraps. Change to lavender, wrap 8 times. Then using lt. blue, wrap 5 times, leaving ¼" space between wraps. Change to yellow, wrap 16 times. Using lt. blue, wrap outside cord without stitching to inside cord and run it underneath where loop #2 meets center (see figure #4). Begin stitching to inside cord at top of loop #1. At point on inside cord where raspberry changes to green, change to green and wrap 10 times, leaving ¼" space between wraps. Change to lt. blue, wrap outside cord, running it underneath at center cross (see figure #4). Change to lavender, wrap 8 times, stitching to inside cord. Using lt. blue, wrap 5 times, leaving ¼" space between wraps; change to lavender, wrap 8 times. Change to green; wrap, leaving ¼" space between wraps until you are 1" from where you started; cut cord at end. Continue to wrap tightly and stitch securely until you have covered end of cord. Knot and cut thread. Sew on button or bead.

"CHANGE HOLDER" NECKLACE

(page 17)

MATERIALS: Felt fabric, 3"x5"; DMC Art 115 pearl cotton, size 3 (same color as felt), 64" length (see Buyer's Guide, page 136); one ⅜" button; tapestry needle; thread to match felt.

DIRECTIONS: Following directions on page 83, cut out patterns from felt. Stitch ⅛" from all edges on pattern piece #1. Stitch two more rows, each ⅛" apart, along outside edge only. On pattern piece #2, stitch ⅛" from edge around entire piece. Stitch two more

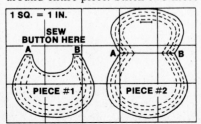

rows, each ⅛" apart. With wrong sides facing, pin, then stitch together, directly on outside row of stitching. Slash buttonhole. Sew on button. Fold length of DMC pearl cotton in half and secure folded half on hook or other stable object. Holding cut ends together, twist in one direction until string is uniformly taut. Fold twisted string in half, securely knotting cut ends and end from hook together. As string folds back on itself, it will form a permanent twist. Adjust twist evenly. Thread folded end of twisted string through tapestry needle. From inside of purse flap, draw string through at point A. From outside of purse flap, draw string through at point B. Remove needle and knot end.

GREEN TASSEL NECKLACE

(page 17)

MATERIALS: DMC Art 115 pearl cotton, size 3, #702 Green: 70 yds.; DMC Art 115 pearl cotton, size 3, #797 Blue: 4 yds. (see Buyer's Guide, page 136); tapestry needle.

DIRECTIONS: Cut 28 lengths, each 90" long, of green pearl cotton. Knot one end. Secure knotted end on hook or other stable object. Holding other ends, twist in one direction until strings are uniformly taut. Fold twisted string in half. Holding all cut ends securely, remove original knot, and knot all ends together. As string folds back on itself, it will form a permanently twisted rope. Adjust twist evenly along rope. **To form tassel:** Cut 20" strand of blue pearl cotton and thread tapestry needle. Fold twisted rope in half. Measuring 15" from this fold, tie one end of blue thread tightly around both thicknesses of green rope. Closely wind single strand around both thicknesses for ½". Insert needle back through wrapped section and trim. Cut off green rope 3" below wrapped section to form tassel. **To make decorative wrapped sections:** On each side of necklace, measure up 3½" from tassel and wrap a 1⅛" section using a 40" strand of blue; 1" above, wrap a ½" section using a 20" blue strand.

SOLID PURPLE AND MULTI-COLORED CHOKERS

(page 17)

MATERIALS: DMC Art 115 pearl cotton, size 3, #552 purple: 60 yds. *For Multi-colored Choker:* 15 yds. each of #321 red, #797 blue, #444 yellow, #702 green (see Buyer's Guide, page 136). One 1" brass S-hook for each choker; tapestry needle; pliers.

DIRECTIONS: Cut 27 lengths, each

80" long, of DMC pearl cotton. Knot one end. Secure knotted end on hook or other stable object. Holding other ends, twist in one direction until strings are uniformly taut. Fold twisted string in half. Holding all cut ends securely, remove original knot and knot all ends together. As string folds back on itself, it will form a permanently twisted rope. Adjust twist evenly along rope. To make center knots: Knot rope 5" from folded end. Make second knot 2" from first knot and third knot 2" from second knot. To attach hook: With pliers, spread open both ends of S-hook ¼". Make a slip knot 5" from last knot. Insert one open end of S-hook into loop of slip knot before pulling knot tight. Close end of S-hook that is in knot. Cut a 40" single strand of pearl cotton and thread through tapestry needle. Holding excess rope from slip knot against necklace, tie one end of threaded strand tightly around both thicknesses, firmly up against slip knot. Closely wind single strand around both thicknesses for ½". Insert needle back through wrapped section and pull out through knot. Cut strand. Trim away remaining rope ends where they emerge from wound section.

STUFFED HEART NECKLACE

(page 17)

MATERIALS: Piece of fabric, 4"x8"; strip of felt, 12"x1"; straight pins; DMC Art 115 pearl cotton, size 3, 64" length (see Buyer's Guide); stuffing (nylon stocking, cotton balls, polyester fiberfill, etc.); tapestry needle.

DIRECTIONS: Enlarge and cut out heart pattern, following directions on page 83. Cut out 2 hearts from fabric. Press felt strip in half lengthwise. Beginning at point A, pin felt strip to right side of one heart section, matching raw edges of felt along outer edge of heart. Cut off excess length of felt strip at point A. Stitch on seam line. Pin second heart piece to first heart piece, right sides together. Stitch through all thicknesses, leaving a 1" opening along one side of heart. Clip seam allowance. Turn heart right side

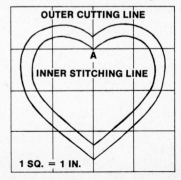

out. Fold length of DMC pearl cotton in half and secure folded end on hook or other stable object. Holding cut ends together, twist in one direction until string is uniformly taut. Fold twisted string in half, securely knotting cut ends and end from hook together. As string folds back on itself, it will form a permanent twist. Adjust twist evenly. Thread folded end of twisted string through tapestry needle. At point A, draw string through heart from inside to outside and return to inside ⅛" away. Knot end. Stuff heart. Slipstitch opening closed.

STUFFED BUTTERFLY PENDANT

(page 17)

The size and shape of this necklace were determined by the printed motif taken from a scrap of fabric. In this case we used a butterfly which formed a rectangular shape. Other possibilities might include flowers, small animals, fruit or geometric design. (We suggest that no dimension exceed 3" or 4".)

MATERIALS: Piece of fabric (not to exceed 3" or 4"); piece of solid color fabric for backing (same size as motif fabric); strip of felt, 1" wide and as long as outer edge of motif fabric; DMC Art 115 pearl cotton size 3, 64" length (see Buyer's Guide, page 136); straight pins; stuffing (nylon stocking, cotton balls, polyester fiberfill, etc.); tapestry needle.

DIRECTIONS: Press felt strip in half lengthwise. Pin felt strip to right side of motif fabric, matching raw edges of felt along entire outer edge of motif. Cut off any excess felt. Stitch felt to motif, allowing ⅛" seam allowance. Pin backing fabric to motif, right sides together. Stitch through all thicknesses, leaving a 1" opening along one side of motif. Clip seam allowance; turn right side out. Fold length of DMC pearl cotton in half and secure folded end on hook or other stable object. Holding cut ends together, twist in one direction until string is uniformly taut. Fold twisted string in half, securely knotting cut ends and end from hook together. As string folds back on itself, it will form a permanent twist. Adjust twist evenly. Thread folded end of twisted string through tapestry needle. At appropriate point, draw string through motif from inside to outside and return to inside ⅛" away. Knot end. Stuff motif. Slipstitch opening closed.

FAIR ISLE SWEATER AND HAT

(page 19)

Instructions are for Size 6-8. Changes for Sizes 10-12 and 14-16 are in paren-

theses.

MATERIALS: Bucilla Spice (1¾ oz. balls): *For Sweater:* 10 (12,14) balls of Winter White (A), 1 of Brown (B), 1 of Turquoise (C), 1 of Rust (D). *For Hat:* 2 balls of (A), 1 of (B), 1 of (C), 1 of (D). Circular needle, Size 10; double-pointed needles, 1 set Size 8, OR ANY SIZE NEEDLES WHICH WILL OBTAIN THE STITCH GAUGE BELOW; tapestry needle.

GAUGE: 3 sts = 1"; 9 rows = 2 ".

FINISHED MEASUREMENTS: Bustline: 32(36,40)".
Back at underarm: 17(18½,20)".
Sleeve at underarm: 15(16,17)".

DIRECTIONS—SWEATER: (Note: Work back and forth on circular needle to yoke.)

BACK: With Size 10 needle and A, cast on 48(52,56) sts. **Row 1—wrong side:** * K 1, p 1; rpt from * across. **Row 2:** * K 1, p 1; rpt from * across. Rpt these 2 rows until 2¼ ins. from beg. Work st st - k 1 row, p 1 row until 17 ins. from beg, or desired length to underarm.

Armhole Shaping: Bind off 3 sts at beg of next 2 rows; 42(46, 50) sts. Sl sts to holder for yoke. Break yarn.

FRONT: Work as for Back.

SLEEVES: With Size 10 needle and A, cast on 30(32,34) sts. Work ribbing as for Back until 3 ins from beg. Work st st, inc 6 sts evenly spaced across first row; 36(38,40) sts. Work 3 rows even. Inc 1 st each side of next row. Rpt inc every 8th row 3 more times; 44(46,48) sts. Work even until 17½ ins from beg, or desired length to underarm; end on wrong side.

Cap Shaping: Bind off 3 sts at beg of next 2 rows; 38(40,42) sts. Sl rem sts to holder for yoke. Break yarn. Work other sleeve in same way.

YOKE: From right side, with A, k across 42(46,50) sts of back, 38(40,42) sts of one sleeve, 42(46,50) sts of front, 38(40,42) sts of other sleeve; 160 (172,184) sts. Join. K around for 3 rnds, inc 2 sts evenly spaced on 2nd rnd; 162(174,186) sts. Mark end of rnd. Work pat.

Pat—Rnd 1: K * 1 B, 5 A; rpt from *, end 1 B, 5 A. **Rnd 2:** K 2 B, * 3

A, 3 B; rpt from *, end 1 B. **Rnd 3:** K 3 B, * 1 A, 5 B; rpt from *, end 1 A, 2 B. **Rnd 4:** K * 1 C, 5 A; rpt from *, end 5 A. **Rnd 5:** K 2 C, * 3 B, 3 C; rpt from *, end 1 C. **Rnd 6:** K 3 C, * 1 B, 5 C; rpt from *, end 2 C. **Rnd 7:** K * 1 A, 5 C; rpt from *, end 5 C. **Rnd 8:** K 2 A, * 3 C, 3 A; rpt from *, end 1 A. **Rnd 9:** K 3 A, * 1 C, 5 A; rpt from *, end 2 A. **Rnd 10:** With A only, k. **Rnds 11, 12, 13 and 14:** K 2 D, * 3 A, 3 D; rpt from *, end 1 D. **Rnd 15: Dec Rnd** - With A only, k around, dec 18 sts evenly spaced; 144(156,168) sts. **Rnd 16:** K 3 A, * 1 C, 5 A; rpt from *, end 2 A. **Rnd 17:** K 2 A, * 3 C, 3 A; rpt from *, end 1 A. **Rnd 18:** K 1 A, * 5 C, 1 A; rpt from *, end 5 C. **Rnd 19:** K 3 C, * 1 B, 5 C; rpt from *, end 2 C. **Rnd 20:** K 2 C, * 3 B, 3 C; rpt from *, end 1 C. **Rnd 21:** K * 1 C, 5 B; rpt from *, end 5 B. **Rnd 22:** K 3 B, * 1 A, 5 B; rpt from *, end 2 B. **Rnd 23:** K 2 B, * 3 A, 3 B; rpt from *, end 1 B. **Rnd 24:** K * 1 B, 5 A; rpt from *, end 5 A. **Rnd 25: Dec Rnd** - With A only, k around, dec 48 sts evenly spaced; 96(108,120) sts. **Rnd 26:** K 2 A, * 3 D, 3 A; rpt from *, end 1 A. **Rnd 27:** K 1 A, * 3 D, 3 A; rpt from *, end 2 A. **Rnd 28:** K * 3 D, 3 A; rpt from *, end 3 A. **Rnds 29, 30, 31 and 32:** With A only, k around. **Rnd 33:** With A only, k around, dec 24(36,48) sts evenly spaced; 72 sts. Work even for 3(4,5) rows. With dp needles and A, work around in k 1, p 1 ribbing for 16 rows. Bind off loosely in ribbing.

FINISHING: Sew seams. Turn neck ribbing in half to wrong side and sew loosely in place. Block.

HAT: (Note: Work back and forth on circular needle.) With Size 10 needle and A, cast on 61 sts. **Row 1—wrong side:** P 1, * k 1, p 1; rpt from * across. **Row 2:** K 1, * p 1, k 1; rpt from * across. Rpt Rows 1 and 2 until 3" from beg, end on right side. P 1 row. Beg pat. Following chart, work k rows from right to left and P rows from left to right, end with Row 31. With A, p 1 row. **1st Dec Row:** K 1, * k 2 tog, k 1; rpt from * across; 41 sts. Rpt first

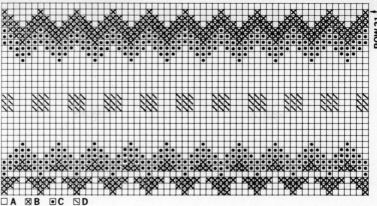

ROW 31

□ A ⊠ B ⊡ C ◩ D

Rpt first dec row, every 2nd row, twice more; 19 sts. P 1 row. **2nd Dec Row:** K 1, * k 2 tog, rpt from * across; 10 sts. Break yarn, leaving an 18″ end for sewing. Thread into tapestry needle and draw through sts on needle, draw up tightly and fasten; with same strand, sew back seam. Fold ribbing in half to wrong side and sew loosely.

LAVENDER SWEATER

(page 20)

Directions are given for size Small (8-10). Changes for sizes Medium (12-14) and Large (16-18) are in parentheses.
MATERIALS: Belding/Lily's Sugar & Cream Yarn (100 yd. skeins): 7(8,10) skeins of Lavender; crochet hook, Size J OR ANY SIZE HOOK WHICH WILL OBTAIN THE STITCH GAUGE BELOW.
GAUGE: 10 dc = 3″; 2 rnds = 1″.
MEASUREMENTS:

Sizes:	Small (8-10)	Medium (12-14)	Large (16-18)
Bust:	33″	36″	40″
Width across back or front at underarm:	16½″	18″	20″
Width across sleeve at upper arm:	11½″	12½″	13¼″

DIRECTIONS—YOKE: Starting at neck edge (excluding edging), ch 104(108,108). Being careful not to twist chain, join with sl st to first ch to form a circle.
Foundation Rnd: Ch 1, sc in same st as joining, sc in each ch around. Join with sl st to first sc. Ch 3, turn. Always count ch-3 as 1 dc. **Rnd 1 (wrong side):** Sk joining, dc in each of next 25(27,27) sc—**back**; ch 1 for raglan seam, dc in each of next 26 sc—**sleeve**; ch 1, dc in next 26(28,28) sc—**front**; ch 1, dc in next 26 sc—**sleeve**; ch 1. Join to top of ch 3—4 raglan ch-1 sps. Ch 3, turn. **Rnd 2:** In next ch-1 sp make dc, ch 1 and dc; * dc in each dc to next ch-1 sp, in ch-1 sp make dc, ch 1 and dc; rpt from * 2 more times; dc in each rem dc. Join with sl st to top of ch-3 —inc made at each side of each section (8 incs in all); there are now 28(30,30) dc on back and front and 28 dc on each sleeve. Ch 3, turn. **Rnd 3:** Sk joining, * dc in each dc to within next ch-1 sp, in ch-1 sp make dc, ch 1 and dc; rpt from * 3 more times; dc in next dc. Join to top of ch-3. Ch 3, turn. **Rnd 4:** Sk joining, * dc in each st to next ch-1 sp, in ch-1 sp make dc, ch 1 and dc; rpt from * 3 more times; dc in each rem st. Join as before —32(34,34) dc on back and front; 32 dc on each sleeve. Ch 3, turn. Rpt last Rnd (Rnd 4), 2(4,5) more times—36(42,44) dc on back and front, 36(40,42) dc on each sleeve. At end

of last rnd, ch 1, turn. **First Popcorn Rnd:** Sc in same st as joining, * tr in next dc, pushing tr just made to right side of work to form popcorn, sc in next dc; * placing one st in each dc, continue to work 1 tr and 1 sc across to next ch-1 sp; ch 1, sk next sp; rpt from * around, ending with tr in last dc. Join to first sc. Ch 3, turn. **Next Rnd:** Work same as Rnd 4. Ch 3, turn. **Next Rnd:** Sk joining, * dc in each st to next ch-1 sp, 2 dc in next sp, ch 1, dc in each dc across sleeve, ch 1, 2 dc in next sp; rpt from * once more; dc in each rem dc. Join to top of ch-3 —2 dc increased at each side of back and front only. Ch 3, turn. Rpt last rnd 3 more times—54(60,62) dc on back and front; 38(42,44) dc on each sleeve. There are 5 rnds from popcorn rnd. **Second Popcorn Rnd:** Rpt First Popcorn Rnd. Ch 3, turn. **For Size 16-18 Only:** Work a dc rnd, increasing 2 sts at each side of back and front only—54(60,66) dc on back, front.
For All Sizes: Cut yarn, fasten. Turn. **To Divide Sections—Body—Rnd 1:** Attach yarn in ch-1 sp preceding back sts, ch 2, dc in each dc across back, *holding back on hook last loop of each dc, make dc in next sp, sk sleeve sts, dc in next sp, yarn over hook, draw through all 3 loops on hook—2-joint dc made at underarm;* dc in each dc across front, work a 2-joint dc at underarm as before, sk ch-2. Join with sl st to top of first dc—110(122,134) sts. Ch 3, turn. **Rnd 2:** Sk joining, dc in each st around. Join with sl st to top of ch-3. Ch 3, turn. Rpt last rnd 2(2,1) more times. Ch 3, turn. There are 4 dc rnds from last popcorn rnd. **Next Rnd:** Sk joining, *holding back on hook last loop of each dc, make dc in each of next 2 sts, yarn over hook draw through all 3 loops on hook—dec made at side edge;* dc in each of next 53(59,65) dc, dec over next 2 sts, dc in each rem st. Join to top of ch-3. Ch 1, turn. **Third Popcorn Rnd:** Sc in same st as joining, * tr in next st, sc in next st; rpt from * around, ending with tr in last st. Join to first sc. Ch 3, turn. **Next 5 Rnds:** Working same as Rnd 2 of Body, make a dec directly above each of the 2 previous decs in every other rnd twice; then work 1 rnd even—104(116,128) sts. **Fourth Popcorn Rnd:** Rpt Third Popcorn Rnd. **Next 4 Rnds:** Working as Rnd 2, inc 1 dc at each side edge every other row 2 times (to inc, make 2 dc in same st). Now, rpt Rnd 2 until length from underarm is approximately 9(10,10)″, ending with a wrong-side row. At end of last rnd, ch 1, turn.
Edging—Rnd 1: Sc in joining, sc in each st around. Join to first sc. Ch 1, turn. **Rnds 2 and 3:** Rpt last rnd. **Rnd 4:** Work same as Third Popcorn Rnd. Ch 1, turn. **Rnd 5:** Sl st in same st as joining, * ch 3, sc in 3 ch from

hook for picot, sk next st, sl st in each of next 3 sts; rpt from * around. Join. Cut yarn and fasten.
SLEEVES—Rnd 1: With wrong side of last rnd on sleeve facing, attach yarn to top of 2-joint dc at underarm, ch 1, sc in same st, dc in each dc around sleeve. Join with sl st to first sc. Ch 2, turn. **Rnd 2:** Sk joining, dc in each dc around, sk ch-2 at beg of rnd. Join to top of next dc—38(42,44) sts. Ch 3, turn. **Rnd 3:** Sk joining, dc in each st around. Join with sl st to top of ch-3. Rpt last rnd 2(2,1) more times. Ch 1, turn. **Next 5 Rnds:** Work a popcorn rnd same as Third Popcorn rnd of Body; ch 3, turn, then work 4 rnds same as Rnd 3 of Sleeve. Ch 1, turn. Rpt last 5 rnds 2 more times. Work 1(3,4) more rnds same as Rnd 3 of Sleeve, end with wrong-side row. **Edging:** Work same as Edging for Body. Work other sleeve in same way.
Neck Edging: With wrong side facing, attach yarn in first ch of starting chain at neck edge. **Rnd 1:** Working along opposite side of starting chain, sc in same st where yarn was attached, sc in each ch around. Join to first sc. Ch 1, turn. **Rnd 2:** Sc in same sc as joining, sc in each sc around. Join. Ch 1, turn. **Rnds 3 and 4:** Work same as Rnd 4 and 5 of Body Edging. Cut yarn and fasten.
FINISHING: Pin sweater to measurements on a padded surface; cover with a damp cloth and steam very lightly. Remove when completely dry.

LIGHT GOLD SWEATER

(page 21)

Directions are given for size Small (8-10). Changes for sizes Medium (12-14) and Large (16-18) are in parentheses.
MATERIALS: Belding/Lily's Sugar & Cream Yarn (in 100 yd. skeins): 7(8,9) skeins of Lt. Gold; crochet hook, Size J OR ANY SIZE HOOK WHICH WILL OBTAIN THE STITCH GAUGE BELOW.
GAUGE: 10 dc = 3″; 2 dc rows = 1″.
MEASUREMENTS:

Sizes:	Small (8-10)	Medium (12-14)	Large (16-18)
Bust:	33″	36″	40″
Width across back or front at underarms:	16½″	18″	20″
Width across sleeve at upper arm:	11½″	12½″	14″

DIRECTIONS—YOKE: Starting at neck edge (excluding neck border), ch 88(90,90).
Row 1 (right side): Dc in 4th ch from hook, dc in each of next 5 ch—**left front**; ch 1 for raglan seam, dc in each of next 24 ch—**sleeve**; ch 1, dc in each of next 24(26,26) ch—**back**; ch 1, dc

in each of next 24 ch—**sleeve**; ch 1, dc in each of rem 7 ch—**right front**—4 raglan ch-1 sps. Ch 3, turn. Always count ch-3 as 1 dc. **Row 2:** Sk first dc, * dc in each dc to next ch-1 sp, in next ch-1 sp make dc, ch 1 and dc; rpt from * 3 more times; dc in each rem dc, dc in top of ch-3—1 dc inc made at each side of back and sleeves and 1 dc inc at raglan edge of each front. Rpt last row 6(8,10) more times—14(16,18) sts on each front, 38(42,46) sts on each sleeve and 38(44,48) sts on back. Ch 3, turn. **Next Row:** Sk first dc, * dc in each dc to next ch-1 sp, 2 dc in next ch-1 sp, ch 1, dc in each dc across sleeve, ch 1, 2 dc in next sp; rpt from * once more; dc in each rem dc, dc in top of ch-3—2 dc increased at each side of back and at raglan seam edge of each front; no incs made on sleeves. Ch 3, turn. Rpt last row 3(3,4) more times—22(24,28) sts on each front; 38(42,46) sts on each sleeve and 54(60,68) dc on back. At end of last row, ch 8(10,8) for base of front neck opening. Join with sl st to top of ch-3 at beg of row, being careful not to twist chain. Cut yarn and fasten. Turn. *Hereafter work in rnds.*

To Divide Sections—Body—Rnd 1: Attach yarn in ch-1 sp preceding back sts, ch 2, dc in each dc across back, *holding back on hook last loop of each dc, dc in next ch-1 sp, sk sleeve sts, dc in next ch-1 sp, yarn over hook, draw through all 3 loops on hook—**2-joint dc made at underarm;** dc in each dc across front sts, including ch sts at center front, make 2-joint dc at underarm as before, sk ch-2. Join with sl st to top of first dc—108(120,134) sts. Ch 3, turn **Rnd 2:** Sk joining, dc in each dc around. Join to top of ch-3. Ch 3, turn **Rnds 3 and 4:** Rpt Rnd 2. Ch 3, turn. **Rnd 5:** Sk joining, *holding back on hook last loop of each dc, make dc in each of next 2 dc, yarn over hook, draw through all 3 loops on hook—**dec made at side edge;** dc in each of next 52(58,65) dc, dec over next 2 dc, dc in each rem dc. Join to top of ch-3—dec made at each side. Ch 3, turn. **Rnd 6:** Sk joining, dc in each st around. Join to top of ch-3. Ch 3, turn. **Rnd 7:** Work same as last rnd, but dec one st above each of 2 previous decs. Ch 3, turn. **Rnds 8 and 9:** Rpt Rnds 6 and 7—102(114,128) sts. Ch 3, turn. Rpt Rnd 6 only 4(5,6) times. Cut yarn and fasten. Turn. **Side Slits—First Panel—Row 1:** Sk first 6 sts on last rnd, attach yarn to next dc, ch 3, dc in same st, dc in each of next 38(44,50) dc, 2 dc in next dc; do not work over rem sts—42(48,54) sts. Ch 3, turn. **Row 2:** Dc in first dc, dc in each dc across, 2 dc in top of ch-3. Ch 3, turn. **Row 3:** Rpt last row. Ch 3, turn. **Row 4:** Sk first dc, dc in each dc across, dc in top of ch-3. Cut yarn

and fasten. Turn. **Second Panel—Row 1:** Sk next free 11(11,12) sts on last rnd of body, attach yarn to next dc and continue to work same as Row 1 of First Panel. Ch 3, turn. Rpt Rows 2,3 and 4 of First Panel.

SLEEVES—Rnd 1: With wrong side of last rnd on sleeve facing, attach yarn in top of 2-joint dc at underarm, ch 1, sc in same st, dc in each dc around sleeve. Join with sl st to first sc. Ch 2, turn. **Rnd 2:** Sk joining, dc in each dc around, sk ch-2. Join with sl st to top of first dc—38(42,46) sts. Ch 3, turn. **Rnd 3:** Sk joining, dc in each dc around. Join to top of ch-3. Ch 3, turn. **Rnd 4:** Rpt last rnd. Ch 3, turn. **Rnd 5:** Sk joining, dec over next 2 dc, dc in each dc around to within last 2 dc, dec over last 2 dc. Join to top of ch-3. Ch 3, turn. Rpt last 3 rnds (Rnds 3,4 and 5) 2(3,4) more times—32(34,36) sts. Ch 3, turn. Rpt Rnd 3 only until length from underarm is 11(12,12)″, ending with a wrong-side row. Ch 1, turn.

Sleeve Border—Rnd 1: Sc in same st as joining, * tr in next st, pushing tr just made to right side, sc in next st; rpt from * around, ending with tr in last st. Join to first sc. Ch 3, turn. **Rnd 2:** Sk joining, * holding back on hook last loop of each dc, make 5 dc in next tr, yarn over hook, draw through 5 loops on hook, yarn over, draw through rem 2 loops on hook—**cluster made;** ch 1, sk next sc; rpt from * around, ending with ch 1, sk ch-3. Join with sl st in top of first cluster. Ch 1, turn. **Rnd 3:** Sc in same st as joining, * ch 3, sl st in top of last sc made for picot, sc in next sp, sc in next cluster, sc in next sp, ch 3, complete picot, sc in next cluster, in next sp and in next cluster; rpt from * around, ending last rpt with sc in last sp. Join to first sc. Cut yarn and fasten. Work other sleeve in same way.

Bottom Border—1st Row: With wrong side facing, attach yarn at side edge of first row on first panel, working along ends of rows, work 2 sc over end of each of 4 rows, make 5 sc in corner st, sc in each st across last row to next corner, 5 sc in corner st, 2 sc over end of each of 4 rows. Ch 1, turn. **Row 2:** Sc in first sc, * tr in next sc, sc in next sc; rpt from * across last row, ending with sc in last 1(or 2) sc; sk next free dc on last rnd of body, sl st in each of next 3 dc on body. Ch 1, turn. **Rnd 3:** Sk 1(or 2) sc, * make cluster in next tr, ch 1, sk next sc; rpt from * across last row, ending with ch 1, sk next 4 free dc on last rnd of body, sl st in next dc. Ch 1, turn. **Rnd 4:** Sc in first cluster, starting from *, work same as Rnd 3 of Sleeve Border across, ending with sc in last cluster, sl st in next dc on last rnd of body. Cut yarn and fasten. Work border on second panel in same way.

Neck Border—Rnd 1: With wrong side facing, attach yarn to first ch at base of front neck opening, work 5(7,7) sc evenly spaced across chain, continue to sc evenly along front opening and neck edges, making 3 sc in same st at each outer corner, and having an even number of sts. Join to first sc. Ch 1, turn. **Rnd 2:** Work same as Rnd 1 of Sleeve Border. Ch 3, turn. **Rnd 3:** Sk next 1(2,2) st, make cluster in next st, sk 1(2,2) st, dc in next st, ch 1; skipping all sc, make cluster and ch 1 in each tr around. Join to top of ch-3. **Rnd 4:** Sk joining, sc in next sp, sc in cluster; rpt from * on Rnd 3 of Sleeve Border around, ending with sc in sp before dc, sk dc, sc in last cluster. Join to first sc. Cut yarn and fasten.

FINISHING: Pin sweater to measurements on a padded surface; cover with a damp cloth and steam lightly with a warm iron. Remove when completely dry.

AMERICAN INDIAN IRIS MOTIF BELT AND NECKPIECE

(pages 25-26)

Directions are given for Belt to measure approximately 3″x34″ and Neckpiece to measure approximately 4½″x5″.

MATERIALS: Columbia-Minerva Crewel Yarn (see chart, page 94, for colors and yardage); heavy cardboard; scissors; masking tape; needle; small hole puncher or manicure scissors.

For Belt: 10 mesh mono-interlocking canvas, 6″x36″; black felt, cut 1¼″ larger in both directions than finished needlepoint for ⅝″ seam allowances.

For Neckpiece: 10 mesh mono-interlocking canvas, 7¼″x8″; white felt, cut 1¼″ larger in both directions than finished needlepoint for ⅝″ seam allowances; 1 piece red silk cording, 36″ long.

(**Note:** The following directions indicate sufficient yardage to complete the items using the continental stitch [see page 100 for diagram and instructions]. If other stitches are used, you may not have enough yarn to complete the items. As you work, refer to the color photograph on pages 34-35, as well as the directions that follow.)

GENERAL DIRECTIONS—Color Pattern Chart: For many designs, the easiest and most accurate method of working is to follow a Color Pattern Chart. Keep in mind that each square on the Chart represents one stitch on the canvas. The method of counting stitches is your guarantee of a perfect copy of the design. Both designs are worked in the Continental Stitch throughout. The Color Pattern Chart shows yarn colors used in each part of the design. Each square on the Chart equals one stitch on your canvas. Colors are indicated by symbols.

Transferring the Design: Following directions on page 83, enlarge the pattern onto white paper. (The belt pattern is only half the design. "Flop" the pattern to obtain complete design.) Tape the pattern to a window with strong light shining through. Center the canvas over the pattern; tape in place. With waterproof marking pen, trace the pattern onto the canvas. Remove pattern and canvas from window. Bind canvas edges with masking tape to prevent raveling.

Sorting the Yarn: Refer to the Color Pattern Chart for the number of yards of each color. For easier selection of colors while working, cut a series of 1½″ slits across an edge of heavy cardboard for each yarn color. Draw color symbol above each slit and thread the corresponding color yarn through. This method will allow you to choose the correct color yarn as you stitch. **Cutting the Yarn:** Cut lengths to about 18″, as longer pieces may fray. **Threading Needle:** Wrap yarn once around shaft of needle. Pinch yarn tightly and withdraw needle. Squeezing folded yarn flat between finger and thumb, press eye of needle down over yarn. Now pull yarn through eye. (**Note:** The yarn is a loosely twisted 3-ply yarn. Separate and work 2-ply throughout. Use a single strand of gold thread when working design.) **Working the Yarn:** No knots are used in needlepoint. To start the first strand, hold short end of yarn at back and work over this yarn "float" for several stitches. To end or begin new strands, weave yarn into wrong side of stitches previously worked. If yarn becomes twisted while working, drop needle and allow to resume natural twist. Work with light, even tension so stitches lay evenly and cover canvas well.

DIRECTIONS—BELT: The chart for the belt is half the design. After stitching the motifs on one half the belt, turn the chart upside down to work the second half of the pattern.

Working Motifs: Begin the first motif 2″ from the top and 3″ from the upper right corner of the canvas as indicated by the letter "A" on the Chart, using black yarn. Carefully count the stitches on the chart to work the motif. Continue in a similar manner to work all five motifs.

Hole Punching: Use hole puncher or manicure scissors to make each of the six holes for the belt ties as follows: Center holes—⅞″ from the center green bar of the first and last motifs on each end, indicated by the letter "C". Top and bottom holes—position top hole one inch above center

hole and bottom hole one inch below center hole, indicated by letters "B" and "D".

Working Background: Work background in Gray yarn. Be sure there are the same number of stitches of Gray on the extreme left and right sides of the belt.

Border: Work border in Forest Green, three rows on each of the four sides of the belt.

NECKPIECE: The chart for the neckpiece is completed as is.

Center Column: Find center row of the canvas. Working with Gold thread, stitch 3 stitches across, 1¼″ from the top of the canvas. Continue center Gold column as indicated on Chart for 34 rows.

Design: Work design on each side of center column, leaving White for last. Work inner border in Gold.

Top: Directly above Gold column, work the Navy yarn and then work outward on each side to finish top of design. Continue working center border in White.

Bottom: Work three rows again in Gold at center bottom. Work colored yarn outward to edges.

Sides and Top: Embroider last rows

BELT

	COLOR NAME	NO. OF YARDS	REFERENCE NUMBER
▲	RED-ORANGE	13	R-50
⊞	MUSTARD	5	427
⊠	FOREST GREEN	44	528
⊙	TURQUOISE	8	738
▣	BLACK	13	050
☐	GRAY	56	186

NECKPIECE

	COLOR NAME	NO. OF YARDS	REFERENCE NUMBER
▲	RED	4	R10
△	ORANGE	4	424
◲	YELLOW	4	450
▦	NAVY	4	365
⊡	BLUE	4	752
☐	WHITE	8	005
⊠	GOLD THREAD	14	GOLD CAMELOT

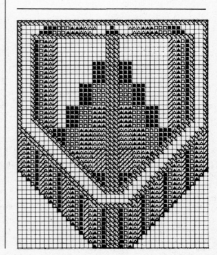

of Gold above stripes, on the sides and on the top to complete the neckpiece.

BLOCKING—Belt and Neckpiece: A needlepoint canvas may become distorted while working. Blocking will return it to its original shape. Measure length and width of canvas. On a blocking board, draw a rectangle using these measurements, making sure corners are true right angles. Mark center of each side of rectangle and mark center of each side of canvas. Moisten a turkish towel with cold water (towel should be damp, not dripping). Roll needlepoint in towel and leave overnight. Place canvas on board, matching center marks. Using rust-proof tacks, tack center points. Place tacks about 1″ away from stitching. Working out from centers, tack canvas every inch. Pull piece into shape as you work, matching edge of canvas to lines of rectangle. Leave on board until thoroughly dry. If removed while damp, canvas will revert to its original shape.

FINISHING—Belt: Pin needlepoint and fabric together with right sides facing. Baste and then machine stitch around three sides. Turn right side out, then slipstitch closed. Be sure sides are securely sewn. Stitch edges of holes to felt using green sewing thread and tiny stitches. Then thread a 3-ply, yard length of Forest Green yarn through each hole. Bring yarn through only half way, make all ends the same length. Gather all strands together and make a knot close to the belt. Make an additional knot at the ends of each pair of 3-ply lengths of yarn. Trim excess, if any.

Neckpiece: Pin needlepoint and fabric back together with right sides facing. Baste and then machine stitch around sides and bottom. Turn right side out, then slipstitch closed. Be sure sides are securely sewn. Tie a knot at one end of the red cording. Stitch the knot to the side at the top corner, using red sewing thread and tiny stitches to attach the cording. Measure desired length and make a second knot, trim any excess, and attach to second side in a similar manner.

(**Note:** Dry clean only.)

INDIAN JEWELED T-SHIRTS

(page 27)

MATERIALS: T-shirts with round necks; decorative neckline appliqués in a neutral color (Wright's); glass bugle beads and caviar beads for the top shirt; flat pressed powder turquoise beads and navy beads and navy bugle beads for the bottom shirt (Sheru bead); embroidery floss to attach beads (see Buyer's Guide, page 136).

DIRECTIONS: Appliqués should be embroidered to emphasize their shape and pattern.

SUN APPLIQUÉS: We used bugle beads to accent the saw-tooth edge and outer spokes of the sun circle. Massed bugle and caviar beads are worked at top with DMC embroidery floss. Buttonhole Stitches and beads outline center; eight rows of Chain Stitch are worked over the spokes beyond it.

SQUASH FLOWER APPLIQUÉ: Cover each circular motif with a round bead; bugle beads and Bucilla's "Glossilla" embroidery thread accent remaining areas.

To attach to shirt: Pin around neckline; slipstitch with matching thread.

INDIAN VEST

(page 27)

Directions are given for size Small (8-10). Changes for sizes Medium (12-14) and Large (16-18) are in parentheses.

MATERIALS: Bernat Sesame "4" (4 oz. balls): 2 oz. each of #7533N Scarlet (A), #7504N Goldenrod (B), #7563N Lopino Blue (C), #7540N Oyster White (D), #7539N Gothic Red (E), #7553N Orange (F), #7556N Sunset (G), #7589N Kelly Green (H) for each size; crochet hook, Size I OR ANY SIZE CROCHET HOOK WHICH WILL OBTAIN THE STITCH GAUGE BELOW.

GAUGE: 3 dc = 1″; 2 dc rows = 1″.

MEASUREMENTS:

Sizes:	Small (8-10)	Medium (12-14)	Large (16-18)
Bust:	34″	37″	40″
Width across back at underarms:	17″	18″	20″
Width across each front at underarm (excluding edging)	8½″	9½″	10″

DIRECTIONS—BODY: Starting at entire lower edge with A, ch 105(113,121) to measure 35(38,41)″. **Row 1 (wrong side):** Dc in 4th ch from hook, dc in each ch across—103(111,119) dc, counting chain at beg of row as 1 dc. Ch 3, turn. **Row 2:** Sk first dc, dc in each dc across, dc in top of end chain. Cut A; attach B, with B ch 1, turn. **Row 3:** With B, sc in each dc across, sc in top of ch-3. Cut B; attach A; with A, ch 3, turn. **Row 4:** With A, sk first sc, dc in each sc across—103(111,119) dc, counting ch-3 as 1 dc. Ch 3, turn. Always count ch-3 as first dc of following row. **Row 5:** Rpt Row 2. Cut A; attach C and ch 3, turn. **Row 6:** Place a strand of D along top edge of last row, with C, working over D, sk first dc, dc in next dc; * holding back on hook last loop of dc, dc in next dc, drop C; pick up D and draw a loop through the 2 loops

on hook—**color change made;** *with D, working over C and holding back on hook last loop of dc, make dc in next dc, drop D, pick up C and draw a loop through the 2 loops on hook—another color change made;* with C, working over D, dc in each of next 2 dc; rpt from * across, ending with C dc in each of last 2 dc, dc in top of ch-3. Cut both colors; attach E and ch 3, turn. (**Note:** When 2 or more colors are needed in same row, carry color, or colors, not in use inside sts. Always change color in last dc of each color group. Cut and attach colors as needed.) **Row 7:** With E, work 1 dc row (same as Row 2). **Rows 8 through 11:** Continuing to work in dc's rows, work colors as follows: 1 row F, 1 row G, 1 row B, 1 row H. **Row 12:** With D, work 1 sc row. Drop D (do not cut); attach E and ch 3, turn. **Row 13:** With E, working over D, sk first st, dc in each of next 2 sts, changing to D in last dc, * with D make 1 dc in next st, changing to E, with E, dc in each of next 3 sts, changing to D; rpt from * across, ending with E, dc in each of last 3 sts. Cut both colors; attach C, ch 3, turn. **Row 14:** With C, work 1 dc row. Change to D, ch 3, turn. **Row 15:** With D, working in dc's, inc 1 dc at center of row (to inc, work 2 dc in same st)—104(112,120) dc. **Rows 16 through 22:** Following Chart For Pattern Motif, between lines indicating Size being made; rpt each row on Chart from right to left 4 times in all and continue in same manner until all 7 rows on Chart have been completed. **Row 23:** With D only, work 1 dc row.

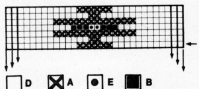

□ D ☒ A ⦿ E ■ B

To Divide Fronts and Back: At end of last row, attach C, ch 3, turn.

RIGHT FRONT—Row 1: Sk first dc, dc in each of next 25(27,29) dc; drop loop from hook; attach a separate strand of C in same st as last dc made; ch 5(7,9) for sleeve; cut this strand and fasten, pick up dropped loop and dc in each of next 5(7,9) ch—31(35,39) dc; do not work over rem sts. Change to E, ch 3, turn. **Row 2:** Rpt Row 13 of Body. **Row 3:** With D, work 1 sc row. **Row 4:** With H, work 1 dc row. Cut yarn and fasten. Turn.

Neck Shaping—Row 5: From front edge, sk first 9(10,11) sts, attach B to next st, ch 3, dc in each st across—22(25,28) sts. Change to G, ch 3, turn. **Row 6:** With G, sk first st, dc in each dc to within last 2 dc and ch-3, *holding back on hook last loop of each dc, make dc in each of next 2 dc, yarn over hook,* *draw through all 3 loops on hook—dec made at neck edge;* dc in top of ch-3. Change to F, ch 3, turn. **Row 7:** Sk first dc, dec over next 2 sts, dc in each rem st—20(23,26) sts. Change to E, ch 3, turn. **Row 8:** With E, work same as for Row 6 of Neck Shaping. Change to C, ch 3, turn. **Row 9:** With C, working over D, sk first dc, dec over next 2 dc, dc in next dc, changing to D in last dc, * 1 dc D, 3 dc C, rpt from * across, ending last rpt with 3(1,1) dc C. Change to A, ch 3, turn. With A, decreasing 1 dc at neck edge on next row only, work 2(3,4) rows —17(20,23) sts. Now, working even, make 1 sc row with B; 2(3,4) dc rows with A, ending last row at neck edge. Ch 3, turn.

Shoulder Shaping: Continuing with A, sk first dc, dc in each of next 6(7,9) dc, hdc in each of next 3 sts, sc in next st, sl st in next st; do not work over rem sts. Cut yarn and fasten.

BACK—Row 1: With right side facing, attach C to same st on last row of Body where last dc of Row 1 of Right Front was worked, ch 7(9,11), dc in 4th ch from hook, dc in each of next 3(5,7) ch, dc in same dc where yarn was attached, dc in each of next 52(56,60) dc; drop loop from hook, attach a separate strand of C in same st as last dc made, ch 5(7,9) for other sleeve; cut this strand and fasten; pick up dropped loop and dc in each of next 5(7,9) ch—63(71,79) sts, counting chain at beg of this row as 1 dc; do not work over rem sts. **Row 2:** Rpt Row 13 of Body. Change to D, ch 1, turn. **Row 3:** With D, work 1 sc row. **Rows 4 through 8:** Working in dc's rows, use colors as follows: 1 row H, 1 row B, 1 row G, 1 row F, 1 row E. Change to C, ch 3, turn. **Row 9:** Rpt Row 6 of Body. Change to A, ch 3, turn. With A, work 2(3,4) dc rows; with B, work 1 sc row; with A work 1(2,3) dc rows. Ch 3, turn.

Shoulder Shaping—Row 1: Continuing with A, sk first dc, dc in each of next 14(17,20) dc, dec over next 2 dc, dc in next dc; do not work rem sts. Ch 3, turn. **Row 2:** Sk first dc, dec over next 2 sts, dc in next 5(6,7) dc, hdc in each of next 2 sts, sc in next st, sl st in next st; do not work over rem sts. Cut yarn and fasten. Sk next 27(29,31) dc on last row of back made before shoulder shaping; attach A to next dc, ch 3 and work other back shoulder to correspond with opposite side, reversing shaping.

LEFT FRONT: Work to correspond with Right Front, reversing shaping.

FINISHING: Pin vest to measurements on a padded surface; cover with a damp cloth and allow to dry; do not press. Sew shoulder seams.

Edging—Rnd 1: With wrong side facing, attach E to a shoulder seam. Making 3 sc in same st at each corner,

sc evenly along entire outer edge of vest, being careful to keep work flat. Join with sl st to first sc. Ch 1, turn. **Rnd 2:** Sc in same sc as joining, sc in each sc around, making 3 sc in center sc of 3-sc group at each corner. Join to first sc. Ch 1; do not turn. **Rnd 3:** From right side, sc in same sc as joining, working from left to right, * sc in next sc to the right; rpt from * around. Join. Cut yarn and fasten. **TIE (Make 4):** With E, make a chain 45″ long. Sl st in 2nd ch from hook, sl st in each ch across. Cut yarn and fasten. Sew a tie securely to each neck corner. Sew a tie to center of each front edge.

INDIAN COAT

(page 28)

MATERIALS: Simplicity pattern #7936; Pendleton "Chief Joseph" green blanket, 64″x80″; scissors; straight pins; thread to match.

DIRECTIONS: Pin pattern, following diagram, having front edge of A and lower edges of A and D along bound edges. (This finishes front and lower edges of coat.) Cut out all pieces except sleeves (C). Rip out remaining binding on blanket, then cut out sleeves. Use binding for remaining unfinished outer edges of coat, sides and lower edges of pockets and lower edge of sleeves. Put coat together, following pattern directions.

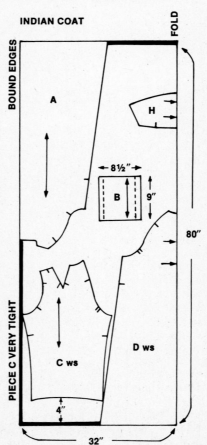

INDIAN COAT

STRIPED HOODED SWEATER WITH TASSELS

(page 29)

"FOR EXPERIENCED KNITTERS ONLY"

Directions are given for size Small (8-10). Changes for sizes Medium (12-14) and Large (16-18) are in parentheses.

MATERIALS: Reynolds Classique Wool (50 gr.balls): 7(8,9) balls Navy (A); Reynelle Tweed (4 oz. skeins): 2(3,4) skeins Green (B); Reynolds Persian Type Crewel Yarn (10 yd. card): 20(21,22) cards Chartreuse (C); Reynolds Velourette Chenille (30 gr. balls): 2(2,3) balls Purple (D); Reynolds Constellation Metallic Yarn (30 gr.balls): 2(3,3) balls Black & Gold (E); knitting needles, 1 pair No.8 OR ANY SIZE NEEDLES WHICH WILL OBTAIN THE STITCH GAUGE BELOW.

GAUGE: Garter Stitch using A—4 sts = 1″; 10 rows (5 ridges) = 1″.

MEASUREMENTS:

Sizes:	Small (8-10)	Medium (12-14)	Large (16-18)
Bust:	33″	37″	41″
Width across back at underarms:	13″	15″	17″
Width across each front at underarms:	10″	11″	12″
Width across sleeve at upper arm:	11½″	12″	13½″

(**Note:** The sweater back and fronts including hood sections, are worked all in one piece, starting and ending at center front edges.)

DIRECTIONS: Starting at center Right Front edge with A, cast on 120(124,128) sts; place a marker on needle, cast on 50 more sts for hood —170(174,178) sts on needle. Slip marker in every row.

RIGHT FRONT—Rows 1 and 2: With A, k 2 rows. Mark row 1 for right side. Drop A; attach E. **Rows 3 and 4:** With E, k 2 rows. Cut E; pick up A. (**Note:** Entire sweater is worked in stripes of garter st (k each row); cut and attach colors as needed.) **Rows 5 and 6:** With A, k 2 rows. **Rows 7 through 10:** Using all 3 strands of crewel yarn, with C, k 4 rows. **Rows 11 through 14:** With A, k 4 rows. **Rows 15 and 16:** With D, k 2 rows. **Rows 17 through 20:** With A, k 4 rows. **Rows 21 through 24:** With B, k 4 rows. **Rows 25 and 26:** With E, k 2 rows. Rpt last 6 rows (Rows 21 through 26) 3(4,5) more times; then rpt Rows 21 through 24 once more. **Next Row:** With E, k 50; do not work over rem sts; turn. With E, bind off the 50 sts of hood, knitting sts; remove marker—120(124,128) sts.

Right Front Shoulder Shaping and Peplum: Attach A. **Rows 1 through 8:** With A, k 8 rows. Now work in short rows. **Row 9 (first short row):** With C, k 70(74,78); do not work over rem sts; turn. **Rows 10 and 11:** K 2 rows over 70(74,78) sts. **Row 12:** K to within last 2 sts, *k 2 tog*—**dec made at shoulder;** cut C. **Row 13:** With A, k across last short row; cut A; attach A again in first st of rem 50 sts on needle; k rem 50 sts for Peplum. **Rows 14 through 21:** Working over the 50 sts of peplum only, k 8 more rows, ending at lower edge. **Row 22:** With A, k across all sts—119(123,127) sts. **Rows 23 through 30:** Working in garter st over all sts, make 2 rows E, 2 rows A, 2 rows D, 2 rows A. **Rows 31 through 38:** Rpt Rows 23 through 30. **Row 39 (short row):** With C, k 69(73,77); do not work over rem sts; turn. **Rows 40 and 41:** With C, k 2 rows. **Row 42:** K to within last 2 sts, *k 2 tog*—**another dec made at shoulder edge. Row 43:** With A, k across last short row, cut A; attach A again to first st of rem 50 sts on needle; k these 50 sts. **Rows 44 through 52:** Rpt Rows 14 through 22—118(122,126) sts. **Row 53:** With A, bind off 23(27,31) sts for armhole edge, k to end of row.

Underarm Section: Continuing with A, k 7(9,11) rows, ending at armhole edge. **Next Row:** With C, k 45; do not work over rem sts; turn. **Next 3 rows:** With C, k 3 rows over 45 sts. **Next 10 Rows:** Rpt Rows 13 through 22 of Right Front Shoulder Shaping and Peplum—95 sts. With A, k 6(8,10) more rows, ending at armhole edge. At end of last row, cast on 23(27,31) sts for armhole edge—118(122,126) sts. This completes underarm section.

BACK—First Shoulder Shaping and Peplum—Row 1 (short Row): With C, k 68(72,76); do not work over rem sts; turn. **Rows 2 and 3:** With C, k 2 rows. **Row 4:** K across to last st, inc in last st. **Rows 5 through 14:** Rpt Rows 13 through 22 of Right Front Shoulder Shaping and Peplum—119(123,127) sts. **Rows 15 through 30:** Working in

garter st, make (2 rows D, 2 rows A, 2 rows E, 2 rows A) twice. **Row 31:** With A, k 69(73,77); turn. **Rows 32 and 33:** K 2 rows over 69(73,77). **Row 34:** K to last st, inc in last st. **Rows 35 through 44:** Rpt Rows 13 through 22 of Right Front Shoulder Shaping and Peplum—120(124,128) sts. **Rows 45 through 52:** With A, k 8 rows.

Center Back Stripe and Hood Section—Row 1: With B, k across. **Row 2:** K across, place a marker on needle, cast on 40 sts for hood—160(164,168) sts. Slip marker on every row. **Rows 3 and 4:** With B, k 2 more rows. **Rows 5 and 6:** With E, k 2 rows. **Rows 7 through 10:** With B, k 4 rows. Rpt last 6 rows (Rows 5 through 10) 3(4,5) more times. **Next Row:** With E, k 40 sts of hood; turn. Bind off these 40 sts, knitting sts. Remove marker.

Left Shoulder Shaping: Rpt directions for Right Front Shoulder Shaping and Peplum from Row 1 to end of underarm section—118(122,126) sts.

LEFT FRONT—Shoulder Shaping: Rpt directions for Back—First Shoulder Shaping and Peplum from Row 1 to end of Row 52. **Row 53:** With B, k across. **Row 54:** K across, place a marker on needle, cast on 50 sts for hood—170(174,178) sts. **Rows 55 and 56:** With E, k 2 more rows. Continuing in garter st, make (2 rows E, 4 rows B) 4(5,6) times. Then, work 4 rows A, 2 rows D, 4 rows A, 4 rows C, 2 rows A, 2 rows E, 2 rows A. Bind off all sts.

SLEEVES: Starting at upper section of underarm seam, with A, cast on 49(51,53) sts. **Row 1 (right side):** K across. **Row 2:** Inc in first st, k across—50(52,54) sts. **Row 3:** K across; on same needle cast on 12 sts—62(64,66) sts. **Row 4:** K across all sts. **Rows 5 through 8:** Rpt Rows 3 and 4 alternately 2 times—86(88,90) sts. Work 1(3,5) rows even in garter st, ending

at lower edge.

Top Shaping—Row 1: With D, k across to last st, inc in last st—mark this end for top edge. **Row 2:** Inc in first st, k across. Continue in garter st throughout. **Rows 3 through 8:** Continuing to inc one st at top edge *every* row, work 2 rows A, 2 rows E, 2 rows A—94(96,98) sts. **Rows 9 through 16:** Rpt last 8 rows (Rows 1 through 8)—102(104,106) sts. Increasing one st at top edge every row, make 4 rows C, 6(8,10) rows A—112(116,120) sts. *For center section—* **Next Row:** With B, k across; at end of row, cast on 68 sts for saddle shoulder and hood. **Following 2 Rows:** With B, k across all sts—180(184,188) sts. Working even in garter st across all sts, make (2 rows E, 4 rows B) 4(4,5) times. **Next Row (short row):** With E, k 50; turn. With E, bind off these 50 sts. Turn. *Now work other half of sleeve as follows:* **Row 1:** Attach B to first st on needle, bind off first 18 sts (mark this bound-off edge for saddle shoulder; mark corresponding 18 sts on opposite edge). Cut B; attach A and k across rem sts. Now, decreasing one st at top edge in *every* row, make 6(8,10) rows A, 4 rows C, (2 rows A, 2 rows E, 2 rows A, 2 rows D) twice—86(88,90) sts. With A, working even, make 0(2,4) rows, ending at lower edge. **Next Row:** Bind off 12 sts, k across. **Next Row:** K across. Rpt last 2 rows 2 more times. Bind off rem sts.

Tassel (make 10): Cut 5 strands of 3-strand C yarn, each 30″ long. Hold strands together and fold in half to form a loop. With right side facing, insert a large size crochet hook from back to front through lower end of a short C stripe on sweater and draw loop through; draw loose ends through loop on hook and pull tightly to form a knot. From wrong side, sew ends of the A short rows directly

HOW TO ESTIMATE YARDAGE

The fabrics we sew today come in many widths. Since the space on the pattern envelope is limited, at times the fabric width chosen may not be included in the yardage chart provided for each pattern.

The Fabric Conversion Chart reprinted below was developed by Rutgers, The State University of New Jersey, Cooperative Extension Service, to help estimate the yardage for different fabric widths.

FABRIC CONVERSION CHART

FABRIC WIDTH	32″	35″-36″	39″	41″	44″-45″	50″	52″-54″	58″-60″
Yardage*	1 7	1¾	1½	1½	1 3	1¼	1 1	1
	2¼	2	1¾	1¾	1 5	1½	1 3	1¼
	2½	2¼	2	2	1¾	1 5	1½	1 3
	2¾	2½	2¼	2¼	2 1	1¾	1¾	1 5
*Add an additional ¼ yd. for wide span conversion in fabric, for nap or one directional prints, for styles with sleeves cut in one piece with body of garment.	3 1	2 7	2½	2½	2¼	2	1 7	1¾
	3 3	3 1	2¾	2¾	2½	2¼	2	1 7
	3¾	3 3	3	2 7	2¾	2 3	2¼	2
	4	3¾	3¼	3 1	2 7	2 5	2 3	2¼
	4 3	4¼	3½	3 3	3 1	2¾	2 5	2 3
	4 5	4½	3¾	3 5	3 3	3	2¾	2 5
	5	4¾	4	3 7	3 5	3¼	2 7	2¾
	5¼	5	4¼	4 1	3 7	3 3	3 1	2 7

Reprinted courtesy of: New Jersey Cooperative Extension Service, Rutgers, The State University

below tassel to end of C stripe.

FINISHING: Pin sections to measurements on a padded surface; cover with a damp cloth and allow to dry; do not press.

To Assemble: Sew sleeve seams. Fold fronts over back section, with underarm C stripes at folds. Fit sleeves into armholes, adjusting the (marked) 18-st sections of saddle shoulders of sleeves to fit over back and front shoulder edges (see diagram). Leaving

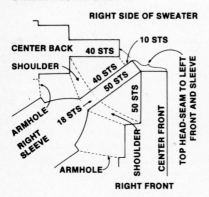

STRIPED HOODED SWEATER

RIGHT SIDE OF SWEATER

CENTER BACK

SHOULDER

40 STS

10 STS

40 STS

50 STS

18 STS

ARMHOLE

RIGHT SLEEVE

50 STS

SHOULDER

CENTER FRONT

TOP HEAD-SEAM TO LEFT FRONT AND SLEEVE

ARMHOLE

RIGHT FRONT

all hood sections free, sew sleeves in place, including saddle shoulder seams. Sew side edge of each front portion of hood to corresponding edge of sleeve portion. Sew each side edge of back portion to first 40 sts of corresponding sleeve portion. Fold remaining 10 sts of each sleeve portion over top edge of back, with corners at center back; sew in place. Sew center top seam.

GARTER STITCH SWEATER AND HAT FOR WOMEN AND MEN

(page 30)

Directions are given for Woman's size Small (8-10). Changes for Woman's sizes Medium (12-14) and Large (16-18) and Man's sizes Medium (42-44) and Large (46-48) are in parentheses. Woman's Large size can be used for Man's Small size. A / separates Women's and Men's sizes. Hat will fit all sizes.

MATERIALS: Bernat's Danish Bulky (2 oz. balls) *For Sweater:* 9(10,11/18,20) balls of Birch White or desired color. *For Hat:* 3 balls same color; knitting needles, 1 pair No. 13 OR ANY SIZE NEEDLES WHICH WILL OBTAIN THE STITCH GAUGE BELOW; crochet hook, Size H; for women's sweater, 4 buttons, 1″ in diameter; one st holder.

GAUGE: 5 sts = 2 ″; 10 rows (5 ridges) = 2″.

MEASUREMENTS:

Sizes: Women's   Men's
Small Medium Large / Medium Large
(8-10) (12-14) (16-18)/ (42-44) (46-48)
Bust or chest:
33″   36″   40″ /   44″   48″

Width across back or front at underarms:
16½″   18″   20″ /   22″   24″
Width across sleeve at upper arm:
13″   13½″   14″ /   16″   17″

DIRECTIONS—SWEATER BACK: Starting at lower edge, cast on 42 (45,50/55,60) sts. Work in garter st (k each row) for 50(52,54/64,68) rows—25(26,27/32,34) ridges.

Underarm Shaping—Row 1: K 1, inc in next st, k across to within last 2 sts, inc in next st, k 1—inc made at each end. **Row 2:** K across. Rpt last 2 rows alternately 4 more times—52(55,60/65,70) sts.

For Women's Sizes Only—Sleeves: Continuing in garter st, cast on 12(13,14) sts at beg of next 2 rows—76(81,88) sts.

For All Sizes: Place a marker at each end of last row. Work even in garter st until length from markers is 5½(6¼, 7/8, 8½)″.

Neck Shaping—Row 1: K 30(32,34/-22,24), place these sts just worked on a st holder; bind off next 16(17,20/-21,22) sts; k rem sts. **Rows 2-3:** Working in garter st over 30(32,34/22,24) sts on needle only, dec one st at neck edge in each of the 2 rows. Work 1 row even. Bind off rem 28(30,32/-20,22) sts for shoulder. Slip sts from holder onto a needle; attach yarn at neck edge and work to correspond with opposite side.

FRONT: Work same as for Back until length from underarm markers is 4½(5¼,6/7,7½)″.

Neck Shaping: Work same as Back Neck Shaping until Row 3 has been completed. Work even in garter st over 28 (30,32/20,22) sts until length from markers is same as on Back to bound-off edge. Bind off all sts. Slip sts from holder onto a needle; attach yarn at neck edge and work to correspond with opposite side.

For Men's Sizes Only—Sleeves: Starting at top edge, cast on 40 sts for medium size (42 sts for large size). Work in garter st for 19 rows (10 ridges).

Row 20 (Dec Row): K 2, k 2 tog, k across to within last 4 sts, k 2 tog, k 2—one st dec made at each end. Working in garter st, rpt dec row every 20th row 3 more times—32(34 for larger size) sts rem. Work even in garter st until total length of sleeve is 23″ (including a 4″ cuff). Bind off.

Finishing For Men's Sizes: Pin pieces to measurements on a padded surface; cover with a damp cloth and allow to dry; do not press. With a large-eyed darning needle and same material, sew side, shoulder and sleeve seams. Sew in sleeves, adjusting to fit. Using crochet hook, from right side work one rnd of sl sts loosely along lower edge of sweater, along entire neck

edge and along lower edge of each sleeve. Turn 4″ cuff to right side at lower edge of each sleeve.

Finishing For Women's Sizes: Pin pieces to measurements on a padded surface; cover with a damp cloth and allow to dry; do not press. With a large-eyed darning needle and same material, leaving first 7 ridges free for slits, sew side and underarm of sleeve seams. Starting at sleeve edge, sew 6″ shoulder seams, leaving rem edges of shoulder open.

Button Loops: Using crochet hook, attach yarn with sl st to first st (close to neck edge) on a front shoulder edge, ch 6, sl st in next st. Break off and fasten; sk next 5 sts on same edge and work another loop over following 2 sts as before. Work 2 button loops on other front shoulder edge in same manner. Sew buttons opposite button loops. From right side, with crochet hook, work 1 rnd of sl sts along entire lower edge, including slit edges. Break off and fasten. Work 1 rnd of sl sts along outer edge of each sleeve.

HAT: Starting at outer edge of cuff, cast on 50 sts. Work in garter st (k each row) for 8″ (10″ for man's size).

Top shaping—Row 1: *K 2 tog, k 23; rpt from * once—48sts. **Row 2:** K across. **Row 3:** *K 2, k 2 tog; rpt from * across—36 sts. **Rows 4, 5 and 6:** K across. **Row 7:** *K 1, k 2 tog; rpt from * across—24 sts. **Row 8:** K across. Leaving a 24″ length, break off yarn. Thread darning needle with this end and slip through rem sts; pull tightly and secure on wrong side; sew back seam. With crochet hook, work one rnd of sl sts loosely along cast-on edge. Fold 3″ cuff to right side.

TABARD SWEATER

(page 31)

Directions are given for size Small (8-10). Changes for sizes Medium (12-14) and Large (16-18) are in parentheses.

MATERIALS: Coats & Clark's Red Heart "Fabulend" Knitting Worsted Type Yarn, 4 Ply (4 oz. skeins): 1 skein each of #858 Navy (A), #903 Devil Red (B), #648 Apple Green (C), #515 Dk. Turquoise (D), #224 Baby Yellow (E), #253 Tangerine (F) and #588 Amethyst (G) for each size; crochet hook, Size G OR ANY SIZE HOOK WHICH WILL OBTAIN THE STITCH GAUGE BELOW.

GAUGE: 4 sts = 1″; 2 rows = 1″.

MEASUREMENTS:

	Small (8-10)	Medium (12-14)	Large (16-18)
Sizes:			
Width across back or front at underarms (including edging):	16″	17½″	19″

DIRECTIONS—BACK: Body: Starting at underarm edge (below yoke), with A, ch 65(71,77). **Row 1 (wrong side):** Dc in 4th ch from hook, dc in each ch across—63(69,75) dc, counting chain at beg of row as 1 dc. Cut A; attach B. With B, ch 2; drop B, pick up G and ch one more st; turn. **Row 2:** Place B strand along top edge of last row, sk first dc, *with G, working over B, yarn over hook, draw up a loop in next dc, yarn over hook and draw through 2 loops on hook, drop G, pick up B and draw through rem 2 loops on hook*—**color change made;** * with B, working over G strand dc in each of next 4 dc, *holding back on hook last loop of dc, dc in next dc, drop B, pick up G and draw a loop through the 2 loops on hook*—**another color change made;** with G, working over B, dc in next dc, changing to B as before; rpt from * across, ending with B dc in top of ch at end of row, changing to G. With G, ch 3, turn. Always count ch-3 as 1 dc. **Note:** When 2 colors are used in same row, carry color not in use inside sts; when 3 or more colors are needed in same row, carry background color (A) inside sts, attach and cut other colors as needed. Always change color in last dc of each color group. **Row 3:** With G, working over B, sk first dc, dc in each of next 2 dc, changing to B in last dc, * with B, working over G, dc in each of next 3 dc, with G, working over B, dc in each of next 3 dc; rpt from * across, ending with G, dc in each of next 2 dc, dc in top of ch-3 (do not change color). Ch 3, turn. **Row 4:** With G, sk first dc, dc in each of next 3 dc, * with B, dc in next dc, with G, dc in next 5 dc; rpt from * across, ending with G dc in last 4 sts. Cut both colors; attach A, ch 3, turn. **Row 5:** With A, sk first dc, dc in each dc and in top of ch-3. Cut A; attach C, ch 3, turn. **Rows 6 and 7:** With C, work 2 dc rows (same as Row 5). At end of last row, cut C; attach D, ch 3, turn. **Row 8:** With D, work same as Row 5. Do not cut D. **Row 9:** With D, working over A, sk first dc, dc in next dc, changing to A, * with A, dc in next 2 dc, with D, dc in next 2 dc; rpt from * across, ending with A(D,A) dc in top of turning ch-3. Ch 3, turn. **Row 10:** Using colors as established on last row, sk first dc, dc in each dc across. Cut D, with A, ch 3, turn. **Row 11:** Rpt Row 5. Ch 3, turn. **Row 12:** With A, sk first dc, dc in next 6(5,7) dc, changing to E in last dc, working 1 dc in each dc and carrying A inside sts, make 8(9,9) E dc, 6(7,8) A dc, 8(9,9) B dc and 6(7,8) A dc, 8(9,9) G dc, 6(7,8) A dc, 8(9,9) C dc, 6(6,7) A dc. With A, ch 3, turn. **Row 13:** With A, sk first dc, dc in next 5(5,6) dc, 8(9,9) B dc, 6(7,8) A dc, 8(9,9) E dc, 6(7,8) A dc, 8(9,9) D dc, 6(7,8) A dc,

8(9,9) C dc, 7(6,8) A dc. Ch 3, turn. **Rows 14 and 15:** With A, work 2 dc rows. At end of last row, cut A; attach B. Ch 3, turn. **Row 16:** With B, work same as Row 5. Cut B; attach C, Ch 3, turn. **Row 17:** Using C instead of D, work same as Row 9. Cut both colors; attach E, ch 3, turn. **Row 18:** With E, work as Row 5. Cut E; attach C, ch 3, turn. **Row 19:** Rpt Row 17. Cut both colors. Attach B, ch 3, turn. **Rows 20, 21 and 22:** Working as Row 5, make 1 row B; 2 rows A. Cut A and fasten.

Yoke—Row 1: With right side facing, working along opposite side of starting chain; attach A to first ch, ch 3, dc in each ch across—63(69,75) dc. Ch 3, turn. **Row 2:** With A, sk first dc, dc in next 28(31,34) dc. With C, dc in next 5 dc, with A, dc in next 29(32,35) sts. Ch 3, turn. **Row 3:** Sk first dc, with A dc in next 23(26,29) dc, with C dc in next 15 dc, with A dc in next 24(27,30) sts. Ch 3, turn. **Row 4:** Sk first dc, dc in next 2(2,3) dc, with F dc in next 8(9,9) dc, with A dc in next 8(8,10) dc, with G dc in 8(10,10) dc, with F dc in 9 dc, with G dc in 8(10,10) dc, with A dc in 8(8,10) dc, with C dc in 8(9,9) dc, with A dc in 3(3,4) sts. Ch 3, turn. **Row 5:** Using E in place of F, work same as last row. Ch 3, turn. **Rows 6 and 7:** Rpt Rows 3 and 2 of Yoke. Ch 3, turn. With A only, work 2(3,4) dc rows. Ch 3, turn.

Neck Shaping—Row 1: With A, sk first dc, dc in next 2(2,3) dc, with E dc in next 8(9,9) dc, with A, dc in next 3(3,4) dc; do not work over rem sts—14(15,17) dc. Ch 3, turn. **Row 2:** Using C instead of E, work as last row. With A only, work 3(4,4) dc rows. Cut A and fasten. Sk next 35(39,41) sts on last row before neck shaping, attach A to next dc, ch 3; using any other 2 colors instead of E and C, work to correspond with opposite side.

Neck Border—Row 1: With right side facing, attach C to end st of last row on left side edge of neck; sc evenly along neck edge. Place a marker between 2 sts at each inner corner. Cut C and fasten. **Row 2—(Note:** This row is worked using all colors; make a few sts of each color, having a different number of sts in each color group and changing colors in any desired sequence.) Do not turn; attach any color to first sc at beg of last row, ch 3, * working as directed, dc in each dc to within 3 sts before marker at next corner; *holding back on hook last loop of each dc, make dc in each of next 3 sc, yarn over hook, draw through all 4 loops on hook*—**2-dc dec made;** make another 2-dc dec over next 3 sc; rpt from * once more; dc in each rem sc to end of row. Cut yarn and fasten.

Edging—Rnd 1: Do not turn; attach

A to top of ch-3 at beg of last row, sc in same st, sc in each st across last row; then, making 3 sc in same st at each outer corner, continue to sc evenly along entire outer edge of back. Join with sl st to first sc. **Rnd 2:** Ch 1, turn; with wrong side facing, sc in next sc, drop A to front of work (wrong side), attach B and * with B sc in next sc, drop B to front of work, pick up A and sc in next sc, drop A to front, pick up B; rpt from * around, making 3 sc in center st of 3-sc group of each corner. Join to first sc. Cut both colors and fasten.

FRONT—Body: Work same as Body of Back.

Yoke—Row 1: With right side facing, working along opposite side of starting chain, attach A to first ch, mark center 33(37,41) sts on starting chain. With A, dc in each ch to within center marked sts, changing to C in last dc, making 1 dc in each ch, work 1 dc C, (1 dc A and 1 dc C) 5(6,7) times; (1 dc A, 1 dc B, 1 dc A, 1 dc C) 3 times; (1 dc A, 1 dc C) 5(6,7) times; with A, dc in each rem st—63(69,75) sts. Ch 3, turn. **Row 2:** Sk first dc, working colors as established on last row, dc in each st across. Ch 3, turn. **Neck Shaping—Row 1:** With A, sk first dc, dc in next 13(14,16) dc. Ch 3, turn. **Rows 2 and 3:** Using F instead of E and D instead of C, work same as Rows 1 and 2 of Back Neck Shaping. Ch 3, turn. **Rows 4 through 7:** With A, work 4 dc rows, Ch 3, turn. **Rows 8 and 9:** Work same as Rows 1 and 2 of Back Neck Shaping. With A, work in dc rows until total length from lower edge of body is same as on Back. Cut yarn and fasten. Sk next 35(39,41) sts on last row before neck shaping, attach A to next dc, ch 3; using different colors (any colors you desire) for color blocks, work to correspond with opposite side. Now, starting from **Neck Border,** complete front same as Back.

TIES (Make 2): Using 2 strands of A and 1 strand of B held together, make a chain 50″ long. Cut yarn and fasten.

TASSEL (Make 4): Cut 2 strands A, 1 B and 1 C, each 12″ long. Slip these strands through one end of chain, fold in half; using a separate strand of any of the 3 colors, wind tightly around end of chain and top of tassel, covering about 1″ of folded strands. Tie ends of this strand tog.

FINISHING: Pin each section to measurements on a padded surface; cover with a damp cloth and allow to dry; do not press. Sew shoulder seams. Starting 7(7½,8½)″ below shoulder seams, lace a tie at each side through sts along side edges of back and front, down to within 4″ from lower edge. Adjust to desired fit and tie ends of each tie into a bow.

BASIC NEEDLEPOINT

You'll be able to create and execute your own beautiful needlepoint designs, once you've learned a few stitches. The continental, cross and half cross stitches shown below are the most basic, and after you've mastered these, be adventuresome and try the more complicated stitches. These basic stitches all slant diagonally across one intersection of the canvas mesh, and are easy to learn with a little practice.

IMPORTANT: If you're left handed, reverse all the hand directions we give you, or practice stitches in front of a mirror.

CONTINENTAL STITCH: One of the most durable stitches, it's great for articles which will see a lot of wear and tear. You can use this stitch on either single or double mesh canvas with equally good results, but because of the distortion caused by the stitches you'll **always** have to block your finished canvas.

HOW TO WORK: Bring your needle up at A; work from right to left, put needle down at B; up again at C; down at D. Continue across row in this manner. At the end of the row, put your needle down at H; turn canvas around, bring needle up at A, and continue back across row as before (1). It's important to turn the canvas so your needle will always be in a **slanted** position when making stitches (1). Your needle is parallel to the canvas mesh only when you start a new row (2).

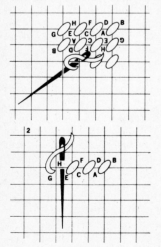

HALF CROSS STITCH: This is a good stitch to use when the article you're making **will not** receive heavy wear (wall hangings, pillows, etc.). It requires less yarn than the continental stitch, but you'll get better results if you work this stitch on the firmer-weave, double thread

(penelope) canvas. (Many experts believe the half cross should **only** be worked on penelope.)

HOW TO WORK: Working from left to right, bring needle up at A and down at B; up at C; then down at D; continue in this manner across row. At the end of the row, put needle down at F, turn canvas; bring up at A, and continue back across row as before.

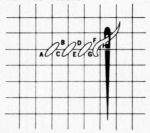

CROSS STITCH: Good for lettering because the finished stitch forms a square; also this stitch should be used when you want additional texture to your canvas.

HOW TO WORK: Start by making a row of half cross stitches; then go back across the same row, slanting stitches in the opposite direction. Or, if you prefer, work individual stitches. No matter how

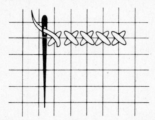

the stitches are worked, **they must all cross in the same direction.**

NEEDLES: Always use blunt-tip "tapestry" needles since they'll never split the mesh threads. The needles come in an array of sizes, so you'll easily find a needle to fit your canvas and threads.

TRANSFERRING A DESIGN: It's easier than you think to transfer a design to canvas. First, cut the canvas about three inches larger on each side than your planned design. Then fold it in half vertically down the center, then horizontally. Unfold canvas and lightly mark the crease lines with a pencil. Fold and mark the design in the same way as you did the canvas. Now tape the design, unfolded, to a window; place and tape canvas over the design, matching centers, and vertical and horizontal lines. Using a **water-proof** marking pen, **starting from the center and working outward,** carefully trace the pattern onto canvas. If you make a mistake, paint over it with white acrylic paint. Remove pattern and canvas from window. Bind canvas edges with masking tape so they will not ravel. Leave canvas as is, or color in design with **waterproof** paints or nylon felt-tip markers.

TO BLOCK NEEDLEPOINT: Cover a table or any other flat board with a piece of brown paper, or old sheet, larger than

your canvas; tack it down flat. With a pencil, mark the size of the canvas on the paper or sheet, making sure all corners are square. Soak canvas in cold water. Note: If you wish to wash needlepoint before hanging, use one of the cold water soaps, or a very mild detergent in cool water. Do not wring; rinse thoroughly to remove all soap. Pull or stretch the canvas **worked side up** until it conforms to the penciled outline. **Using rust proof tacks or nails** (if you aren't sure, ask your hardware dealer), tack down the four corners, ½" outside design edge making sure the corners are at **right angles,** and match the outline you've drawn on the paper or sheet. Then, in the center of each side, nail down four more tacks. Continue around all four sides, until tacks are about ¼" apart. **Let dry thoroughly** — (approximately 48 hours). Remove canvas from board. If you're not going to immediately mount your canvas, roll it around any cardboard tube, with the worked side out. (This will keep stitches from crushing against each other).

STRAIGHT OR UPRIGHT GOBELIN: Worked on single- or double-thread canvas. It is one of the oldest of canvas stitches used to imitate the woven Gobelin tapestries, giving a very effective texture.

HOW TO WORK: Stitches are worked vertically over 2 threads of the canvas. If the yarn does not entirely cover the canvas, lay a strand over the row as a padding and work stitches over.

BASKET WEAVE: Used mainly for backgrounds and filling shapes, can be worked on single- or double-thread canvas. It does not pull the canvas out of shape, looks smooth. It is hard wearing with a firm back which looks woven.

HOW TO WORK: Work on the diagonal with the needle horizontal as rows

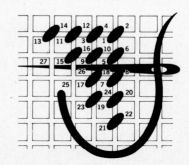

go up from right to left, then vertical as they go down from left to right.

BARGELLO: This stitch looks as complicated as it is beautiful, but actually, it's just a simple up-and-down stitch covering four or more meshes of the canvas (1). There are no hard and fast rules to creating with this stitch. The zigzag stitch is the most common pattern used, and is particularly effective when worked in one or more coordinating colors; or several tones of a single color (2).

HOW TO WORK: Is an *upright Gobelin* usually worked in a zigzag or geometric pattern. The basic stitch is worked over 4 threads of canvas and under 2, rising and falling. It's best to start a bargello pattern by lightly penciling in one row of the design you want to make; work that row; then the rest of the pattern should easily fall into place. Bargello looks best when worked on single-thread (mono) canvas.

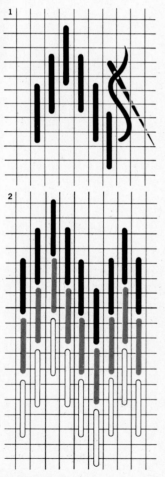

SCOTCH STITCH: The basic stitch is done in squares of 3 meshes, but it can be increased to 4, 5, or 6 meshes.

HOW TO WORK: Starting at the upper left 1, bring needle to front, then over to 2. Bring needle up at 3 and over to 4. Continue, following diagram below to 10. Give canvas a quarter turn to the right. Bring needle up at 11 and over to 12. Continue until double squares are completed.

TENT STITCH: This is basically a slant stitch that gives more backing to the canvas for a firmer finished piece with a more interesting texture on the front.

HOW TO WORK: Starting at the right of canvas (A), bring needle to front. Working from right to left, bring needle down diagonally to row below. Continue until row is completed. Give canvas a half turn. Insert needle 1 row above and bring down diagonally to the left on the next row. Give canvas a half turn at the beginning of each row.

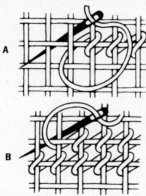

SATIN STITCH: This stitch is the most basic and simplest needlepoint stitch. It can be worked vertically or horizontally over 2, 3, 4, 5 or 6 meshes.

HOW TO WORK: Bring needle up at 1 and over to 2, then down and up at 3. Continue for required number of rows.

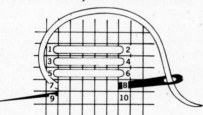

FRENCH KNOT: This stitch is never used as a background stitch, but rather as a stitch to put over the background to add more pattern or texture.

HOW TO WORK: Bring the needle out at A. Swing your yarn to the left of A, circle it down from left to right and hold it flat on the cloth with your left thumb at a place about an inch to the left of A. With your right hand, hold the needle by the eye and slide the point downward "under the bridge", without picking up background. Now think of a clock: Your needle should be pointing to 6 o'clock. Still holding the needle by the eye, turn the point of the needle clockwise, over the yarn held by your left thumb, until it points to 12 o'clock. Continue to hold the yarn down with your left thumb. Insert the point of the needle very close to A but not in the same hole. Now gently pull the yarn with your left thumb and index finger to snug it around the needle. Push the needle straight down with your right hand and pull through gently.

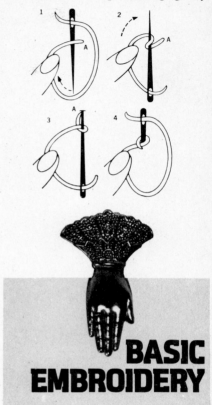

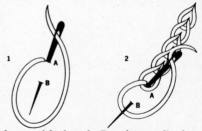

BASIC EMBROIDERY

Embroidery has no rigid rules, and it's great fun to invent your own stitches to create a very personal design. The beginner, though, may be confused by what stitch to use where, so we show a selection of basic stitches: directions on how to do them, and suggestions for the way we think they'll work best. Master these stitches, then experiment on your own!

CHAIN STITCH: Bring the needle up at A, form a loop by holding thread down with thumb. Put the needle down in A and bring up at B (1). Repeat, always inserting needle exactly where the thread came out, inside the last loop (2). For leaves, broad outlines, houses, flower stems and backgrounds.

BACK STITCH: Bring thread up at A, go down at B, and come up again at C;

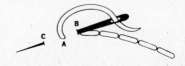

repeat pattern, making sure you go back into the same hole as the previous stitch. Keep stitches uniform. Good for outlining, lines and foundation.

COUCHING: Place thread(s) along sewing line; tack down at even intervals with small stitches. Use for outlining, and to secure very long satin stitches.

CROSS STITCH: Start at lower left corner (left-handed people start at right); work left to right (right to left); making diagonal stitches to end of row

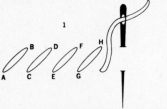

(1); then work back over these stitches

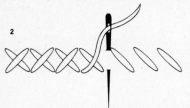

(2). Always keep needle vertical and go into the same holes of the first row of diagonal stitches. Stitches may be worked separately, but all should cross in the same direction. Best used for background, borderwork and filling.

FRENCH KNOT: Bring needle up, wrap around needle once or twice (1);

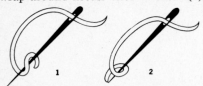

hold taut: then insert needle as close as possible to where thread emerged (2). The size of the knot is determined by the number and size of the threads you use, and how many times you wrap them around the needle. For eyes, seeds, and in clusters to fill spaces.

SATIN STITCH: Bring needle up at one edge of area to be covered (A); in-

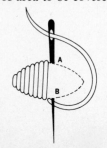

sert at opposite edge (B), keeping stitches together to form a smooth banding.

HERRINGBONE: Bring needle up; make diagonal stitch, keeping thread under needle. Draw thread through;

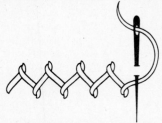

work needle as shown to pick up a vertical stitch; continue pattern. This stitch may be worked close together or far apart.

LAZY DAISY: Bring needle up through fabric, leaving a small loop, then go back and insert needle as close as possible to where thread emerged first; come out at center of loop; go back over loop to anchor it. To make next loop, pass needle beneath work;

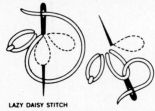

LAZY DAISY STITCH

begin next loop as shown. Several loops around a center point make lovely flowers, leaves or clusters.

BUTTONHOLE OR BLANKET STITCH: The only difference is that *buttonhole stitches* are closer together. Work from left to right. Come out at A. Hold the yarn down with your left thumb, insert the needle at B. Come out at C, just above and close to A, drawing the needle out over the yarn coming from A to form a loop. In at D, out at E.

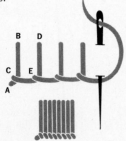

CLOSED BUTTONHOLE STITCH: Made up of 2 *buttonhole stitches* worked from the same hole, the first one from right to left, the second from left to right, making little triangles.

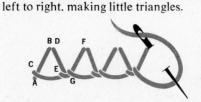

FLY STITCH: Bring the needle out at A. Hold the yarn down with the left thumb, looping it towards the right. Insert at B, coming out at C, below, halfway between A and B. The yarn is looped under the point of the needle from left to right. Pull it through over the loop. Anchor down by inserting at D. You can anchor it with a small stitch, or a long one.

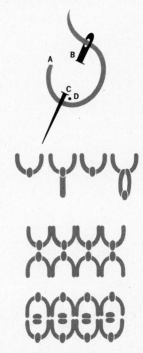

RUNNING STITCH: Run the needle in and out at regular intervals.

FEATHER STITCH: It is really a *blanket stitch* with the stitches slanting instead of at right angles. Work from the top down, towards you.

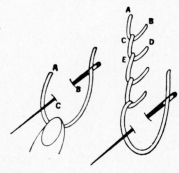

OUTLINE: Come out at A. Holding the thread down with your left thumb, insert the needle at B. Come out at C, halfway between AB. Over to D, still with the thread down, out at B, over to E and out at D. When the yarn is kept *above* the line, it is called an *outline stitch*. When the yarn is kept *down*, the stitch is called a *stem* or *crewel*.

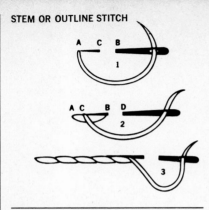

STEM OR OUTLINE STITCH

FELT PILLOWS OR WALL HANGINGS

(page 32)

Materials and instructions given below are for *pillows*. To use designs as wall hangings, be sure to read the instructions at end.

MATERIALS—For all designs: Felt fabric, see individual projects for yardage and colors; Elmer's Glue-All® (see Buyer's Guide, page 136); 22″ zippers; polyester fiberfill stuffing, two 1 lb. packages for each pillow; transparent tape; yardstick; tailor's chalk; single-edged razor blade or mat knife.

RED AND CAMEL BARS
MATERIALS: ¾ yd. camel felt; ½ yd. red felt; ½ yd. blue felt; 22″ camel zipper. **Cut:** Two 22½″x22½″ squares camel; four 1″x22½″ strips blue (A); five 1½″x13″ strips red (B); four ¾″x13″ strips blue (C); four 3″x3″ squares red (D); four ¾″x¾″ squares red (E).

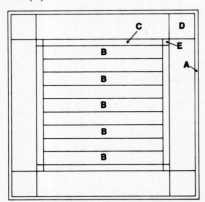

A—1″x22½″ BLUE   D—3″x3″ RED
B—1½″x13″ RED   E—¾″x¾″ RED
C—¾″x13″ BLUE

DIAMOND WITHIN A SQUARE
MATERIALS: ¾ yd. cream felt; ¼ yd. purple felt; ⅛ yd. red felt; 22″ cream zipper. **Cut:** Two 22½″x22½″ squares cream; four 1″x22½″ strips red (A); four 3″x14½″ strips purple (B); four 1″x12½″ strips red (C); four 1″x6¾″ strips red (D); one 6¾″ x 6¾″ square purple (E); four 1″x1″ squares purple.

GREEN BARS VARIATION
MATERIALS: ¾ yd. red felt; ¼ yd.

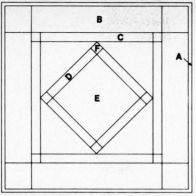

A—1″x22½″ RED   D—1″x6¾″ RED
B—3″x14½″ PURPLE   E—6¾″x6¾″ PURPLE
C—1″x12½″ RED   F—1″x1″ PURPLE

purple felt; ⅛ yd. lime green felt; ½ yd. pink felt; ⅛ yd. turquoise felt; 22″ red zipper. **Cut:** Two 22½″x22½″ squares red; four 1″x22½″ strips pink (A); four ½″x13″ strips pink (B); three 2″x13″ strips lime green (C); four ¾″x13″ strips turquoise (D); four 3″x14½″ strips purple (E).

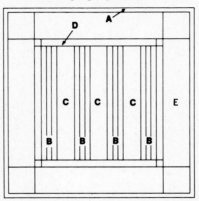

A—1″x22½″ PINK   D—¾″x13″ TURQUOISE
B—½″x13″ PINK   E—3″x14½″ PURPLE
C—2″x13″ GREEN

DIRECTIONS: Measure and cut all pieces *carefully*. The best way to do this accurately is to anchor the felt to a table or other solid surface with tape. Then measure and mark the outline of the pieces with tailor's chalk. Using a yardstick or (better yet) metal-edged ruler as a guide, make smooth cuts along chalked lines with razor blade or mat knife. Place the pre-cut 22½″x1″ (A) strips along the outside edges of one of the 22½″ squares of felt, which will be the top of the pillow. The ends of the strips should overlap. Following the diagrams on this page and using the outside strips as a guide, position all of the appliqué pieces. Anchor the large appliqué pieces by placing a pin in the center. To apply Glue-All®: Begin by gluing the long strips. Carefully lift *one end* of a strip and apply a generous coating of Glue-All® to a section of the back. Return strip to position and *pat gently*. Remove pin. Lift other end as far back as initial

gluing and coat another section. Pat into place. Repeat until the entire strip is cemented. Repeat for all pieces. Small squares can be removed and backs entirely coated, then replaced in position. When positioning long strips which are not against a previously glued strip, mark the placement with tailor's chalk (it will iron out later) and place a yardstick on marking to use as a guide, so that the long edge of the felt will not waver. Allow to dry overnight. For back of pillow, fold the other 22½″ square of felt in half. Cut along the fold line. Insert a 22″ zipper between the two halves, turning back ends of zipper tape so that they do not extend beyond edge of felt. To assemble pillow, pin top and bottom of pillow *wrong* sides together. Stitch ½″ from edge; trim close to seam line. Stuff pillow with fiberfill. (Or, if you wish, make a 21½″ square muslin case for fiberfill, and insert into pillow.)

TO USE DESIGNS AS WALL HANGINGS: Omit fiberfill and zippers from materials. You will need a 22½″ square of foam-core board (available in art supply stores). Instead of cutting two 22½″ squares of felt for top and bottom of pillow, cut one 26½″ square, and draw a 22½″ square in the center. Glue design as for pillows. Place finished design face-down on table and center foam-core board over it. Fold felt border to back, mitering corners, and secure with wide cloth tape or masking tape.

THREE FELT VESTS

(page 33)

MATERIALS—For all designs: Butterick pattern #5137; felt fabric, see individual projects for yardage and colors (see Buyer's Guide, page 136); straight pins; single-edged razor blade or mat knife; metal-edged ruler; yardstick; transparent tape; tailor's chalk; 1 yd. 18-inch wide Stitch Witchery® fusible webbing.

BEIGE MULTI-COLOR VEST
MATERIALS: ½ yd. beige felt; ⅛ yd. red felt; ¼ yd. blue felt.
DIRECTIONS: Following GENERAL DIRECTIONS, cut vest from beige felt. Cut red felt into the following pieces: 1 strip, 34″ x ½″ (A); 4 strips, 14″ x ½″ (B); 2 strips, 2⅜″ x ½″ (C); 2 squares, 1¾″ x 1¾″ (D). Cut blue felt into the following pieces: 2 strips, 14″ x 1¾″ (E); 2 strips, 3¼″ x 1¾″ (F); 4 strips, 15½″ x ½″ (G); 2 strips, 5″ x ½″ (H); 4 squares, ½″ x ½″ (I). Apply strips and squares to vest, following GENERAL DIRECTIONS. (**Note:** Separate strips by ⅜″ for design.)

RED-GREEN FELT VEST
MATERIALS: ½ yd. red felt; ¼ yd.

purple felt; ⅛ yd. turquoise felt; ⅛ yd. lime green felt; ⅛ yd. pink felt.
DIRECTIONS: Following GENERAL DIRECTIONS, cut vest from red felt. Cut purple felt into the following pieces: 1 strip, 32¾″ x 1⅛″ (A); 2 strips, 14″ x 1⅛″ (B); 4 strips, 15″ x 1⅛″ (C); 2 strips, 5″ x 1⅛″ (D); 2 strips 3½″ x 1″ (J). Cut turquoise felt into the following pieces: 2 strips, 14″ x ½″ (E); 2 strips, 15″ x ½″ (F); 2 strips, 3″ x ½″ (G). Cut lime green felt into 6 strips, 5½″ x 1⅞″ (H). Cut pink felt into 6 strips, 5½″ x ⅝″ (I). Apply strips to vest, following GENERAL DIRECTIONS. (**Note:** Separate diagonals by ¾″.)

PURPLE MULTI-COLOR VEST

MATERIALS: ½ yd. purple felt; ½ yd. red felt; ⅛ yd. cream felt.
DIRECTIONS: Following GENERAL DIRECTIONS, cut vest from purple felt. Cut red felt into the following pieces: 1 strip, 34″ x ½″ (A); 4 strips, 14″ x ½″ (B); 2 strips, 15½″ x ½″ (C); 2 strips, 5″ x ½″ (D); 2 squares, 1⅜″ x 1⅜″ (E); 2 L's, 4¼″ x 4¼″ x ½″ (F); 2 rectangles, 4½″ x 1¾″ (G). Cut cream felt into the following pieces: 2 triangles, 5¼″ x 3⅝″ x 3⅝″ (H); 2 L's, 4¼″ x 4¼″ x ½″ (I); 2 strips, 4″ x ½″ (J). Apply pieces to vest, following GENERAL DIRECTIONS. (**Note:** Separate strips at shoulder by ⅜″.)

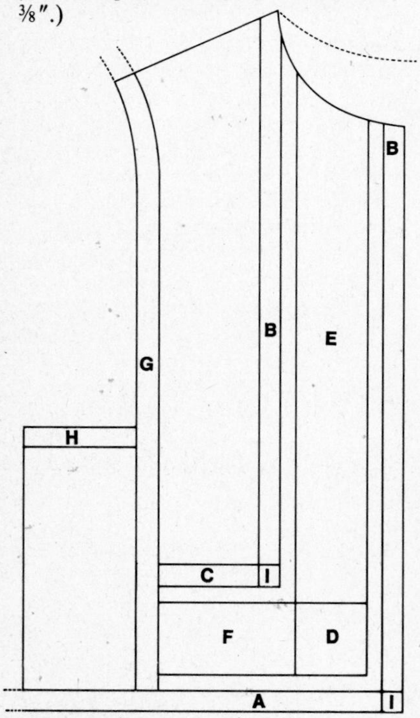

A—34″x½″ RED
B—14″x½″ RED
C—2″x½″ RED
D—1¾″x1¾″ RED
E—14″x1¾″ BLUE
F—3¼″x1¾″ BLUE
G—15½″x½″ BLUE
H—5″x½″ BLUE
I—½″x½″ BLUE

GENERAL DIRECTIONS: Pin vest pattern pieces together, overlapping side edges to eliminate seam allowance, to cut vest in one piece. Place center back of pattern on fold of ½ yd. piece of felt; cut with razor blade or mat knife and metal-edged ruler. To cut contrasting strips, squares and triangles for trim, anchor felt to table or other solid surface with tape. Then measure and mark the outline of each piece with tailor's chalk. Using yardstick or (better yet) metal-edged ruler as a guide, make smooth cuts along chalked lines with razor blade or mat knife. (**Note:** Cut felt carefully in a single thickness—it is imperative that the pieces are accurately cut to line up correctly in the design.) Cut Stitch

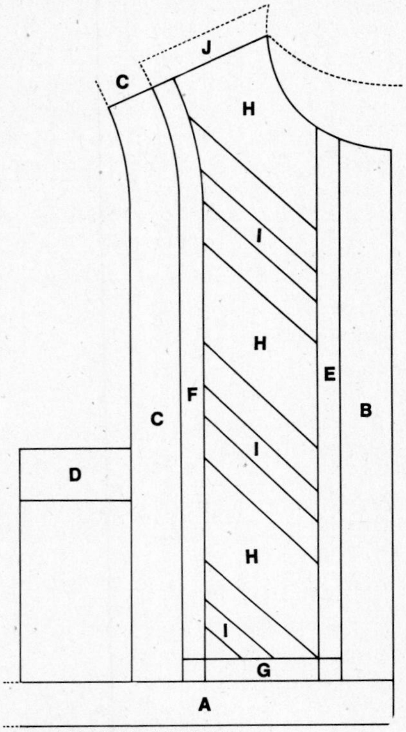

A—32¾″x1⅛″ PURPLE
B—14″x1⅛″ PURPLE
C—15″x1⅛″ PURPLE
D—5″x1⅛″ PURPLE
E—14″x½″ TURQUOISE
F—15″x½″ TURQUOISE
G—3″x½″ TURQUOISE
H—5½″x1⅞″ GREEN
I—5½″x⅝″ PINK
J—3½″x1″ PURPLE

Witchery® to match felt pieces. Place felt pieces on vest, layering them over matching pieces of Stitch Witchery® (see diagrams). Trim any excess from pieces, so they can be pressed flat where edges meet. Start to fuse pieces to vest with strip at bottom edge, then fuse center fronts, lining up edge of strip with vest edge, following package directions. Next fuse front and back armhole edges, extending strip in straight line to meet strip at bottom edge. Iron on strip at underarm edge. Then fit design in on vest fronts. Trim edges at neckline, if necessary. Sew shoulder seams; press open. Secure seams with Stitch Witchery®.

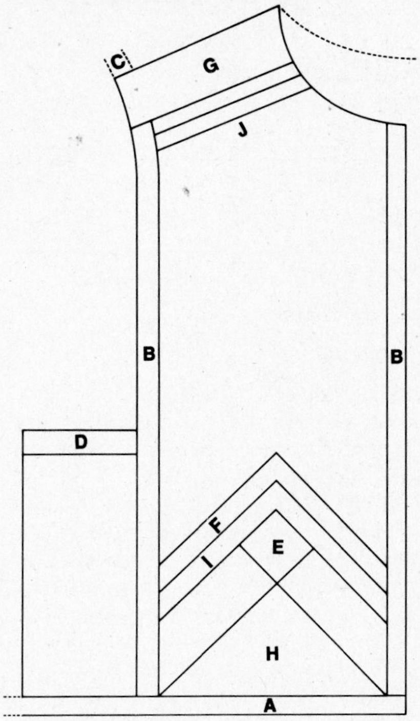

A—34″x½″ RED
B—14″x½″ RED
C—15½″x½″ RED
D—5″x½″ RED
E—1⅜″x1⅜″ RED
F—4¼″x4¼″x½″ RED
G—4½″x1¾″ RED
H—3⅝″x3⅝″x5¼″ CREAM
I—4¼″x4¼″x½″ CREAM
J—4″x½″ CREAM

FOUR T-SWEATERS

(pages 34-37)

Knit-to-measure T-sweaters are perfect for inexperienced knitters. They are constructed from three separately knitted pieces; two interchangeable pieces for front and back (these form the stem of the "T") and a third yoke/sleeve piece (the top of the "T"). We also give you instructions for establishing a gauge and altering size so you can create a garment that fits you perfectly. Following our General Directions are directions for making four interpretations of the basic T-sweater. Refer to diagrams here and on page 42.
GENERAL DIRECTIONS—To measure the stitch gauge: To follow the written instructions for any of these four sweaters, it is important to work according to the stitch gauge specified. To insure the correct gauge, make a sample swatch as follows:

Choose the size knitting needle most likely to give the right tension (approximately No. 10 for knitting worsted; No. 11 for bulky yarn) and cast on 20 sts of knitting worsted (12 to 16 sts of bulky yarns). Knit 10 to 12 rows in stitch pattern (stockinette or garter stitch). Place the swatch on a flat surface and measure in the center of the piece, counting the number of sts within 1″ or 2″. If the gauge is not as specified, *change the size of knitting needles* and try again.

To substitute yarns: Make a sample swatch with the yarn to be used. Measure the stitch gauge as explained above and recalculate the number of sts noted in the instructions by multiplying the number of sts per inch with number of inches to be made.

To alter size measurements given in instructions: Make a sample swatch and measure the stitch gauge. Multiply the number of sts per inch by the number of inches to be made. Change the instructions accordingly.

To alter sleeve length: Styles A, B and C—Add or subtract number of sts per inch, to or from total width of piece (see diagram). Style D—Work White-Blue Stripe area and/or Cuff longer or shorter than specified.

To measure the length: Place knitted piece on a flat surface. Measure across to insure the correct width of piece in all places, *then* measure the length.

To assemble sweaters: Mark Center Front and Center Back on all pieces. Measure 9″ (10″) to either side of Center Front and Back on Top piece. Pin Body pieces to Top within measurement and seam across Chest. Fold sweater Back to Front and sew Sleeves and side seams.

To make matching scarves: Styles A and B—Make half of Sweater Top 52 (or 50)″ x 8″ (see diagram). Style C and D—Make half of Sweater Top but add garter stitch borders to prevent edges from rolling. Add fringe.

STYLE A—RED AND GREEN STRIPE SWEATER

Directions are given for Size 36. Changes for Size 40 are in parentheses. See diagram below.

MATERIALS: Reynold's "Poemes:" 8 (9) balls of Red, 8 (9) balls of Green; knitting needles, No. 10 OR ANY SIZE

STYLE A

NEEDLES WHICH WILL OBTAIN THE STITCH GAUGE BELOW; crochet hook.
GAUGE: 7 sts = 2″, 12 rows = 2″.
STITCH: Garter
DIRECTIONS—FRONT BODY-PIECE 18″ (20″) x 15″: With Red, cast on 52 sts, or number of sts to measure 15″. K 10 rows (2″ including cast-on row). *With Green, k 12 rows—2″. With Red, k 12 rows—2″. To complete 18″: Repeat from * 4 times. Cast off. To complete 20″: Repeat from * 4 times, then k 12 rows—2″ with Green.

BACK BODYPIECE 18″ (20″) x 15″: Make the same as Front but reverse colors.

FRONT AND BACK TOP AND SLEEVES 52″ x 16″: (Drawstring loops will add 1″ to the end of each Sleeve.) With Red, cast on 182 sts—or number of sts to measure 52″. K 10 rows (2″ including cast-on row), then change color and work alternating stripes as on Body.

Front Neck at 8″—last row of 4th stripe: K 77 sts—22″, cast off 28 sts —8″, k 77 sts—22″. **Next row:** With Red, k 77 on Left Front, cut thread, k 77 on Right Front.

Back Neck: K 77, cast on 28, k 77. Continue as before, alternating colors every 2″, ending with a Green stripe at 16″.

DRAWSTRING LOOPS: Insert crochet hook into edge at seam, ch 3, *sk 3 knitted rows along edge, dc in the 4th k row, ch 1. Rpt from * around edge, end ch 1 into first ch 3 loop.

DRAWSTRINGS: Ch to length desired, turn, sk 1 ch, sl st 1 into every ch. Thread through loops.

STYLE B—VARIEGATED STRIPED SWEATER WITH SCARF

Directions are given for Size 36. Changes for Size 40 are in parentheses. See diagram, this page.

MATERIALS: 9 or 10 balls (total) in the following: Paternayan's Tapestry Yarn 4 Ply (4 oz. skns) Yellow #460, Blue #351, Lavender #647, Pink #290, Green #533, Orange #962, White #040, Paterna Persian Crewel 3 Ply (3 oz skns) Purple #738; knitting needles, No. 8 OR ANY SIZE NEEDLE WHICH WILL OBTAIN THE STITCH GAUGE BELOW.
GAUGE: 5 sts = 1″.
STITCH: Garter. Stripe at random. For Striping detail, see picture on cover and pages 44-45.
DIRECTIONS—FRONT AND BACK BODY (Make 2): Cast on 90 (100) sts, or number of sts to measure 18 (20)″ across. Work even until piece measures 15″.
FRONT TOP and SLEEVES: Cast on 250 sts—or number of sts to measure 50″. Work even 8″.
Neck: K 105 sts—21″, cast off 40 sts —8″, k 105 sts—21″. **Next row:** K 105

STYLE B
DIRECTION OF KNIT →

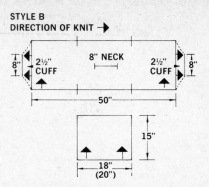

sts—21″, cast on 40 sts—8″, k 105 sts —21″.

BACK TOP and SLEEVES: Work as Front 8″. Cast off.

CUFF: Pick up sts at end of Sleeve by inserting knitting needle into the first (last) st of every 2nd garter stitch ridge. K 2½″. Cast off.

SCARF: Cast on 250 sts—50″. Work even 8″. Cast off. **Fringe:** Cut strands of yarn in lengths of 1 yd. Fold each strand in half twice and loop through edge of Scarf, matching colors of stripes.

For striping detail, see picture on cover and photographs on pages 44-45.

STYLE C—BLACK AND WHITE CHECKERBOARD SWEATER

Directions are given for Size 36. Changes for Size 40 are in parentheses. See diagram, page 42.

MATERIALS: Brunswick's Germantown Knitting Worsted (4 oz. skns): 3 skns White, 2 skns Black; knitting needles, No. 8 OR ANY SIZE NEEDLE WHICH WILL OBTAIN THE STITCH GAUGE BELOW.
GAUGE: 10 sts = 2″; 12 rows = 2″; squares = 2″x2″; stripes = 2″ wide.
STITCH: Checkerboard and Stripes —stockinette stitch; Cuffs and Borders—garter stitch.

DIRECTIONS—FRONT BODY-PIECE 18 (20)″ x 15″: With White, cast on 90 (100) sts, or number of sts to measure 18 (20)″: 9 (10) squares x 2″ = 18 (20)″.

Border: K 1″ in garter stitch.

Checkerboard Pattern: Work with 9 or 10 small balls of yarn, one of each color for each square. (Tie with rubber bands, or use bobbins.) Or, you can work with one ball of each color, floating or weaving the color not in use at the back of fabrics. Cross threads when changing color. For 18″ Chest—right side of work: (k 10 White, k 10 Black) 4 times, k 10 White. For 20″ chest—right side of work: (k 10 White, k 10 Black) 5 times. Wrong side of work: p sts in same color as knitted on previous row. Repeat these 2 rows to complete 12 rows, 2″, then reverse colors. For 18″ Chest - right side: (k 10 Black, k 10 White) 4 times, k 10 Black. For 20″ Chest - right side: (k 10 Black, k 10 White) 5 times. Wrong side: p sts in same color as knitted on previous row. Repeat 24 rows—4″ pattern as above, until piece measures 15″ in length (7 squares x 2″ + 1″ border). Cast off.

BACK BODYPIECE: Make the same as Front but reverse colors of checkerboard.

STRIPED FRONT and BACK SLEEVES: With Black—cast on 170 sts—or number of sts to measure 34″. Work 12 rows—2″ in stockinette stitch. Alternate colors every 2″ until 3½ stripes—7″ have been completed of Front.

1″ Neckband and 8″ Opening: Rows 7, 9 and 11 of White stripe, right side: K 170. Rows 8, 10 and 12: P 60, k 50, p 60. **Row 13:** place 60 sts on either side of neck on holders and work on sts, for Neck only, k 50 sts with White. **Row 14:** K 5, knit and cast off 40, k 5. **Row 15:** K 5 only on either side of Neck. **Row 16:** K 5, cast on 40, k 5.

1″ Back Neckband: work 6 rows of White, place sts on holder.

Left and Right Sleeves: With Black—work 6 rows—1″ on either side of White Neckband.

Back: Place all sts on same needle and continue 2″ striped pattern until 8 stripes—16″ are completed. Cast off.

Cuffs: With White—cast on 26 sts—or number of sts to measure 5″. Work even in garter stitch until piece measures—16″. Sew Cuffs to end of Sleeve.

STYLE D—WHITE PULLOVER WITH STRIPES AND DIAMOND PATTERN
Directions are given for Size 36. Changes for Size 40 are in parentheses. See diagrams, this page.

MATERIALS: Columbia-Minerva's Nantuk Bulky: 10 (11) skns Winter White, 2 skns Sapphire, 1 skn Scarlet, 1 skn Kelly, 1 skn Bright Yellow; knitting needles, No. 11 OR ANY SIZE NEEDLE WHICH WILL OBTAIN THE

STYLE D
DIRECTION OF KNIT

18″ (17″) 18″ 18″ (17″)
20″
16″

SEAM 13″ 12″ 8″

18″ (20″)

STITCH GAUGE BELOW.
GAUGE: 3 sts = 1″.
STITCH: Stockinette stitch with Garter stitch Borders.
FRONT and BACK BODYPIECES: 18″ (20″) x 20″: With White—cast on 57 (63) sts—or number of sts to measure 18 (20)″.
Border: K 4 rows—1″ in garter stitch. **Row 5:** K 57 (63). **Row 6** - wrong side: K 4, p 49 (55), k 4. Repeat Rows 5 and 6 until piece measures 8″, then continue in stockinette stitch only until piece measures 20″. Cast off.
LEFT SLEEVE: With White—cast on 51 sts—or number of sts to measure 16″.
Cuff: Work in garter stitch—4″.
Blue-White Stripe: Work 9″ right side of work—k 5 Blue, (k 5 White, k 5 Blue) 4 times, k 6 White. Work with 10 balls of yarn, one for each stripe. (Tie with rubber bands.) Or, you can work with one ball of each color, floating or weaving the color not in use at the back of the fabrics. Cross threads when color changing. Wrong side: P sts in same color as knitted on previous row. **Green, Red and Yellow Band 6″:** Work charted design. With White—work 2 rows ½″. **Blue-White Stripe ½″ only:** Work as above for 2

rows only. With White—work 2″.
Neck Borders and Opening: Right side of work—k 57 (63). Wrong side: P 21, k 8, p 22. Repeat twice, then divide Sleeve in half for Neck Opening and work 2 parts.
Back: Right side—k 26, turn. Wrong side: K 4, p 22. Repeat for 8″, end completing the right side.
Front: Right side—K 25. Wrong side: P 21, k 4. Repeat for 8″, end completing the right side.
Back and Front: Wrong side—P 21, k 8, p 22. Right side: K. Repeat twice.
Right Shoulder and Sleeve: Work to correspond to Left Sleeve.

THE KNITTED SWEATER AND HAT

(pages 40-41)

Directions are given for size Small (8-10). Changes for sizes Medium (12-14) and Large (16-18) are in parentheses. Hat will fit all sizes.
MATERIALS: Columbia-Minerva Knitting Worsted (4 oz. skeins): *For Sweater:* 5(6,7) skeins of desired color. *For Hat:* 1 skein; knitting needles, 1 pair No. 10 OR ANY SIZE NEEDLES WHICH WILL OBTAIN THE STITCH GAUGE BELOW; crochet hook, Size G.
GAUGE: 4 sts = 1″; 14 rows (7 ridges) = 2″.
MEASUREMENTS:

Sizes:	Small (8-10)	Medium (12-14)	Large (16-18)
Bust:	34″	37″	40″
Width across back or front at underarms:	17″	18½″	20″
Width across sleeve at upper arm:	14″	15½″	17″

DIRECTIONS—BACK: Starting at lower edge cast on 68(74,80) sts. Work even in garter st (k each row) until total length is 16(16½,17)″ or desired length to underarm. Place a marker at each end of last row for underarms. Continue in garter st until length from markers is 7(7¾,8½)″. Bind off.
FRONT: Work same as Back.
SLEEVES: Starting at lower edge, cast on 48(50,52) sts. Work in garter st until total length is 16″. Continuing to work in garter st, inc one st at each end of next row, then every 4th row until there are 58(64,68) sts. Work even in garter st until total length is 20(21,21½)″ from beg. Bind off.
POCKET: Starting at top edge, cast on 20 sts. Work in k 1, p 1 ribbing for 1″. Work even in garter st until length is 5″ from beg. Bind off.
FINISHING: Pin each piece to measurements on a padded surface; cover with a damp cloth and allow to dry; do not press. Starting at side edges, sew approximately 3½(4,4¼)″ shoulder seams. Leaving 6″ slits at lower

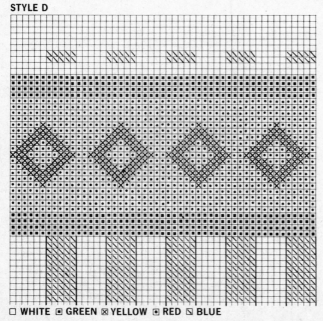

□ WHITE ▣ GREEN ⊠ YELLOW ▩ RED ◨ BLUE

edge, sew side seams up to underarm markers; sew sleeve seams. Fit sleeves into armholes and sew in place. Sew pocket to upper right front as illustrated. From right side, using crochet hook and holding yarn on wrong side, work 1 row of sl sts along each seam. Cut yarn and fasten at end of each row. Fold lower portion of each sleeve to right side for cuffs.
HAT: Starting at lower edge, cast on 66 sts. Work in k 1, p 1 ribbing for 1″. Now work in garter st (k each row) until total length is 9″ from beg.
Top Shaping—Row 1: * K 2 tog, k 9; rpt from * across—6 decs made. **Row 2:** K across—60 sts. **Row 3:** * K 2 tog, k 8; rpt from * across—54 sts. **Row 4:** K across. Continuing to work in garter st, dec 6 sts evenly spaced on next row, then every other row (having one st less after each dec than on previous dec row) until 12 sts rem. Leaving a 24″ length, cut yarn. Using a darning needle, slip rem sts onto end of yarn; draw sts closely together and fasten securely on wrong side; sew back seam.

CABLE PULLOVER AND HAT

(page 42)

Directions are given for size Small (8-10). Changes for sizes Medium (12-14) and Large (16-18) are in parentheses. Hat will fit all sizes.
MATERIALS: Bernat Sesame "4" (4 oz. balls):—*Pullover:* 4(5,6) balls of White. *Hat:* 2 oz. of White; knitting needles, 1 pair No. 8 OR ANY SIZE NEEDLES WHICH WILL OBTAIN THE STITCH GAUGE BELOW. One double-pointed needle, No. 8.
GAUGE: Pattern—5 sts= 1″; 6 rows = 1″.
MEASUREMENTS:

Sizes:	Small (8-10)	Medium (12-14)	Large (16-18)
Bust:	33″	36″	41″
Width across back or front at underarms:	16½″	18″	20½″
Width across sleeve at upper arm:	11½″	13″	13″

(Note: Pullover is worked in vertical rows, from side to side.)
DIRECTIONS—PULLOVER—
BACK: Starting at right side edge, cast on 86(88,90) sts. **Underarm Section—Row 1 (right side):** (K 2, yo, sl 1, k 1, psso, p 2) 4 times; k 16, (p 2, k 2, yo, sl 1, k 1, psso) 4 times; *k 22(24,26)*—**waist band—Row 2:** K 22(24,26), work (p 2, yo, p 2 tog, k 2) 4 times; p 16, (k 2, p 2, yo, p 2 tog) 4 times. Rpt last 2 rows (Rows 1 and 2) 0(2,2) more times. *Next Row:* * Place 2 sts on dp needle and hold in front of work, k next 2 sts, k 2 sts from dp needle—**front cable made;** p 2,

(front cable, p 2) 3 more times; k 16, p 2, *place next 2 sts on dp needle and hold in back of work, k next 2 sts, k 2 sts from dp needle*—**back cable made;** (p 2, back cable over next 4 sts) 3 more times; k to end of row. **Next 7 Rows:** Rpt Row 2 once; then rpt Rows 1 and 2 alternately 3 times—there are 10(14,14) rows in all.
YOKE—First Armhole and Shoulder Shaping: At end of last row, place a marker on needle; on same needle cast on 34(38,43) sts for armhole edge.
Row 1: K to marker, slip marker; across body sts work (front cable over 4 sts, p 2) 4 times; *place next 4 sts on dp needle and hold in front, k next 4 sts, k 4 sts from dp needle, place next 4 sts on dp needle and hold in back, k next 4 sts, k 4 sts from dp needle*—**large double cable made;** (p 2, back cable over 4 sts) 4 times; k 22(24,26) for waist band—120(126,133) sts.
Row 2: K 22(24,26), work (p 2, yo, p 2 tog, k 2) 4 times; p 16, (k 2, p 2, y o, p 2 tog) 4 times; slip marker, k rem sts. Slip marker in every row.
Row 3: K to marker, (k 2, yo, sl 1, k 1, psso, p 2) 4 times; k 16, (p 2, k 2, yo, sl 1, k 1, psso) 4 times; k to end of row. **Rows 4 through 7:** Rpt last 2 rows (Rows 2 and 3) twice. **Row 8:** Work as Row 2 to marker, k to within last st, inc in last st—inc made at shoulder. **Row 9:** K to marker, (front cable) 4 times; k to end of row —121(127,134) sts. **Rows 10 through 15:** Rpt Rows 2 and 3 of Armhole and Shoulder Shaping, 3 times. **Row 16:** Work same as Row 2 to last st, inc in last st—122(128,135) sts.
(**Note:** Last 16 rows form pattern over body stitches; waist band and yoke are worked in garter stitch (k each row) throughout.)
Working even (omit all shoulder increases), repeat Rows 1 through 16, 3(3,4) more times, and ending at shoulder edge.

Second Shoulder and Armhole Shaping:—Row 1: *K 2 tog*—dec made at shoulder edge; k to marker; complete row same as Row 1 of First Armhole and Shoulder Shaping. **Rows 2 through 8:** Rpt Rows 2 through 8 of First Armhole and Shoulder, but omitting inc at end of Row 8. **Row 9:** Dec at beg of row, complete row same as Row 9 of pattern—120(126,133) sts. **Rows 10 through 16:** Working even (omit inc at shoulder), work same as Rows 10 through 16 of First Armhole and Shoulder Shaping. **Next Row:** From shoulder edge, bind off 34(38,43) sts; complete row in pattern.
Underarm Section: Work 9(13,13) rows even over rem 86(88,90) sts to correspond with opposite underarm section. Bind off, knitting k sts and purling p sts.

FRONT: Starting at left side edge, work same as for Back until Row 16 of First Armhole and Shoulder Shaping has been completed. Being careful to keep continuity of pattern over body sts, and continuing to work waist band and yoke in garter st throughout, work 8(8,12) more rows even, ending at shoulder.
Neck Shaping:—Next Row: From shoulder edge, bind off 10 sts, k to marker, complete row in pattern— 112(118,125) sts. Work even in pattern over these sts for 31(31,39) more rows, ending at neck edge. At end of last row, cast on 10 sts for side edge of neck. Work even over 122(128,135) sts for 8(8,12) rows. Starting from Second Shoulder and Armhole Shaping, complete Front same as Back.
SLEEVES: Starting at underarm seam, cast on 112 sts for all sizes.
Underarm Section:—Row 1 (right side): (K 2, yo, sl 1, k 1, psso, p 2) 4 times; k 16, (p 2, k 2, yo, sl 1, k 1, psso) 4 times; k 48 for lower section of sleeve. Having 48 sts in garter st (k each row) for lower section of sleeve, instead of 22(24,26) sts of waist band, continue to work same as for Back Underarm Section until 10(14,14) rows have been completed.
Cap Shaping: At end of last row, place a marker on needle, on same needle cast on 12(15,18) sts. **Row 1:** Work same as Row 1 of First Armhole and Shoulder Shaping of Back— 124(127,130) sts. **Row 2:** K 48, (p 2, yo, p 2 tog, k 2) 4 times; p 16, (k 2, p 2, yo, p 2 tog) 4 times; slip marker, k to within last 2 sts, inc in each of last 2 sts **Row 3:** K to marker, (k 2, yo, sl 1, k 1, psso, p 2) 4 times; k 16, (p 2, k 2, yo, sl 1, k 1, psso) 4 times; k 48. **Rows 4 through 16:** Rpt last 2 rows (Rows 2 and 3) 6 times, then rpt Row 2 once more—140(143,146) sts. **Rows 17 through 32:** Working even (omit all incs) over 140(143,146) sts, rpt Rows 1 through 16 of First Armhole and Shoulder Shaping of Back. **Rows 33 through 48:** Continuing to work same as for Rows 1 through 16, dec 2 sts (to dec 2 sts, k 2 tog twice) at cap edge of sleeve on next row, then at same edge every other row 8 times in all—124(127,130) sts. **Row 49:** From cap edge, bind off 12(15,18) sts; complete row same as Row 1 of First Armhole and Shoulder—112 sts. **Underarm Section:** Work 9(13,13) rows to correspond with opposite underarm section. Bind off, knitting k sts and pushing p sts.
FINISHING: Pin each piece to measurements on a padded surface; cover with a damp cloth and allow to dry; do not press. Sew front shoulders to corresponding edges of back, sew side and sleeve seams, matching cables. Fit sleeves into armholes and sew in place. Turn 2½″ cuff to right side at

lower edge of each sleeve.

HAT: Starting at center back, cast on 46 sts. **Row 1 (right side):** K 6, (k 2, yo, sl 1, k 1, psso, p 2) 4 times, k 16. Mark end of this row for lower edge. **Row 2:** P 16, (k 2, p 2, yo, p 2 tog) 4 times; do not work over rem sts. Turn. **Row 3:** (K 2, yo, sl 1, k 1, psso, p 2) 4 times, k 16. **Rows 4 and 5:** Rpt Rows 2 and 3. **Row 6:** P 16, (k 2, p 2, yo, p 2 tog) 4 times; k 6—46 sts. **Row 7:** K 6, * place next 2 sts on dp needle and hold in front, k next 2 sts, k 2 sts from dp needle—**front cable made**; rpt from * 3 more times; *place next 4 sts on dp needle and hold in front, k next 4 sts, k 4 sts from dp needle; place next 4 sts on dp needle and hold in back, k next 4 sts, k 4 sts from dp needle—**large double cable made.** **Rows 8 through 13:** Rpt Rows 2 and 3, 3 times. **Row 14:** Rpt Row 6. **Row 15:** K 6, (front cable, p 2) 4 times; k 16. **Rows 16 through 21:** Rpt Rows 2 and 3, 3 times. **Row 22:** Rpt Row 6. Rpt last 16 rows (Rows 7 through 22) 7 more times; then rpt Rows 7 through 14 once more. Bind off, knitting k sts and purling p sts. With a darning needle and same yarn, garter top edge closely together, secure; then sew back seam, matching cables.

LOOP JACKET WITH KNITTED SLEEVES

(page 42)

Directions are given for size Small (8-10). Changes for sizes Medium (12-14) and Large (16-18) are in parentheses.

MATERIALS: Bernat Sesame "4" (4 oz. balls): 4(5,5) balls of White (A) and Bernat Catkin by Jaeger (1¾ oz. balls): 11(12,14) balls White (B); crochet hook, Size I OR ANY SIZE HOOK WHICH WILL OBTAIN THE STITCH GAUGE BELOW; knitting needles, 1 pair No. 8 OR ANY SIZE NEEDLES WHICH WILL OBTAIN THE STITCH GAUGE BELOW; 6 large hooks and eyes.

GAUGE: Crochet (using one strand each of A and B held tog)—3 sts = 1"; 6 rows = 2". Knit (using A only) —5 sts = 1"; 8 rows (4 ridges) = 1".

MEASUREMENTS:

	Small	Medium	Large
Sizes:	(8-10)	(12-14)	(16-18)
Bust:	33"	36"	40"
Width across back at underarms:	16½"	18"	20"
Width across each front at underarm:	8¼"	9"	10"
Width across sleeve at upper arm:	12"	13"	14"

(**Note:** Body is crocheted all in one piece without side seams, using one strand each of the 2 yards (A and B)

held together. Sleeves are knitted with a single strand of A.)

DIRECTIONS—BODY: Starting at entire lower edge with crochet hook and one strand each of A and B held together, ch 100(110,122) to measure 34(37,41)". **Row 1:** Cut a piece of cardboard 2" wide and about 3" long, hold cardboard in back of work, sk first ch from hook, * insert hook in next ch, wind yarn from back to front around the 2" width of cardboard, yarn over hook and draw loop through, yarn over hook, draw through the 2 loops on hook—**loop st made**; rpt from * across chain—99(109,121) loop sts. Ch 1, turn. **Row 2 (right side):** Sc in first st, * ch 1, sk next st, sc in next st; rpt from * across. Ch 1, turn. **Row 3:** Make loop st in each sc and in each ch across—99(109,121) loop sts. Rpt last 2 rows (Rows 2 and 3) for pattern until length is approximately 11(12,12½)" from beg, ending with Row 3. Ch 1, turn.

RIGHT FRONT—Row 1: Sc in first st, * ch 1, sk next st, sc in next st; rpt from * 9(10,12) more times; do not work over rem sts—21(23,27) sts, including ch sts. Ch 1, turn. **Row 2:** Rpt Row 3 of Body. Rpt Rows 2 and 3 of Body until length from Row 1 of Right Front is 6½(7¼,8)", ending with a right-side row. Ch 1, turn.

Neck Shaping—Row 1: Work loop st in each of first 13(13,15) sts; do not work over rem sts. Ch 1, turn. **Row 2:** Sk first 2 sts, sc in next st, * ch 1, sk next st, sc in next st; rpt from * across to end of row—11(11,13) sts. Ch 1, turn. **Row 3:** Work loop st in each sc and in each ch across. Ch 1, turn. **Row 4:** Rpt Row 2 of Body. Ch 1, turn.

Shoulder Shaping: Sl st in each of first 5(5,6) sts (including ch sts), loop st in each of rem 6(6,7) sts. Cut yarn and fasten.

BACK: With right side facing, sk next free 7(9,9) sts on last row worked before Right Front for underarm, attach double strand to next st, sc in same st, work (ch 1, sk next st, sc in next st) 21(22,24) times; do not work over rem sts—43(45,49) sts. Ch 1, turn. Work even in pattern over these sts until length of armhole is same as on Right Front up to shoulder, ending with a right-side row. Ch 1, turn.

Shoulder Shaping—Row 1: Sl st in each of first 5(5,6) sts (including ch sts), make loop st in each st to within last 5(5,6) sts, sl st in next st. Ch 1, turn. **Row 2:** Sk sl st, make sl st in each of next 5(5,6) sts, sc in next st, (ch 1, sk next st, sc in next st) 11(12,12) times; do not work over rem sts. Cut yarn and fasten.

LEFT FRONT: With right side facing, sk next 7(9,9) sts on last row worked before Right Front for underarm, attach double strand to next st,

sc in same st; work to correspond with Right Front, reversing shaping.

SLEEVES: Starting at lower edge with A only and knitting needles, cast on 38(40,44) sts. Working in garter st (k each row) throughout, work 9 rows even. Inc one st at each end of next row, then every 10th row until there are 60(66,70) sts. Work even until total length is 17(17½,18)".

Top Shaping— Continuing in garter st, bind off 4(5,5) sts at beg of next 2 rows. Dec one st at each end every other row until 20 sts rem. Bind off 2 sts at beg of next 4 rows. Bind off rem 12 sts.

Cuff: With 1 strand each of A and B held together and crochet hook, ch 30(32,34). Work same as Body until Row 3 has been completed—29(31,33) sts. Rpt Rows 2 and 3 of Body 3 more times. Cut yarn and fasten.

FINISHING: Sew shoulder seams. **Collar—Row 1:** With wrong side facing, using double strand as for Body and crochet hook, attach yarn to corner st on left front neck edge; working along entire neck edge, make a loop st in each st and in side edge of each row across neck to corner st on right front edge (be sure to have an odd number of sts). Ch 1, turn. Rpt Rows 2 and 3 of Body 3 times. Cut yarn and fasten. Sew side and sleeve seams. Sew short edges of each cuff together. With wrong side of cuff facing, sew starting ch of cuff to lower edge of each sleeve, easing in cuff edge to fit. Turn cuffs to right side. Sew in sleeves, adjusting to fit. Sew hooks and eyes to wrong side along front edges, having first set at top corners of collar, second set at base of collar and other 4 sets evenly spaced along rem front edges.

WHITE "BOBBLE-N-LACE" CARDIGAN WITH DRAWSTRING WAIST

(page 43)

"FOR EXPERIENCED KNITTERS ONLY"

Directions are given for size Small (8-10). Changes for sizes Medium (12-14) and Large (16-18) are in parentheses.

MATERIALS: Tahki's Donegal Homespun Tweeds (4 oz. skeins): 6(7,8) skeins of #826; knitting needles, 1 pair No. 8 OR ANY SIZE NEEDLES WHICH WILL OBTAIN THE STITCH GAUGE BELOW; circular needle, No. 8 (29" length); 1 dp needle, No. 8; crochet hook, Size F.

GAUGE: 9 sts = 2"; 6 rows = 1".

MEASUREMENTS:

	Small	Medium	Large
Sizes:	(8-10)	(12-14)	(16-18)
Bust:	35"	38"	41"
Width across			

back at underarms:	17"	19"	20"
Width across each front at underarm:	9"	9½"	10½"
Width across sleeve at upper arm:	12"	12½"	13½"

DIRECTIONS—CARDIGAN—

BACK: Starting at lower edge, cast on 78(86,92) sts. **Bottom Band—Row 1 (right side):** P 1(5,1), * k 6, p 2, *k 2, yo, sl 1, k 1, psso*—lace strip started; p 2; rpt from * 4(4,5) more times; k 4,p 1(5,1). **Row 2:** K 1(5,1) * *place next 2 sts on dp needle and hold in front, p 1, p the 2 sts from dp needle, place next st on dp needle and hold in back, p 2, p st from dp needle*—**this makes double cable on right side;** *k 2, p 2, yo, p 2 tog*—**lace strip;** k 2; rpt from * 4(4,5) more times; place 2 sts on dp needle and hold in front, p 1, p 2 from dp, place next st on dp needle and hold in back, p 2, p 1 from dp needle, k 1(5,1). **Row 3:** Rpt Row 1. **Row 4:** K 1(5,1) * p 2, p 2 tog, but keep sts on needle, p first st again, drop both sts off needle, p 2, k 2, p 2, yo, p 2 tog, k 2; rpt from * 4(4,5) more times; p 2, p 2 tog, keeping both sts on needle, p first st again, drop both sts off needle, p 2, k 1(5,1). **Rows 5 through 18:** Rpt last 4 rows (Rows 1 through 4) 3 times; then rpt Rows 1 and 2 once more. **Row 19:** Working same as Row 1, dec one st at each end—76(84,90) sts.

Body—Row 20: P 0(4,0), * k 6, p 8; rpt from * 4(4,5) more times; k 6, p 0(4,0). **Row 21:** K 0(4,0), * p 6, k 8; rpt from * 4(4,5) more times; p 6, k 0(4,0). **Row 22:** Rpt Row 21. **Row 23:** Rpt Row 20. **Rows 24 through 81:** Rpt Rows 20 through 23 for Body pat 14 more times; then rpt Rows 20 and 21 once more.

Underarm Shaping—Row 82: Bind off 6(8,9) sts, keeping continuity of pat, work across to within last 6(8,9) sts, bind off rem sts. Place rem 64(68,72) sts on a large st holder and put aside.

RIGHT FRONT: Cast on 42(44,48) sts. **Bottom Band—Row 1 (right side):** P 1(2,4), work (k 6, p 2, k 2, yo, sl 1, k 1, psso, p 2) 2 times; k 6, p 2, k 2, yo, sl 1, k 1, psso, p 1(2,4) **Row 2:** K 1(2,4), * p 2, yo, p 2 tog, k 2, place next 2 sts on dp needle and hold in front, p next st, p 2 from dp needle, place next st on dp needle and hold in back, p 2, p 1 from dp needle, k 2; rpt from * across, ending last rpt with k 1(2,4). **Row 3:** Rpt Row 1. **Row 4:** K 1(2,4), * p 2, yo, p 2 tog, k 2, p 2, p 2 tog but keep sts on needle, p first st again, drop both sts off needle, p 2, k 2; rpt from * across, end last rpt with k 1(2,4). **Rows 5 through 18:** Rpt last 4 rows (Rows 1 through 4) 3 times; then rpt Rows 1 and 2 once more. **Row 19:** Work same

as Row 1 but end with yo, sl 1, k 2 tog, psso, p 0(1,3)—41(43,47) sts. **Body—Row 20(wrong side):** Work (p 8,k 6) twice; place a marker on needle, k 13(15,19)—**front panel. Row 21:** P 13(15,19), slip marker, (p 6, k 8) twice. Slip marker in every row. **Row 22:** (K 8, p 6) twice; k 13(15,19). **Row 23:** P 3(4,6), *in next st (k 1, p 1) twice, turn, p 4, turn, (p 2 tog) twice; turn, k 2 tog*—**bobble made;** p 5, make bobble in next st, p 3(4,6), work (k 6, p 8) twice. **Row 24:** Work as Row 20 to marker; k 3(4,6), p 1, k 5, p 1, k 3(4,6). **Row 25:** P 1(2,4), bobble in next st, p 1, *place next st on dp needle and hold in front, p next st, k st from dp needle*—**left twist;** p 3, *place next st on dp needle and hold in back, k next st, p st from dp needle*—**right twist;** p 1, bobble in next st, p 1(2,4); complete row as Row 21. **Row 26:** Work as Row 22 to marker; k 1(2,4), p 1, k 2, p 1, k 3, p 1, k 2, p 1, k 1(2,4). **Row 27:** P 1(2,4), make (left twist, p 1) twice; (right twist, p 1) twice; p 0(1,3), complete row as Row 23. Continue to work as Rows 20 through 23 for rib pat over the 28 sts of body section. **Row 28:** Work in rib pat to marker; k 2(3,5), p 1, k 2, p 3, k 2, p 1, k2(3,5). **Row 29:** P 1(2,4), inc in next st, left twist, p 1, sl 1, k 2 tog, psso, p 1, right twist, inc in next st, p 1(2,4); complete row in rib pat. **Row 30:** Work rib pat to marker, k 4(5,7), place next st on dp needle and hold in back, k 1, p st from dp needle, p 1, place next st on dp needle and hold in front, p 1, k st from dp needle, k 4(5,7). **Row 31:** P 4(5,7), inc in next st, sl 1, k 2 tog, psso, inc in next st, p 4(5,7), complete row in rib pat. (**Note:** Continue to rpt Rows 20 through 23 over the 28 sts of body section for rib pat. Hereafter directions are given for Front Panel Only.) **Row 32:** Work to marker, k 6(7,9), p 1, k 6(7,9). **Row 33:** P 3(4,6), bobble in next st, p 2, k 1, p 2, bobble in next st, p 3(4,6). **Row 34:** K 3(4,6), p 1, (k 2, p 1) twice; k 3(4,6). **Row 35:** P 1(2,4), bobble in next st, p 1, left twist, p 1, k 1, p 1, right twist, p 1, bobble in next st, p 1(2,4). **Row 36:** K 1(2,4), p 1, k 2, (p 1, k 1) twice; p 1, k 2, p 1, k 1(2,4). **Row 37:** P 1(2,4), left twist, p 1, left twist, k 1, right twist, p 1, right twist, p 1(2,4). Keeping continuity of rib pat over body section, rpt last 10 rows (Rows 28 through 37) for Front Band bobble pat 4 more times; then rpt Rows 28 through 31 once more. There are 81 rows in all.

Underarm Shaping—Row 82: Bind off 6(8,9) sts; work to marker, k 6(7,9), p 1, k 6(7,9)—35(35,38) sts. Place rem sts on a separate st holder and put aside.

LEFT FRONT: Work same as Right Front until the 19 rows of Bottom Band have been completed.

Body—Row 20: *K 13(15,19)—front panel;* place marker on needle, (k 6, p 8) twice. **Row 21:** (K 8, p 6) twice; p 13(15,19). Work to correspond with Right Front, reversing pat, position of front band as established, and underarm shaping.

SLEEVES: Work same as Right Front until 18 rows of Bottom Band have been completed. **Row 19:** Rpt Row 1—42(44,48) sts. **Row 20 (Inc Row):** P 2(3,4), * k in front and in back of each of next 3 sts, p 8; rpt from * across, ending last rpt with p 3(4,5) —54(56,60) sts. **Row 21:** K 3(4,5), p 6, (k 8, p 6) 3 times; k 3(4,5). **Row 22:** Rpt Row 21. **Row 23:** P 3(4,5), * k 6, p 8; rpt from * across, ending last rpt with p 3(4,5). **Row 24:** Rpt Row 23. Rpt last 4 rows (Rows 21 through 24) for sleeve pat until total length is approximately 17(17½,18)" from beg, end with a right-side row. **Underarm Shaping:** Keeping in pat, bind off 6(7,9) sts at each end of row. Place rem 42 sts on a st holder. Make other sleeve in same manner.

YOKE: With wrong side of all pieces facing, slip sts onto circular needle in the following order: Left Front, Sleeve, Back, Sleeve, Right Front— 218(222,232) sts on needle (be careful to have underarm bound-off sts in the right position). **Row 1:** With right side facing, attach yarn to front edge at beg of Right Front; p 3(4,6), bobble in next st, p 2, k 1, p 2, bobble, p 4(3,5), work (p 2 tog) 2(3,2) times; p 2, *k 2, yo, sl 1, k 1, psso,—lace strip started;* * p 7(7,8), p 2 tog, bobble, p 5, bobble, p 7(7,9), (k 2 tog) 1(1,0) time; k 2, yo, sl 1, k 1, psso; rpt from * across all sections to within last 20(22,24) sts, p 4(3,5), work (p 2 tog) 2(3,2) times; p 2, bobble, p 2, k 1, p 2, bobble, p 3(4,6)—202(204,222) sts. Do not join. Turn. Work back and forth on circular needle as if working on straight needles. **Row 2:** K 3(4,6), p 1, (k 2, p 1) twice; k 8(8,9), * *p 2, yo, p 2 tog—lace strip;* k 8(8,9), p 1, k 5, p 1, k 8(8,9); rpt from * across to within last 22(23,26) sts, p 2, yo, p 2 tog, k 8(8,9), (p 1, k 2) twice; p 1, k 3(4,6). **Row 3:** P 1(2,4), bobble, p 1, left twist, p 1, k 1, p 1, right twist, p 1, bobble, p 6(6,7), * k 2, yo, sl 1, k 1, psso, p 6(6,7), bobble, p 1, left twist, p 3, right twist, p 1, bobble, p 6(6,7); rpt from * across to within last 22(23,26) sts, k 2, yo, sl 1, k 1, psso, p 6(6,7), bobble, p 1, left twist, p 1, k 1, p 1, right twist, p 1, bobble, p 1(2,4). **Row 4:** K 1(2,4), p 1, k 2, (p 1, k 1) twice; p 1, k 2, p 1, k 6(6,7), * p 2, yo, p 2 tog, k 6(6,7), p 1, k 2, p 1, k 3, p 1, k 2, p 1, k 6(6,7); rpt from * to within last 22(23,26) sts, p 2, yo, p 2 tog, k 6(6,7), p 1, k 2, (p 1, k 1) twice; p 1, k 2, p 1, k 1(2,4). **Row 5:** P 1(2,4), left twist, p 1, left twist, k 1, right twist, p 1, right twist,

* p 6(6,7), k 2, yo, sl 1, k 1, psso, p 6(6,7), left twist, p 1, left twist, k 1, right twist, p 1, right twist; rpt from * across to within last 1(2,4) st, p 1(2,4). **Row 6:** K 2(3,5), p 1, k 2, p 3, k 2, p 1, * k 7(7,8), p 2, yo, p 2 tog, k 7(7,8), p 1, k 2, p 3, k 2, p 1; rpt from * across, end with k 2(3,5). **Row 7:** P 1(2,4), * inc in next st, left twist, p 1, sl 1, k 2 tog psso, p 1, right twist, inc in next st, p 6(6,7), k 2, yo, sl 1, k 1, psso, p 6(6,7); rpt from * across to within last 2(3,5) sts, inc in next st, p 1(2,4). **Row 8:** K 4(5,7), * place next st on dp needle and hold in back, k 1, p st from dp needle, p 1, place next st on dp needle and hold in front, p 1, k st from dp needle, k 9(9,10), p 2, yo, p 2 tog, k 9(9,10); rpt from * across to last 4(5,7) sts, k rem sts. **Row 9:** P 4(5,7), * inc in next st, sl 1, k 2 tog, psso, inc in next st, p 9(9,10), k 2, yo, sl 1, k 1, psso, p 9(9,10); rpt from * across to last 5(6,8) sts, inc in next st, p rem 4(5,7) sts. **Row 10 (Dec Row):** K 6(7,9), p 1, * k 5, k 2 tog, k 4(4,5), p 2, yo, p 2 tog, k 4(4,5), k 2 tog, k 5, p 1; rpt from * across, end with k 6(7,9)—14 sts decreased. **Row 11:** P 3(4,6), * bobble in next st, p 2, k 1, p 2, bobble in next st, p 7(7,8); k 2, yo, sl 1, k 1, psso, p 7(7,8); rpt from * across to last 3(4,6) sts, p 3(4,6)—188(190,208) sts. **Row 12:** K 3(4,6), * work (p 1, k 2) 2 times; p 1, k 7(7,8), p 2, yo, p 2 tog, k 7(7,8); rpt from * across to last 3(4,6) sts, k 3 (4,6). **Row 13:** P 1(2,4), * bobble, p 1, left twist, p 1, k 1, p 1, right twist, p 1, bobble, p 5(5,6), k 2, yo, sl 1, k 1, psso, p 5(5,6); rpt from * across to last 1(2,4) st, p 1(2,4). **Row 14:** K 1(2,4), * p 1, k 2, (p 1, k 1) twice; p 1, k 2, p 1, k 5(5,6), p 2, yo, p 2 tog, k 5(5,6); rpt from * across to last 1(2,4) st, k 1(2,4). **Row 15:** P 1(2,4), * left twist, p 1, left twist, k 1, right twist, p 1, right twist, p 5(5,7), k 2, yo, sl 1, k 1, psso, p 5(5,6); rpt from * to last 1(2,4) st, p 1(2,4). **Row 16:** Making k 6(6,7) instead of k 7(7,8) before and after each lace strip, work same as Row 6. **Rows 17,18 and 19:** Having one st less before and after each lace strip, work same as Rows 7, 8 and 9. **Row 20 (Dec Row):** K 6(7,9), p 1, * k 4, k 2 tog, k 4(4,5), p 2, yo, p 2 tog, k 4(4,5), k 2 tog, k 4, p 1; rpt from * across to last 6(7,9) sts, k 6(7,9)—174(176,194) sts. **Rows 21 through 25:** Having one st less before and after each lace strip, work same as Rows 11 through 15. **Rows 26 through 29: Having 2 sts less before and after each lace strip,** work same as Rows 6 through 9. **Row 30 (Dec Row):** K 6(7,9), p 1, * k 2 tog, k 5(5,6); k 2 tog, p 2, yo, p 2 tog, k 2 tog, k 5(5,6), k 2 tog, p 1; rpt from * across, end with k 6(7,9)—2 decs made before and after each lace strip—146(148,166) sts. **Rows 31 through 35: Having 3 sts**

less before and after each lace strip, work as for Rows 11 through 15. **Rows 36 through 39: Having 4 sts less before and after each lace strip,** work same as Rows 6 through 9. **Row 40 (Dec Row):** K 6(7,9), p 1, * k 2 tog, k 3(3,4), k 2 tog, p 2, yo, p 2 tog, k 2 tog, k 3, k 2 tog, p 1; rpt from * across, end with k 6(7,9)—118(120,138) sts. **Rows 41 through 49:** Keeping continuity of bobble pat and lace strip throughout, work 9 rows even.
FOR LARGE SIZE ONLY—Row 50 (Dec Row): Keeping in pat, dec one st before and after each lace strip—124 sts. Work 9 rows even in pat over these sts.
FOR ALL SIZES—Next Row (Dec Row): K 0(1,3), work (k 2 tog) 3 times; p 1, *(k 2 tog) twice; k 1, p 2, yo, p 2 tog, (k 2 tog) twice; k 1; rpt from * across, end with (k 2 tog) 3 times; k 0 (1,3)—84(86,90) sts. **Next Row:** Bind off, working sts as follows: P 3(4,6), k 1, (p 1, p 2 tog, sl 1, k 1, psso, k 2 tog, p 1, k 2 tog, k 1) 7 times; p 3(4,6).
FINISHING: Pin cardigan to measurements on a padded surface; cover with a damp cloth and allow to dry; do not press. Sew side, sleeve and underarm seams.
BUTTON LOOPS: With right side facing, mark with pins the position of 13 button loops evenly spaced along right front edge, having first pin ¼" above lower edge and last pin ¼" below neck edge. Using crochet hook, attach yarn in end st of first row on right front edge, sl st in end of next row, * ch 5, sk about ½" along front edge, sl st evenly to within next pin; rpt from * 11 more times; ch 5, sk ½", sl st to corner at neck edge. Continue to sl st evenly along neck edge and along left front edge, down to lower corner. Cut yarn and fasten.
BUTTON (Make 13): With crochet hook, ch 4. Join with sl st to form ring. **Rnd 1:** 6 sc in ring. Do not join. **Rnd 2:** Sc in each sc around. Stuff button with some cotton. **Rnd 3:** (Sk next sc, sc in next sc) 3 times. Leaving 10" length for sewing, cut yarn and fasten. Using a darning needle and end of yarn, sew sts of last rnd closely together, sew button opposite a button loop.
DRAWSTRING: Make a chain approximately 80" long. Cut yarn and fasten. Run drawstring under each lace strip along last row of bottom band.
CLUSTER FOR DRAWSTRING (Make 2): Ch 5; join with sl st to form ring for base of cluster; sc in ring, * ch 15, sl st in 5th ch from hook to form another ring. Working in ring just made, (with chain inside ring) rpt the 3 rnds of Button (do not cut yarn), sl st in first sc, sl st in each of rem ch sts of ch-15; 1 sc in starting ring; rpt from * 4 more times. Join with

sl st to first sc made in starting ring. Cut yarn and fasten. Sew a cluster to each end of drawstring.

KNITTED HAT

(page 43)

Hat will fit all sizes.
MATERIALS: Tahki's Donegal Homespun Tweeds (4 oz. skein): 1 skein # 826; knitting needles, 1 pair No.10 OR ANY SIZE NEEDLES WHICH WILL OBTAIN THE STITCH GAUGE BELOW.
GAUGE: 7 sts = 2"; 5 rows = 1".
DIRECTIONS: Starting at outer edge of cuff, cast on 68 sts. Work in k 1, p 1 ribbing for 3½". Now work pat as follows: **Row 1:** * P 1, k 1; rpt from * across. **Row 2:** Rpt Row 1. **Row 3:** * K 1, p 1; rpt from * across. **Row 4:** Rpt Row 3. Rpt last 4 rows (Rows 1 through 4) for pat until length is approximately 9" from beg, ending with Row 4 of pat.
Top Shaping—Row 1: * (P 1, k 1) 6 times; p 2 tog, k 2 tog; rpt from * 3 more times; (p 1, k 1) 2 times—8 decs made. **Row 2:** Same as Row 1 of pat —60 sts. **Row 3:** *(K 1, p 1) 5 times; k 2 tog, p 2 tog; rpt from * 3 more times; (k 1, p 1) 2 times—52 sts. **Row 4:** Same as Row 3 of pat. **Row 5:** *(P 1, k 1) 4 times; p 2 tog, k 2 tog; rpt from * 3 more times; (p 1, k 1) 2 times. **Row 6:** Same as Row 1 of pat—44 sts. **Row 7:** (K 2 tog, p 2 tog) 11 times. Leaving a 24" length, cut yarn. Using a darning needle, draw end of yarn through rem sts, pull tightly together and fasten securely on wrong side. Sew back seam. Fold ribbing to right side for cuff.

"NEW HAMPSHIRE SPRING" VEST

(pages 44-45)

MATERIALS: McCall's pattern #5477; ¾ yd. sweater-knit fabric or an old flat-knit sweater; ¾ yd. lightweight cotton or cotton/polyester fabric for backing; ¾ yd. lightweight solid or print fabric for lining; 45"x60" (baby and craft size) polyester quilt batting; scraps of polyester fiberfill; DMC cotton embroidery floss and Paternayan crewel wool in greens, peach, yellow, lavender and blue; variegated loop mohair yarn for edging; steel crochet hook, Size 1; crewel embroidery wool to match vest fabric; 6 buttons in a floral or other appropriate motif; dressmaker's carbon; ballpoint pen.
DIRECTIONS: Following directions on page 83, enlarge embroidery design. To cut vest in one piece, lap pattern pieces for vest front and vest back at side seams, matching ends of

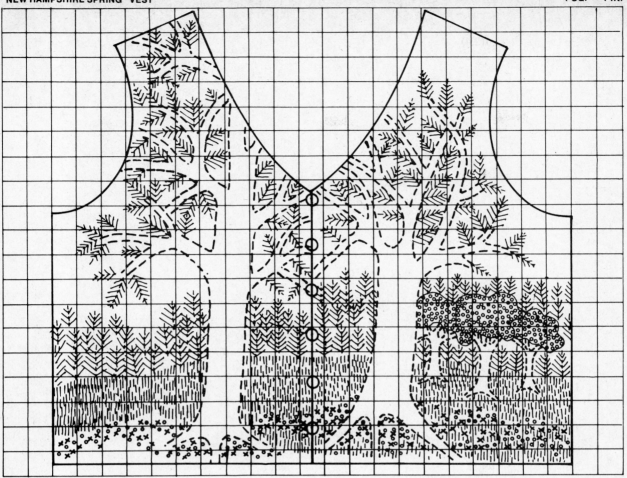

seam lines; tape together. Cut vest, batting, backing and lining from lapped pattern pieces, placing center back on fold. Pin batting and backing to wrong side of vest. Baste from center outward to edges, then baste around all edges. Trace tree shapes onto vest, using dressmaker's carbon and ballpoint pen. If necessary, add extra branches to tops of trees, so design fills entire vest front. With 3 or 4 strands of embroidery floss, stitch around outlines of tree trunks and branches, using running stitch. On wrong side of vest, make small holes through backing and batting within tree outlines, and stuff trunks *lightly* with fiberfill. To stuff branches, roots and small tree trunks, use scraps of yarn and a yarn needle, running needle through back of work, along length of branch and out again. Trim away excess yarn. By hand, sew up holes that were cut for stuffing. Embroider other details of vest as indicated on chart, using crewel wool and cotton embroidery floss. (See photo on page 52 for color suggestions; see page 101 for embroidery stitch diagrams.) If necessary, add more background stitches, so that design covers entire front of vest. Stitch shoulder seams in vest. Press under ½″ on front, neck, bottom and armhole edges, clipping curves where

necessary. Repeat for lining. With crewel wool to match vest, blanket stitch through fold around all edges of vest. Edge vest with crocheted shell stitch as follows: *Do 5 or 6 double crochet stitches into one blanket stitch at vest edge. Skip over 1″ along edge and do one single crochet. Repeat from * around vest edge and armholes. Pin lining into vest, wrong sides together. Slipstitch around all edges to secure lining to vest. Remove basting stitches. (If desired, do scattered embroidery stitches, e.g. feather stitch, only through lining and backing layers, to further secure lining to vest.) Sew buttons on left front, under openings between shell stitches.

NEEDLEPOINT TABARD VEST

(page 46)

MATERIALS: McCall's pattern #5136 (to order pattern, see backviews, page 23); ¾ yd. #12 mono mesh canvas; fabric of your choice (corduroy, suede cloth, or wool) for front lining, back and binding, 1¼ yds.; Persian or tapestry wool: 2 skns. terracotta, 1 skn. cream; small amounts of leftover wools for flowers and bargello, in colors of your choice; heavy brown paper; transparent tape; straight pins.

DIRECTIONS: Trace outline of vest front onto canvas, making sure that straight neck edge is on grain of canvas. Trace ⅝″ seam line. Cut out vest on cutting line; tape or stitch edges to keep from raveling. Draw an 8½″ square in center of vest front, 1½″ below neck edge. Work needlepoint in square according to stitch diagram, page 112. Fill in rest of canvas (except ⅝″ seam allowance) with bargello as noted in stitch diagram.

To prepare canvas for sewing: Wet finished canvas thoroughly. Shake off excess water. *Do not squeeze.* Roll in a terry cloth towel. Make outline of vest pattern on heavy brown paper. Tape paper to wooden table or board. Pin finished piece onto the paper and stretch to fit outline. Let needlepoint dry for at least 24 hours at room temperature. To construct garment, use the finished needlepoint as you would fabric.

FINISHING: Cut lining for vest front according to pattern. Cut 3 strips for binding 2½″ wide and 18″ long. Seam needlepoint to front lining at neck edge; turn and press. Baste lining to needlepoint at side and bottom seam lines; trim close to basting. Bind sides and bottom with binding strips. Attach back according to pattern directions.

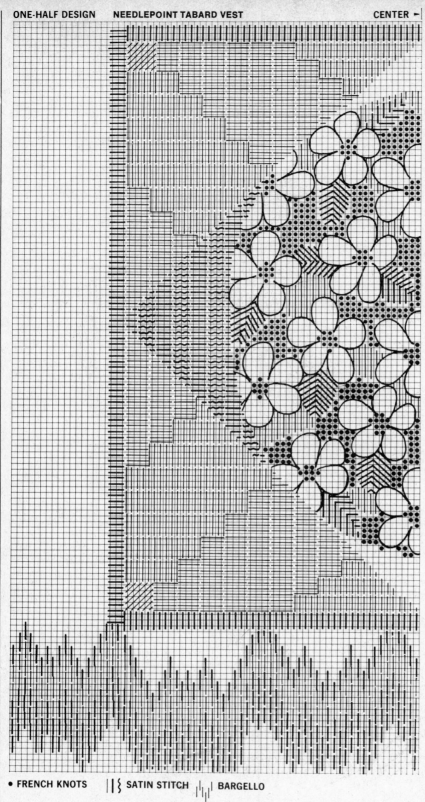

● FRENCH KNOTS ||||| SATIN STITCH ||||| BARGELLO

DECORATED BOXES

(pages 48-49)

We used various household boxes and tins: a wooden artist's box, tin cash box, cigar boxes and tins, tea canister, cookie can, hatbox, gift box, etc.

MATERIALS—_For cardboard or wooden boxes:_ Rubber cement or white glue; Crystal Clear Krylon Spray Paint® (see Buyer's Guide, page 136); flat spray paint to cover printed matter; medium sandpaper for wooden boxes. _For metal boxes:_ Rubber cement or Scotch Extra Strength Adhesive® (see Buyer's Guide); Crystal Clear Krylon Spray Paint® (if using rubber cement, finish box with Satin Finish polyurethane; see Buyer's Guide); flat spray paint to cover printed matter. (**Note:** White glue will _not_ work on metal.)

To decorate boxes: Various papers and stickers; wallpaper (ours from Brunschwig & Fils; see Buyer's Guide); wrapping paper; marble paper; self-adhesive paper; a map of your favorite city; postcards; sheets of paper dolls; decorative paper trims (ours from Brandon's Memorabilia; see Buyer's Guide); printed initials and decorations; fabrics; lace doilies; fabric trims and tapes; ribbons.

DIRECTIONS: Prepare the box for decorating by first removing all labels. They usually lift off when moistened with water. If the surface of the box is unusually rough, sanding it with medium sandpaper should smooth it down for a cleaner surface. _Make sure the box is clean._ If there is printed matter on the box which might show through paper or fabric, give it several _thin_ coats of spray paint. Thin coats don't run and drip. (Be sure to wait until each coat is dry before beginning another coat.) When the surface you plan to work on is going to be a painted surface, be extra careful with your paint job. Make sure that the box is completely dry before adding any decorations. Glue your decorations to the box. When your decorations are complete, seal the box for water resistance and extra strength with a final coat of Crystal Clear Krylon Spray Paint.® Remember, if using rubber cement on a metal box, finish instead with Satin Finish polyurethane.

NEEDLEPOINT JUMPER AND NEEDLEPOINT DRESS

(page 47)

MATERIALS: ½ yd. 36″ interlocked mono or single mesh #12 canvas for each; pencil; sharp scissors; transparent tape; heavy brown paper; DMC wool or comparable Persian yarn (see color code, pages 113-114 for colors and amounts; colors given are for DMC wool); corduroy fabric, check yardage from pattern envelope. _For Jumper:_ Simplicity pattern #7372. _For Dress:_ Butterick pattern #4916 (to order pattern #4916, see backviews, page 23).

DIRECTIONS—How To Prepare Canvas: Trace the outline of pocket or bodice with pencil onto the canvas. Make a second outline around first outline, allowing 2″ space between outlines. Cut around second outline. Tape or machine-stitch outside edges to prevent raveling. To work needlepoint, follow color code and stitch guide, pages 113-114.

How To Prepare For Sewing: Wet finished canvas thoroughly. Shake off excess water. _Do not squeeze._ Roll in towel. Make outline of pocket or bodice pattern on heavy brown paper. Tape paper to wooden table or board. Pin finished piece onto the paper and

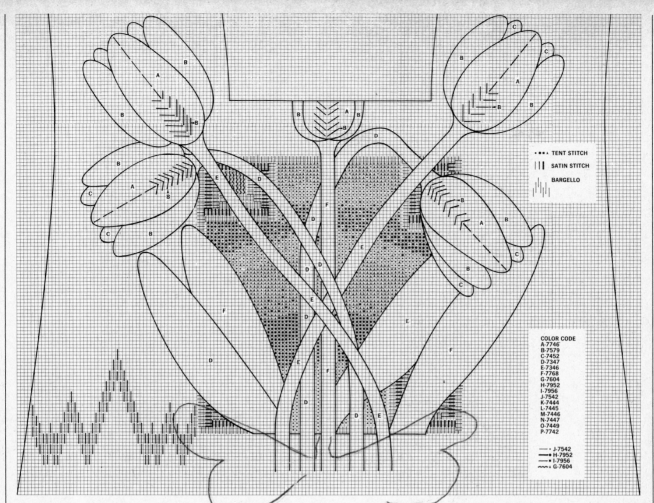

stretch to fit outline. Let dry 24 hours at room temperature. To construct garment, use the finished needlepoint as you would fabric, following the pattern directions.

BLACK, GOLD AND SILVER SEQUIN JACKET

(page 50)

MATERIALS: Bernat Berella 3-Ply Fingering (1 oz. skein): 12 skeins of Black; knitting needles, 1 pair each of No. 2 and No. 3; crochet hook, Size D OR ANY SIZE NEEDLES OR HOOK WHICH WILL OBTAIN THE STITCH GAUGE BELOW; 5 buttons; 5 strands of gold and 4 strands of silver sequins.

GAUGE: 7 sts = 1 inch.

(**Note:** Jacket is worked in st. st. [knit 1 row, purl 1 row]. Only the knitted rows are shown on the chart, page 114. The back rows are purled throughout [worked without sequins]. When knitting the stitch with the sequin, place sequin close to work and knit into the back of stitch. Wind 12 bobbins of gold and 5 bobbins of silver.)

BACK: With No. 2 needles, cast on 119 sts and work in st st for 1 inch, end with a knit row. **Next row:** Knit (hemline). Change to No. 3 needles and work in st st, following chart, page 114, to center st, then omitting center st, work back to beginning of chart. P second row and all even rows without sequins (not shown on chart). Work in this way until top of chart is reached; rep first through 14th row of chart for pat until piece measures 16 inches from hemline.

Armholes: Bind off 6 sts at the beg of next 2 rows. Dec 1 st at armhole edge every other row 5 times. Work on rem 97 sts until armholes measure 7 inches.

Shoulders: Bind off 8 sts at the beg of next 2 rows. **Next row:** Bind off 8 sts, work across next 19 sts, turn. Dec 1 st at beg of next row and every row at neck edge 2 times more, at the same time bind off 8 sts at shoulder edge every other row 2 times. Bind off center 31 sts and work other side to correspond.

LEFT FRONT: With No. 2 needles, cast on 60 sts and work in st st for hem as on Back. Change to No. 3 needles and work in pat, following chart to center st, which marks the center front edge. Work in pat until piece measures 14 inches from hemline, end at side edge.

Neck shaping: Work in pat to within last 2 sts, k 2 tog. Keeping continuity of pat dec one st at front edge every 4th row, 17 times in all. At the same time when piece measures 16 inches from hemline, end at side edge shape armhole: bind off 6 sts at the beg of next row, dec 1 st at same edge every other row 5 times. Continue to dec 1 st at neck edge as before until 32 sts remain. Work until armhole measures 7 inches. End at armhole edge.

Shoulder: Bind off 8 sts at the beg of next row and every other row 4 times in all.

RIGHT FRONT: Work as for Left Front, reversing pat and shapings.

SLEEVES: With No. 2 needles, cast on 57 sts and work hem as for Back. Change to No. 3 needles and work in pattern starting at sleeve sign and working to center st, then omitting center st, work back to beg of row. Work inc 1 st at both ends every 1¼ inches 12 times. Work on 81 sts until sleeve measures 17 inches, from hemline.

Top: Bind off 6 sts at the beg of next 2 rows. Dec 1 st at both ends every other row until piece measures 4 inches. Bind off 2 sts at the beg of next 4 rows. Bind off rem sts.

FINISHING: Steam pieces very lightly from wrong side through a damp cloth. Sew side and shoulder seams. Turn all hems to inside and stitch.

Front and Neck Band—Row 1: With right side facing, work a row of sc along right front edge across back of neck and left front edge. Ch 1, turn.

BLACK, GOLD AND SILVER SEQUIN JACKET

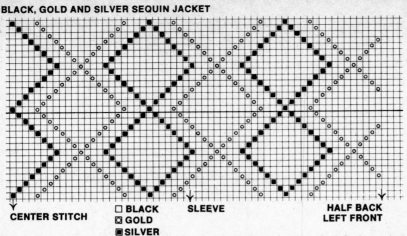

CENTER STITCH   SLEEVE   HALF BACK
LEFT FRONT

□ BLACK
◨ GOLD
▣ SILVER

Row 2: Sc in each sc across. With pins mark the position of 5 buttons on right front edge, having first pinmark 1 inch from hemline and the last pinmark ½ inch from first row of neck shaping. **Row 3:** * Sc in each sc to within next pin, ch 3, skip 3 sc, sc in next sc. Rpt. from * 4 more times, sc in each rem sc across. **Row 4:** Sc in each sc and ch across. Work one more row. Break off. Sew sleeve seams. Turn under hem and stitch in place. Sew in sleeves. Sew on buttons.

WHITE AND GOLD RIB CARDIGAN

(page 51)
Directions are given for size Small (8-10). Changes for sizes Medium (12-14) and Large (16-18) are in parentheses.
MATERIALS: Columbia-Minerva Nantuk Sports Yarn (2 oz. skeins): 6(8,9) skeins of White (A) and Camelot; (1 oz. ball): 1 ball Gold (B); "Boye" circular knitting needles, No. 4 and No. 5 (24″ length) OR ANY SIZE NEEDLE WHICH WILL OBTAIN THE STITCH GAUGE BELOW; knitting needles, 1 pair No. 5 (or same size as large circular needle).

NEEDLEPOINT DRESS

COLOR CODE

A-7895 PURPLE	E-7363 OLIVE	I-7446 RUST	M-7402 LIGHT GREEN
B-7241 BLUE PURPLE	F-7604 PALE TURQUOISE	J-7211 PALE PINK	N-7232 PINK BEIGE
C-7896 PINK PURPLE	G-7952 MED. TURQUOISE	K-7453 BEIGE	O-7447 MED. DARK RUST
D-7257 WINE	H-7444 ORANGE RUST	L-ECRU	P-7449 DARK RUST

▲▲ •• TENT STITCH || SATIN STITCH   BARGELLO
× FRENCH KNOTS

GAUGE: No. 5 needle (slightly stretched)—11 sts = 2″; 8 rows = 1″.

MEASUREMENTS:

Sizes:	Small (8-10)	Medium (12-14)	Large (16-18)
Bust (excluding band):	33″	37″	41″
Width across back at underarms:	16½″	18½″	20″
Width across each front below neck shaping (excluding band):	8¼″	9¼″	10½″
Width across sleeve at upper arm:	12″	13¼″	14″

DIRECTIONS: Pocket Lining (Make 2): Starting at lower edge with straight No. 5 needles and A, cast on 26 sts for all sizes. **Row 1 (wrong side):** K 2, * p 2, k 2; rpt from * across. **Row 2:** P 2, * k 2, p 2; rpt from * across. Rpt these 2 rows alternately until length is 4¾″, ending with a wrong-side row. Break off yarn; place sts on a st holder and put aside.

BODY—Border: Starting at lower edge of entire cardigan with No. 5 circular needle and B, cast on loosely 182(206,226) sts. Do not join. Work back and forth as with straight needles. **Row 1 (wrong side):** K 2, * p 2, k 2; rpt from * across. Cut B; attach A. **Row 2:** With A, k across. **Row 3:** K 2,* p 2, k 2; rpt from * across. **Row 4:** P 2, * k 2, p 2; rpt from * across. Rpt Rows 3 and 4 for rib pat until total length is 1½″ from beg, ending with wrong-side row. Drop A; attach B. **Next Row:** With B, k across. **Next Row:** Rpt Row 3. Cut B; pick up A. **Next Row:** With A, k across —border completed. With A, rpt Rows 3 and 4 of border until length from beg is 4″, ending with Row 3. **Pocket Border—Row 1:** Work in ribbing as established over first 12(12, 16) sts; drop A; attach B and with B k 26; leaving a 36″ length, cut B; attach a separate strand of A and with A, work in ribbing as established to within last 38 (38,42) sts; drop A; attach B and k 26 B, leaving a 36″ length, cut B; attach another separate strand of A and with this strand, work in rib pat to end of row. (**Note:** When changing yarn, twist strand not in use around the other once to prevent making holes in work.) **Row 2:** Working in rib pat as established, work A sts with A and B sts with B, using strands dropped on previous row. Cut extra C and A strands. **Row 3:** (With original A strand work in ribbing to within B sts, continuing with A, k across B sts) 2 times; work in ribbing to end of row. **Rows 4 through 10:** Keeping continuity of rib pat, work 7 more rows, ending with a row on wrong side. **Row 11:** Rpt Row 1 of

Pocket Border. **Row 12:** * With A, work in rib pat to within next B sts; pick up B dropped below, bind off in ribbing next 25 B sts, for pocket opening; pick up A dropped below and bind off one more st; rpt from * once more; complete row in rib pat. Cut extra A strands.

Placement of Pocket Linings—Next Row: Work in rib pat over 12(12,16) sts; slip sts of a pocket lining onto left-hand point of needle, work in ribbing as established across lining sts, then (with same strand) continue in ribbing across body to next pocket opening; join second pocket lining as before and complete row in rib pat—182 (206,226) sts. Continue to work in rib pat until length is 13″ from beg (or 5″ less than desired length to underarms), end with wrong-side row.

Neck Shaping: Keeping continuity of rib pat throughout, dec one st at each end of next row, then every 4th row 10 times in all, ending with a wrong-side row—162(186,206) sts.

To Divide Fronts and Back—Row 1: From right side, work in rib pat over first 31(37,43) sts, place these sts just worked on a st holder for Right Front; bind off next 8 sts for underarm; continue in rib pat until there are 84(96,104) sts on right-hand point of needle, place these sts on another st holder for Back; bind off next 8 sts for other underarm; complete row in rib pat—31(37,43) sts on needle. Change to straight needles.

Left Front: Keeping continuity of rib pat throughout, dec one st at armhole edge every other row 3(5,7) times, **at the same time,** continue to dec one st at neck edge every 4th row 4(6,6) more times; then, keeping armhole edge straight, dec one st at neck edge every other row until 18(20,22) sts rem. Work even over rem sts until length from underarm is 7(7½, 8)″, ending at armhole edge.

Shoulder Shaping—Row 1: From armhole edge, bind off in ribbing 6(7,7) sts; complete row. **Row 2:** Work even. Rpt last 2 rows. Bind off in ribbing rem 6(6,8) sts. **Back:** Slip sts from back holder onto a straight needle; attach A. Keeping in rib pat, dec one st at each end every other row 3(5,7) times—78(86,90) sts. Work even until length of armhole is same as on left front.

Shoulder Shaping: Working in rib pat, bind off 6(7,7) sts at beg of next 4 rows; then 6(6,8) sts at beg of following 2 rows. Place rem 42(46,46) sts on a st holder for back of neck.

Right Front: Slip sts from holder onto a straight needle; attach A at armhole edge and work to correspond with Left Front, reversing shaping.

SLEEVES: Starting at lower edge with straight No. 5 needles and B, cast on 42(46,50) sts. Work same as for

Body of Cardigan until bottom border has been completed. With A, rpt Rows 3 and 4 of border 2 times. Keeping continuity of rib pat throughout, inc one st at each end of next row and every 8th row thereafter until there are 66(74,78) sts. Work even in rib pat until length is 17(17½,18)″ from beg or desired length to underarm.)

Top Shaping: Keeping continuity of rib, bind off 4 sts at beg of next 2 rows. Dec one st at each end every other row until 24(26,26) sts rem. Bind off in ribbing 2 sts at beg of next 4 rows. Bind off in ribbing rem sts.

Finishing: Pin pieces to measurements on a padded surface; cover with a damp cloth and allow to dry; do not press. Sew shoulder seams.

Front and Back-of-Neck Band: With right side facing, using No. 4 needle and A, attach yarn to lower right front corner; working along ends of rows, pick up and k one st in end st of each of first 6 rows, * sk next row, pick up and k one st in end of each of next 6 rows; rpt from * along right front edge; slip sts from back holder onto left-hand point of needle, work in ribbing as established across these sts; pick up and k sts along left front edge to correspond with opposite edge. Drop A; attach B. **Row 1:** With B, p across. **Row 2:** P 2, work in k 2, p 2 ribbing across, being careful to keep continuity of rib across back of neck (if necessary, dec 1, 2 or more sts directly before and after back sts), end row with p 2. Cut B; pick up A. **Row 3:** With A, p across. **Row 4:** P 2, work in k 2, p 2 ribbing across. Work in ribbing as established for 7 more rows. Cut A; attach B. K 1 row. Bind off. With right side facing, using B, pick up and k 9 sts along end of front band. Bind off. Finish other end of band in same manner. Sew side and sleeve seams. Sew in sleeves. Sew free edges of pocket linings in place.

WHITE TUBE TOP

(page 51)

Directions are given for tube to fit all sizes.

MATERIALS: Columbia-Minerva Nantuk Sports Yarn (2 oz. skeins): 2 skeins White (A) and Camelot; (1 oz. ball): 1 ball Gold (B); knitting needles, 1 pair No. 5 OR ANY SIZE NEEDLES WHICH WILL OBTAIN THE STITCH GAUGE BELOW; crochet hook, Size F.

GAUGE: (slightly stretched) 11 sts = 2″; 8 rows = 1″.

(**Note:** Tube is worked in one straight piece with a side seam.)

DIRECTIONS: Starting at entire lower edge, cast on 152 sts. Work even in k 2, p 2 ribbing until length is 12½″ from beg, having an even number of rows. Mark first row for right side.

Next Row (Inc Row): Working in ribbing as established, inc one st in every 3rd p rib 12 times—164 sts. Having 3 sts (instead of 2) in every increased rib, work even in ribbing until length is 16½" from beg (or ½" shorter than desired length, ending with a row on wrong side.

Eyelet Row (right side): Keeping in rib pat, in each p rib work as follows: *Yo, p 2 tog—eyelet made.* **Next Row:** Working each yo as one st, work even in ribbing as established. Work 2 more rows in ribbing. Bind off loosely in ribbing.

FINISHING: Sew side seam. With right side facing, using B and crochet hook, work 1 row of sc along top edge, making 1 sc in each st around. Join with sl st to first sc. Cut yarn and fasten. Work sc rnd along lower edge in same way. With B, make a chain 42" long. Run chain through eyelet row. Tie a knot at each end of chain. Tie ends together.

RUSSIAN SKIRT

(pages 52-53)

MATERIALS: 2¾ yds. 45"-wide red cotton fabric for skirt; ½ yd. of 72"-wide black felt; 2¾ yds of 1¼"-wide black grosgrain ribbon; 2¾ yds. of 1"-wide green grosgrain ribbon; 2¾ yds. of 2½"-wide gold embroidered ribbon; 2¾ yds. of 1¼"-wide gold embroidered ribbon; 8¼ yds. white crochet-type trim; 4 pkgs. white baby rickrack; 4 pkgs. black baby rickrack; 3 pkgs. white medium rickrack; 2 gross flat silver sequins; 7" skirt zipper; tailor's chalk; yardstick; lightweight cardboard.
(**Note:** Trims used here may be varied depending upon availability of trims in your area. Alternates might be 1"-wide printed bias tape, gold rickrack, strips of calico or other printed fabrics [cut fabric strips ½" wider than finished strip, and press raw edges under ¼"] and printed ribbons.)

DIRECTIONS: Decide on length of skirt; add ½" for waistline seam allowance. Cut two lengths of fabric to this measurement. Cut a waistband 6" wide and 3" longer than your waist measurement. Sew two skirt lengths right sides together along one selvage edge, using ½" seam allowance, to make one side seam. Refer to photo on page 60 for trim placement.

Trim: Begin by marking the bottom 15" of the skirt for the rickrack plaid. Using a yardstick and tailor's chalk, draw parallel lines 7" and 7¼" above lower edge of skirt. Space vertical lines 5" apart; add another set of vertical lines ¼" from each of the previous set. Stitch parallel rows of black and white baby rickrack over

chalk markings. To make black felt saw-toothed trim, cut a 4½"-wide strip across width of felt (72") and a strip 4½"x18¼". Overlap ends ¼" and topstitch to make one long strip 4½"x90". For saw-toothed edge, make a cardboard pattern of a triangle with a 4" base and 3" height (from center of base). Align base of triangle along one edge of felt strip and mark with tailor's chalk. Repeat along entire length of strip. Cut along chalk marks. There should be a 1½" deep straight-edged heading remaining at the top of the saw-toothed strip. Handstitch medium white rickrack along saw-toothed edge. Handstitch sequins inside the rickrack edge, about ¼" apart. Lap green grosgrain ribbon over top edge of black felt, allowing about ¼" overlap; topstitch. Topstitch white medium rickrack over lower edge of green ribbon. Mark a chalk line 14½" above bottom of skirt; topstitch upper edge of green ribbon on line, attaching saw-toothed border to skirt. Topstitch white crochet edging under both long edges of 2½"-wide gold embroidered ribbon. Lap one edge of gold ribbon over black grosgrain; topstitch again at edge of gold ribbon. Lap 1¼" gold ribbon over other edge of black grosgrain; topstitch. Place the five connected rows of trim at upper edge of green grosgrain on skirt; attach to skirt by stitching at top and bottom edges. Cut a 4"-wide strip across the width of black felt (72") and a strip 4"x18¼". Overlap the ends ¼" and stitch to make a long strip 4"x90". Press in half along the length of the strip. Bind the hem edge of the skirt with the folded felt strip and edgestitch through all layers. Topstitch white crochet trim above edge of felt.

FINISHING: Sew second side seam, using ½" seam allowance, leaving 7½" open at top for zipper. Insert zipper. Gather top of skirt to waist measurement and sew on waistband.

RUSSIAN BLOUSE

(page 52)

MATERIALS: See pattern backviews, page 23, for McCalls #5663. Trim: ⅝ yd. of 2"-wide peasant ribbon trim for neckline placket; 1 yd. of ½"-wide peasant ribbon trim for neck; ten white ½" buttons; nine assorted 1 yd. lengths of embroidered peasant ribbon trims and brightly colored flat crochet-type laces of assorted widths for sleeve trims (we used 2", 1", ½", and ¼" widths); two 7"x2½" pieces of black felt for shoulder trim; ½ yd. blue medium rickrack; ½ yd. red medium rickrack; ½ yd. yellow crochet-type edging; ½ yd. red

crochet-type edging.
(**Note:** Trims used here may be varied depending upon availability of trims in your area. Alternates might be 1"-wide printed bias tape, gold rickrack, strips of calico or other printed fabrics [cut fabric strips ½" wider than finished strip, and press raw edges under ¼"] and printed ribbons.)

DIRECTIONS: Cut blouse pieces according to pattern instructions. Refer to photo for trimming placement.

Trim: Begin by trimming both black felt pieces. Pin 8" of crochet lace edging along 7" edges of felt pieces, turning raw edges under felt. Topstitch in place. Stitch on 8" pieces of rickrack in same way. Space five buttons evenly between rickrack on each piece and sew on with bright thread. Center trimmed felt pieces on sleeves 5" down from neckline edge; edgestitch in place. Cut 1 yd. lengths of ribbons and trims in half to make 18" lengths for each sleeve. Space nine rows of assorted trims within 15½" on sleeves. Pin in place; check to make sure trims will meet correctly at sleeve seams before sewing. Topstitch.

FINISHING: Construct blouse according to pattern instructions. After attaching neckline facing, trim neck placket with 2"-wide peasant ribbon trim, mitering bottom edges. Topstitch in place. Finish blouse according to pattern instructions. To trim neckline, cover and back neck binding with ½"-wide peasant ribbon trim. Edgestitch in place.

RED SHORT SWEATER TIE FRONT

(page 53)

Directions are given for size Small (8-10). Changes for sizes Medium (12-14) and Large (16-18) are in parentheses.

MATERIALS: Berga/Ullman, 2 Ply (3½ oz. skeins): 4(5,6) skeins of #2058 Red; knitting needles, 1 pair each No. 1 and No. 2 OR ANY SIZE NEEDLES WHICH WILL OBTAIN THE STITCH GAUGE BELOW; crochet hook, Size E; 6 buttons, ½" in diameter.

GAUGE: On No. 2 needles (slightly stretched) — 8 sts = 1"; 8 rows = 1".

MEASUREMENTS:

Sizes:	Small (8-10)	Medium (12-14)	Large (16-18)
Bust (when stretched):	32"	36"	40"
Width across back at underarm:	16"	18"	20"
Width across each front at underarm:	8½"	9½"	10½"
Width across sleeve at upper arm	11"	12"	13"

(Note: Entire Jacket is worked in k 1, p 1 rib pat.)

DIRECTIONS — BACK: Starting at lower edge with No. 1 needles, cast on 128(144,160) sts. **Row 1:** Work in k 1, p 1 ribbing across. Mark this row for right side. Work in k 1, p 1 ribbing for 2″. Change to No. 2 needles and continue in k 1, p 1 ribbing until total length is 10½(11,11½)″ from beg.

Armhole Shaping: Being careful to keep continuity of rib pat throughout, bind off 4(6,8) sts at beg of next 2 rows. Dec one st at each end every other row 8(9,10) times — 104(114,124) sts. Work even in rib pat over rem sts until length from first row of armhole shaping is 6½(7,7¾)″.

Shoulder Shaping: Keeping continuity of rib pat, bind off in ribbing 8(9,10) sts at beg of next 8 rows. Bind off in ribbing rem 40(42,44) sts for back of neck.

LEFT FRONT: Starting at lower edge with No. 1 needles, cast on 68(76,84) sts. Work in k 1, p 1 ribbing for 2″. Mark Row 1 for right side. Change to No. 2 needles and continue in k 1, p 1 ribbing until total length is 10½(11,11½)″ from beg, ending with a row on wrong side.

Armhole and Neck Shaping — Row 1: Keeping continuity of rib pat throughout, bind off 4(6,8) sts at beg of row; complete row in ribbing. **Row 2:** Dec one st at beg of row — neck edge; work in rib pat to end of row. **Row 3:** Keeping continuity of rib pat, dec one st at each end. Rpt last 2 rows (Rows 2 and 3) alternately 7(8,9) more times — 40(43,46) sts. Now, keeping armhole edge straight, continue to dec one st at neck edge only every row 8(7,6) more times — 32(36,40) sts rem. Work even in rib pat over rem sts until length of armhole is same as on Back, ending at armhole edge.

Shoulder Shaping: From armhole edge, keeping in rib pat, bind off in ribbing 8(9,10) sts at beg of next row, then every other row 4 times in all. With pins, mark position of 6 buttons evenly spaced along left front edge, placing first pin 2″ above lower edge and last pin directly below beg of neck shaping. **To make buttonhole on Right Front:** Starting at front edge, k 1, p 1, bind off next 2 sts for buttonhole, complete row in ribbing as established. On next row, cast on 2 sts over the bound-off sts to complete buttonhole.

RIGHT FRONT: Making buttonholes as directed in line with pins on Left Front, work Right Front to correspond with Left Front, reversing shaping.

SLEEVES: Starting at lower edge with No. 1 needles, cast on 60(64,68) sts. Work in k 1, p 1 ribbing for 2½″. Change to No. 2 needles and continue in ribbing for 1″ more; keeping con-

tinuity of rib pat throughout, inc one st at each end of next row, then every 6th row 14(16,18) times in all — 88(96,104) sts. Work even until total length is 17(17½,18)″ from beg.

Top shaping: Keeping continuity of rib pat, bind off 4(6,8) sts at beg of next 2 rows. Dec one st at each end every other row 8(10,12) times; dec one st at each end every row 16 times. Bind off 3 sts at beg of next 4 rows. Bind off rem 20 sts.

BELT: Starting at one end with No. 1 needles, cast on tightly 24 sts. Work in k 1, p 1 ribbing until belt measures approximately 54(56,58)″. Bind off tightly in ribbing.

Tab For Belt (Make 3): Starting at a short edge with No. 1 needles, cast on 18 sts. Work in k 1, p 1 ribbing for 2¼″. Bind off in ribbing.

FINISHING: Pin each piece to measurements on a padded surface; cover with a damp cloth and allow to dry; do not press. Sew side, shoulder and sleeve seams. Sew in sleeves. With cast-on edge of each tab at lower edge of jacket, sew one tab to center of each front, and one to center of back.

Edging — Row 1: With right side facing, starting at lower right front corner, with crochet hook, sc evenly along right front edge, across back of neck and down left front edge to lower corner, being careful to keep work flat. Do not turn. **Row 2:** Ch 1, working from left to right, sc in top of last sc made, * sc in next sc to the right; rpt from * across last row. Break off and fasten. Sew buttons opposite buttonholes. Slip belt through tabs and tie at front.

MIRROR-TRIMMED VEST

(page 54)

MATERIALS: See pattern backviews, page 23, for Butterick #5137. Mirrors (to order, use coupon on page 120); Bucilla's "Glossilla" embroidery floss: 3 skeins each of colors 9 (Kelly Green), 23 (Lt. orange), 27 (Turquoise), 30 (Hot Pink), 33 (Yellow) and 34 (Red); dressmaker's carbon; tracing paper; ballpoint pen.

DIRECTIONS: Cut out vest according to pattern instructions. Following directions on page 83, enlarge embroidery motifs below. Trace motifs on tracing paper to obtain 12 copies of the small motif, 14 of the large motif. Pin motifs on vest front as shown in photo. Using dressmaker's carbon and ballpoint pen, transfer motifs to felt. Place mirrors at circles in motifs and attach with buttonhole stitch (see diagrams and instructions below). Fill in rest of motif with satin stitch. Finish assembling vest according to pattern instructions. If pressing is necessary, use dry iron on reverse side to avoid flattening embroidery or shrinking felt.

To attach mirrors with buttonhole stitch—Diagram 1: Up at 1, down at 2; up at 3, down at 4. **Diagram 2:** Up at 5, down at 6 (interweaving as per diagram); up at 7, down at 8. Your framework mesh is now complete.

MIRROR-TRIMMED VEST

1 SQ. = 1 IN.

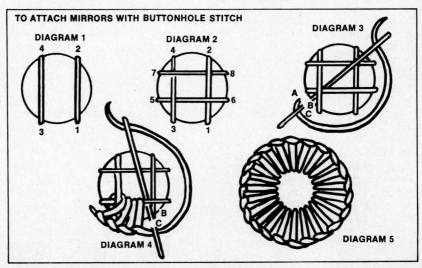

TO ATTACH MIRRORS WITH BUTTONHOLE STITCH

DIAGRAM 1

DIAGRAM 2

DIAGRAM 3

DIAGRAM 4

DIAGRAM 5

Diagram 3: To make the buttonhole or blanket stitch around the mirror: Bring needle up at A. With thread counterclockwise, and needle pointing towards you, slide the needle over and back under framework mesh, inserting the needle at B and up at C. Pull gently. **Diagram 4:** Continue working around mirror counterclockwise using movements B and C. Keep the thread counterclockwise and pull needle *over* thread as you pull gently. **Diagram 5:** Finished mirror.

RED COWL NECK SWEATER

(page 55)

Directions are for size Medium.
MATERIALS: Columbia Minerva "Amy" (art. #2700) 100% brushed acrylic yarn (1 oz. balls): 10 balls Scarlet (#2708); circular needles, Nos. 4(29″), 8(29″), 8(16″) OR ANY SIZE NEEDLES WHICH WILL OBTAIN THE STITCH GAUGE BELOW; 2 yds. ½″ satin ribbon to match.
GAUGE: No. 8 needles—4 sts=1″; 5 rows=1″. **DIRECTIONS:** Starting at bottom of sweater, with No. 4 needle, cast on 132 sts and join. K 2, p 2 in rib for 4″. Change to longer No. 8 needle and work even (knit every row) until piece measures 12″. Divide for Front and Back. Knit 54 sts, k and place next 12 sts on holder. K 54 sts, k and place 12 sts. on holder for underarm. Work up Front and Back separately.
FRONT: Work up even (k one row, p one row) on 54 sts until 7″ above underarm. End on wrong side. Knit 17 sts, place on holder (rt. side); k 20 sts and place on holder for neckline; k 17 sts (left side). Decrease 1 st at neck edge every other row until there are 10 sts. Knit until armhole measures 10″. Place 10 sts on holder for left shoulder. Work rt. side to correspond.
BACK: Work up even on 54 sts (k one row, p one row) for 10″, or until armhole measures same as front. Place 10 sts on holder for shoulder, next 34 sts on holder for neck, 10 sts on holder for other shoulder. Take 10 sts from front and 10 sts from back and weave should together.
SLEEVES: With 16″ No. 8 needle and right side facing you, pick up and knit 72 sts, including 12 sts on holder. Knit even (k every row) until 20½″ from shoulder. Place marker. * k 2, bind off 2, rpt. from * to end of row. Slip marker. * K 2, increase 2 where they were bound off, rpt. from * to end of row. K 1″ even, k 2, p 2 in rib for 5 rows. Bind off in rib.
FINISHING: Weave ribbon through openings, gather in and tie.
COWL COLLAR: With *wrong* side facing you and No. 8 needle, pick up

and knit 92 sts, including sts from holders. Work even for 16″. K 2, p 2 for 5 rows. Bind off in rib.

PENDLETON PLAID PONCHO

(page 61)

MATERIALS: 1 motor robe, 52″x70″. We used Pendleton's Highland Plaid Motor Robe #924.
DIRECTIONS: Cut blanket in half along 70″ length. (You will get 2 pieces 26″x70″, fringed on both ends.) Place the 2 pieces at right angles to each other and lap to get an "L" shape, maching the edges. Topstitch in place with double row of stitching. Run a row of machine stitches on raw edges and finish all sides without fringes with an over-edge stitch.

CHILD'S STRIPED JUMPER

(page 75)

Directions are given for Size 4. Changes are for Sizes 6, 8, 10.
MATERIALS: Coats & Clark's Knitting Worsted, 4 Ply (4 oz. skeins): 1(1,1,2) skein each of Red (A), Orange (B), Yellow (C), Green (D), Blue (E), Purple (F); 1 oz. White (G); crochet hooks, Sizes H and F OR ANY SIZE HOOK WHICH WILL OBTAIN THE STITCH GAUGE BELOW: 1 button, ⅝″.
GAUGE: Size H hook—3 hdc = 1″; 2 hdc rows = 1″.
MEASUREMENTS:

Sizes:	4	6	8	10
Chest:	23″	24″	26″	28″
Width across back or front at underarms:	11½″	12″	13″	14″

DIRECTIONS—BODY: Starting at top edge with Size H hook and A, ch 70(73,79,85) to measure 23(24,26, 28)″. **Row 1:** Sc in 2nd ch from hook, sc in each ch across—69(72,78,84) sc. Ch 1, turn. **Row 2:** Sc in each sc across. Ch 2, turn. **Row 3:** Hdc in each sc across—69(72,78,84) hdc; do not count ch-2 as 1 hdc. Ch 2, turn. **Row 4:** Hdc in each hdc across. Ch 2, turn. Rpt last row 1(1,2,2) time. Ch 2, turn. **Next Row (Inc Row):** Hdc in each of first 17(19,22,25) hdc, (2 hdc in next hdc, hdc in each of next 16 hdc) 2 times; 2 hdc in next hdc, hdc in each rem hdc—3 incs made. Join with sl st to top of first hdc. Joining is at center front of dress. Cut A. *Now work in rnds as follows:* **Rnd 1 (right side):** Do not turn; sk first 36(38,41,44) sts. Attach B to top of next hdc, ch 2, hdc in same st, hdc in each hdc around. Join with sl st to top of first hdc— 72(76,82,88) hdc; do not count ch 2. Joining is at center back. *Hereafter do not turn; work from right side throughout.* **Rnd 2:** Ch 2, hdc in same st as joining and in each hdc around. Join with sl st to top of first hdc. Rpt last rnd 2(2,3,3) more times. **Next Rnd (Inc**

Rnd): Ch 2, hdc in same st as joining, * 2 hdc in next hdc, hdc in each of next 11(11,12,13) hdc; rpt from * 4 more times; 2 hdc in next hdc, hdc in each rem hdc. Join as before— 78(82,88,94) hdc. Cut B; attach C to same st as joining. With C, rpt Rnd 2 of B section 4(4,5,5) times. **Next Rnd (Inc Rnd):** Ch 2, hdc in same st as joining, * 2 hdc in next hdc, hdc in each of next 12(12,13,14) hdc; rpt from * 4 more times; 2 hdc in next hdc, hdc in each rem hdc. Join— 84(88,94,100) hdc. Cut C; attach D to same st as joining. With D, rpt Rnd 2 of B section 4(4,5,5) times. **Next Rnd (Inc Rnd):** Working same as Rnd 2, inc 4 sts evenly spaced around (to inc, make 2 hdc in same st). Join— 88(92,98,104) hdc. Cut D; attach E to same st as joining. With E, rpt Rnd 2 of B section 4(4,5,5) times. **Next Rnd (Inc Rnd):** Working as Rnd 2, inc 0(2,4,6) hdc evenly spaced around. Join—88(94,102,110) hdc. Cut E; attach F to same st as joining. With F, work even as Rnd 2 until total length is approximately 14(16,18,19)″ or desired length. Cut F and fasten.
Edging: Right side facing and Size F hook, attach G to same st as joining, make 3 sc in each hdc around. Join with sl st to first sc. Cut yarn, fasten.
Straps: Working along opposite side of starting chain, sk first 2 sts, attach A to next ch, ch 30(32,34,36) for strap, sk next 25(26,27,28) ch, sl st in next ch; turn, sl st in next ch. **Row 1:** Sc in each ch across strap, sl st in next ch of starting ch. Cut A; attach B in next ch of starting ch, ch 1, turn. **Row 2:** With B, sc in each sc across last row, sl st in next ch of starting chain. Cut B; attach C in next ch and ch 1, turn. Continuing to work same as for last row, make 1 row C, 1 row D, 1 row E and 1 row F. Cut F and fasten. Work other strap to correspond.
Finishing: With right side facing, using Size F hook and color G, work 1 row of sc along entire neck edge, being careful to keep work flat and making sc, ch 5 for button loop and sc all in same st at left corner of front opening. Join with sl st to first sc. Cut yarn and fasten. With G, work 1 row of sc along each armhole edge. Join to first sc. Cut yarn and fasten. Pin dress to measurements on a padded surface, cover with a damp cloth and allow to dry; do not press. Sew button.

NEEDLEPOINT VEST

(page 55)

MATERIALS: 1/2 yard #10 mesh needlepoint canvas; 1 yard fabric for back of vest and lining; 4 buttons— 18 ligne; Columbia Minerva Needlepoint and Crewel Yarn (wool) Art #2931: 25 yards Dark Red (#R50), 36 yards Cranberry (#240), 37 yards Canary (#457), 8 yards Brilliant Green (#559), 15 yards Forest Green (#528), 53 yards Black (#050), 20 yards White (#005).

(Note: Work in continental or basket-weave stitch; stripes in scotch stitch.)

DIRECTIONS: Lay out each side of vest on canvas and stitch. Follow graph on page 119 for stitching and details. Work right side first and do the buttonholes as marked. (Note: First outline the vest entirely with a row of black so you have a guideline for stitching.) Work left side to correspond to right side. Block each piece. Once pieces are blocked, cut out each one, allowing 1/2" seam allowance all around. In fabric, cut out fronts to correspond to needlepoint fronts, allowing 1/2" seam al-

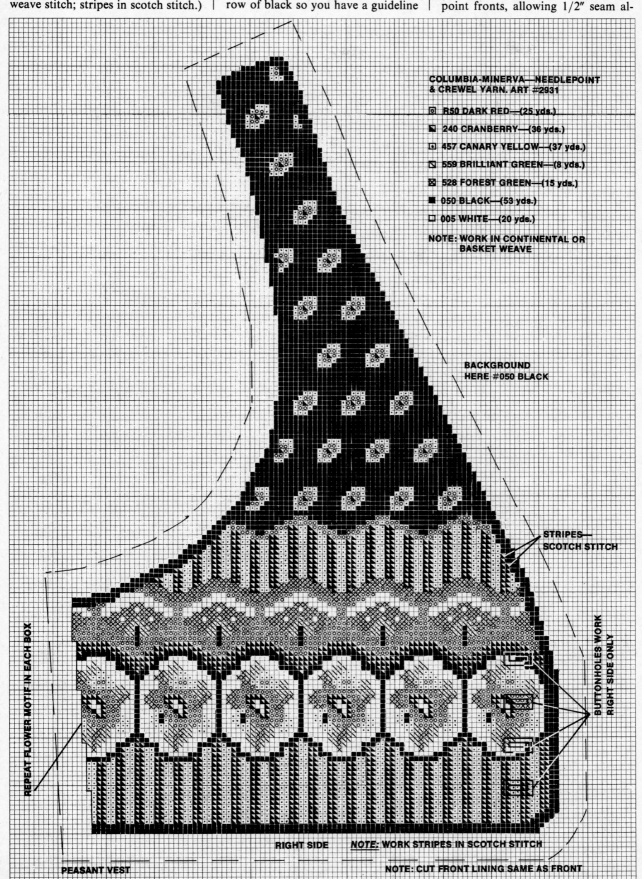

COLUMBIA-MINERVA—NEEDLEPOINT & CREWEL YARN. ART #2931

⊡ R50 DARK RED—(25 yds.)
◪ 240 CRANBERRY—(36 yds.)
⊡ 457 CANARY YELLOW—(37 yds.)
◩ 559 BRILLIANT GREEN—(8 yds.)
⊠ 528 FOREST GREEN—(15 yds.)
■ 050 BLACK—(53 yds.)
□ 005 WHITE—(20 yds.)

NOTE: WORK IN CONTINENTAL OR BASKET WEAVE

BACKGROUND HERE #050 BLACK

STRIPES— SCOTCH STITCH

REPEAT FLOWER MOTIF IN EACH BOX

BUTTONHOLES WORK RIGHT SIDE ONLY

RIGHT SIDE   NOTE: WORK STRIPES IN SCOTCH STITCH

PEASANT VEST

NOTE: CUT FRONT LINING SAME AS FRONT

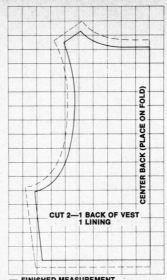

CUT 2—1 BACK OF VEST 1 LINING

CENTER BACK (PLACE ON FOLD)

— FINISHED MEASUREMENT
--- SEAM ALLOWANCE CUTTING LINE

lowance. Following directions, page 83, cut out 2 backs (one for back of vest, one for lining). Join shoulder seams of outside of vest and lining. With right sides of vest and lining facing each other, stitch around neckline and fronts and around armholes. Use needlepoint side as guide for stitching and stitch just inside of last stitched row so no canvas shows when it's turned under. Turn under, press and join side seams. Fold back hem of vest and lining; slipstitch by hand. Cut and finish buttonholes on lining. Sew on buttons.

FAIRY TALE QUILT OR WALL HANGING

(page 66)

Quilt measures approximately 58″ square.

MATERIALS: 1½ yds. 44″-wide red cotton or cotton/polyester fabric for bands; 3½ yds. red/yellow print cotton or cotton/polyester fabric for border and backing; one 72″x90″ sheet of comforter-thickness bonded polyester quilt batting ("Extra-Loft" by Fairfield Processing, see Buyer's Guide); nine different 12½″ squares of solid or printed fabrics for picture backgrounds (see photo for suggestions); scraps of solid and printed fabrics for appliqués; dressmaker's carbon; ballpoint pen; scraps of loose polyester fiberfill; white quilting thread; embroidery floss; gold thread. (**Note:** Prewash all new fabrics.)

DIRECTIONS: (**Note:** For additional directions in cutting and sewing, see descriptions of blocks to follow.) Following directions on page 83, enlarge the nine picture blocks on sheets of paper to 12″ square; add ¼″ seam allowance all around. From red fabric, cut six bands 12½″x4½″, four bands 44½″x4½″ and two bands 52½″x4½″. From red/yellow print fabric, cut two pieces 52½″x26½″, two pieces 52½″x8″ and two pieces

RAPUNZEL   1 SQ. = 1 IN.

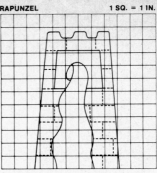

68″x8″. From quilt batting, cut a 60″ square. Trace individual appliqué pieces from each enlarged picture block onto appropriate fabrics, using dressmaker's carbon and ballpoint pen; cut ¼″ outside traced lines (⅛″ for very small pieces, such as apple

LITTLE RED RIDING HOOD

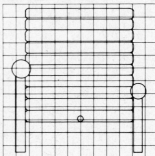

in "Snow White" or basket in "Little Red Riding Hood").

Sewing (¼″ seam allowance): Appliqué each picture block as follows: Clip curved seam allowances on each appliqué shape. Turn under on drawn lines. Pin appliqué pieces to block,

THE PRINCESS AND THE PEA

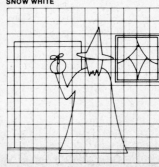

using enlarged picture as a guide. (If you wish, you may trace picture outlines onto block background for exact placement.) Slipstitch turned edges. Finish blocks with hand embroidery as noted in block descriptions. Using diagram on page 121 as a guide,

SNOW WHITE

UGLY DUCKLING

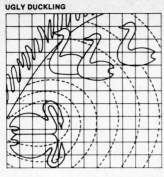

RUMPLESTILTSKIN

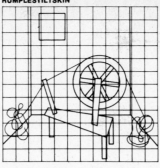

oz. skeins): 1(2,2) skeins of #6332 Navy (A), 1 skein each of #6369 Medium Blue (B), #6303 Kelly Green (C), #6361 Lettuce (D), #6355 Deep Yellow (E),#6306 Orange (F), #6307 Tangerine (G), #6313 Scarlet (H), #6334 Bright Magenta (I), #6371 Purple (J); knitting needles, No. 8 OR ANY SIZE NEEDLES WHICH WILL OBTAIN THE STITCH GAUGE BELOW; 6 buttons, ⅜" in diameter.

GAUGE: 4 sts = 1"; 8 rows (4 ridges) = 1".

MEASUREMENTS:

Sizes:	Small (2-4)	Medium (6-8)	Large (10)
Chest:	26"	29½"	31½"
Width across back at underarms:	12½"	14½"	15½"
Width across each front at underarm (including front band):	7"	8"	8½"
Width across sleeve at upper arm:	10"	11"	12"

assemble quilt top by seaming blocks and strips together. Finished quilt top should be approximately 68" square. Right sides together, seam long edges of two 52½"x26½" backing pieces; press seam open. On the floor or a large table, lay backing wrong side up.

JACK AND THE BEANSTALK

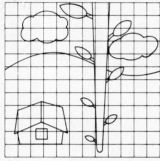

Place batting over this, letting excess batting extend approximately 4" evenly all around backings. Place quilt top over batting, letting top extend evenly around batting. Pin through all layers. Hand baste from center outward to

CINDERELLA

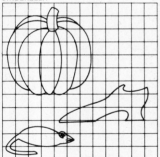

each side and each corner. Quilt (work ⅛" running stitch through all layers) around each appliqué shape, then around edges of each block, quilting center block ("Jack and the Beanstalk") first. Repeat for all other blocks. Quilt 4" squares at intersec-

tions of blocks. Quilt by hand or machine on seam line between solid red band and print border. Turn quilt over. Approximately 3" of batting should extend all around backing. Measure this extension and if necessary trim *batting only* to 3". Red/yellow print border fabric will extend past trimmed batting. Trim

this border to 3½" beyond batting edge all around quilt. Fold border over edge of batting, mitering corners. Turn under raw edge ¼" and slipstitch to backing. Slipstitch mitered corners together.

DESCRIPTIONS OF BLOCKS:
Rapunzel: Tower is solid; "bricks" are quilted. **Ugly Duckling:** Only rings in water are quilted; not the shapes. **Rumplestiltskin:** Make floor different color than walls to provide contrast. Embroider (outline stitch) thread on left of wheel yellow, on right, gold. **Jack & the Beanstalk:** While appliquéing, stuff clouds with extra fiberfill. **Cinderella:** Pumpkin is one solid shape. Lines are outline stitched and quilted. Mouse's ears are satin stitch; whiskers, outline stitch. Glass slipper is cut from sheer white fabric. **Pinocchio:** Pinocchio's seams are running stitch. **Little Red Riding Hood:** Quilt around shapes. **Snow White:** Quilt around shapes. **Princess and the Pea:** Quilt around shapes.

RAINBOW CARDIGAN AND HAT

(page 67)

Directions are given for size Small (2-4). Changes for sizes Medium (6-8) and Large (10) are in parentheses.
MATERIALS: Columbia-Minerva Nantuk Sweater and Afghan Yarn (2

DIRECTIONS—CARDIGAN—BACK: Starting at lower edge with A, cast on 50(58,62) sts. Work in k 1, p 1 ribbing for 15(17,19) rows in all. Mark last row for wrong side. Cut A; attach B. Working in garter st (k each row) throughout, work Rainbow pat as follows: **Rows 1 through 6:** With B, k 6 rows (3 ridges). Cut B; attach C. **Rows 7 through 12:** With C, k 6 rows. Cut C; attach D. Cut and attach colors as needed. **Rows 13 through 18:** 6 rows D. **Rows 19 through 24:** 6 rows E. **Rows 25 through 30:** 6 rows F. **Rows 31 through 36:** 6 rows G. **Rows 37 through 42:** 6 rows H. **Rows 43 through 48:** 6 rows I. **Rows 49 through 54:** 6 rows J. Last 54 rows (Rows 1 through 54) form Rainbow pat. Starting with Row 1, continue in pat until total length is approx. 11(12,13)" from beg, ending with a complete stripe.

Armhole Shaping: Keeping continuity of Rainbow pat throughout, and working in garter st, bind off 2(3,4) sts at beg of next 2 rows. Dec one st at each end every other row 4 times —38(44,46) sts. Work even in pat until length is 4½(5½,6)" from first row of armhole shaping.

Shoulder Shaping: Continuing in the Rainbow pat, bind off 4(5,5) sts at beg of next 4 rows; bind off 4(4,5) sts at beg of following 2 rows. Bind off rem 14(16,16) sts for back of neck.

LEFT FRONT: Starting at lower edge with A, cast on 28(32,34) sts. Work in k 1, p 1 ribbing for 7(9,9) rows. **Next Row:** Work in ribbing across to within last 6 sts; place rem 6 sts on a st holder to be used later for front band. Working over 22(26,28) sts on needle only, continue in ribbing for 8(8,10) more rows. Cut A; attach B. Work Rainbow pat same as for back to underarm, ending at side edge with same color stripe as on Back.

PINOCCHIO

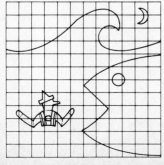

Armhole Shaping: Keeping continuity of Rainbow pat throughout, from side edge bind off 2(3,4) sts at beg of next row. Work one row even. Dec one st at armhole edge on every other row 4 times—16(19,20) sts. Work even in pat until length from first row of armhole shaping is 3(4,4½)″; end at front edge. **Neck Shaping—Row 1:** At front edge, bind off 2(3,3) sts, k to end of row. Dec one st at neck edge every row 2(2,3) times. Work even until length of armhole is same as on back, end at armhole edge. **Shoulder Shaping:** At armhole edge, bind off 4(5,5) sts at beg of next row. Work one row even. Rpt last 2 rows once. Bind off rem sts.

RIGHT FRONT: Work same as Left Front until first 7(9,9) rows of ribbing have been completed. **Next Row:** With A (k 1, p 1) 3 times; place these sts on a st holder; complete row in ribbing. Work in ribbing for 8(8,10) more rows. Cut A; attach B and k across row. Continue to work to correspond with Left Front, reversing shaping. (**Note:** For a Girl's Cardigan, work Left Front Band [button band] first; for a Boy's Cardigan, work Right Front Band [button band] first.)

Button Band: Sl sts from left front holder (or right front holder for a boy's cardigan) onto a needle; attach A and work in k1, p1 ribbing as established until band (slightly stretched) reaches to neck edge; place sts back on holder. Sew band to corresponding front edge. With pins, mark the position of 5 buttons evenly spaced along band, having first pin in line with center of bottom ribbing and 5th pin about 1¼(1½,1¾)″ below neck edge. The 6th button will be placed on neckband. **To make a buttonhole:** Starting at front edge of band, work in ribbing over first 2 sts, bind off next 2 sts; complete row. On next row, cast on 2 sts over bound-off sts. **Buttonhole Band:** Making buttonholes to correspond with pin markers, work band on other front same as Button Band.

SLEEVES: Starting at lower edge with A, cast on 28(30,32) sts. Work in k 1, p 1 ribbing for 15(17,19) rows. Mark last row for wrong side. Working in the Rainbow pat throughout same as for Back, inc one st at each end every 8th(8th, 9th) row until there are 40(44,48) sts. Work even until length is 11(12,13)″ from beg, ending with same color stripe as on back to underarm. **Top Shaping:** Keeping continuity of pat, bind off 2(3,4) sts at beg of next 2 rows. Dec one st at each end every other row until 18(22,24) sts rem, then every 3rd row 0(2,3) times. Bind off 2 sts at beg of next 4 rows. Bind off rem 10 sts.

Pocket (Make 2): Starting at lower edge with B, cast on 18 sts. Work in the Rainbow pat as for Back until 18 rows have been completed. With E, k 1 row; then work in k 1, p 1 ribbing for 4 rows. Bind off in ribbing.

FINISHING: Pin pieces to measurements on a padded surface; cover with a damp cloth and allow to dry; do not press. Sew shoulder seams. **Neckband:** With right side facing, using A, work in ribbing as established over 6 sts on right front holder, pick up and k 44(48,50) sts evenly along neck edge to left front holder; work in ribbing over sts on left front holder—56(60,62) sts. Work in k 1, p 1 ribbing over all sts for ½″. Making a buttonhole in line with previous buttonholes over next 2 rows, continue in ribbing until neckband measures 1¼″. Bind off in ribbing. Sew side and sleeve seams, matching stripes. Sew in sleeves, matching stripes. Sew pocket to center of each front, directly above ribbing. Sew on buttons.

HAT: With A, cast on 62(62,66) sts. Work in k 1, p 1 ribbing for 10 rows. Cut A; attach B. Work in the Rainbow pat same as for Cardigan until total length is 6½(7,7½)″. **Top Shaping—Row 1:** Continuing in pat, k 2 tog, * k 2, k 2 tog; rpt from * across. **Row 2:** K across. **Row 3:** K 1, * k 2 tog, k 1; rpt from * across. **Row 4:** K across. **Row 5:** K 1, * k 2 tog; rpt from * across. **Row 6:** K across. Leaving a 20″ length, break off yarn. Using a darning needle, slip rem sts onto end of yarn, pull tightly together, fasten on wrong side. Sew back seam.

CHILD'S STRIPED SWEATER

(page 67)

Directions are given for Size 4. Changes for Sizes 6, 8 and 10 are in parentheses.

MATERIALS: Lion Brand Knitting Worsted 4 ply (4 oz. skeins): 1 (1,1,1) skein each of #132 Myrtle Green (A), #130 Emerald (B), #157 Pastel Yellow (C), #117 Lemon (D), #134 Brick (E), #133 Tile (F), #114 Cardinal (G), #113 Scarlet (H); knitting needles, No. 10 OR ANY SIZE NEEDLES WHICH WILL OBTAIN THE STITCH GAUGE BELOW.

GAUGE: 4 sts = 1″; 14 rows (7 ridges) = 2″.

MEASUREMENTS:

Sizes:	4	6	8	10
Chest:	24″	25″	27″	29″
Width across back or front at underarms:	12″	12½″	13½″	14½″
Width across sleeve at upper arm:	11½″	12″	13″	14″

DIRECTIONS—BACK: Starting at lower edge with A, cast on 48(50,54,58) sts. Working in garter st (k each row) throughout, work stripe pat as follows: Make 6(8,10,12) rows to form 3(4,5,6) ridges A; cut A; attach B. (**Note:** Cut and attach colors as needed. Make 4 rows B; 6(8,10,12) rows A; 8(8,10,10) rows C; 4 rows D; 8(8,10,10) rows C; 8(8,10,10) rows E; 4 rows F; 8(8,10,10) rows E; 8(8,10,10) rows G; 4 rows H; 8(8,10,10) rows G; 4 rows F; 8(8,10,10) rows E; 6(8,10,12) rows A; 4 rows B; 6(8,10,12) rows A. Bind off all sts. There are 92(100,120,128) rows in all.)

FRONT: Work same as Back.

SLEEVES: Starting at cuff edge with A, cast on 32(34,38,42) sts. Working in garter st (k each row) throughout, with A, work 8(8,10,10) rows for cuff, then continuing with A, work 6(8,10,10) more rows; work 4 rows B; 6(8,10,10) rows A; 8(8,10,10) rows C; 4 rows D; 8(8,10,10) rows C; 8(8,10,10) rows E; 4 rows F. **Underarm Shaping:** Starting with next E stripe and working next 24 rows in stripe pat to correspond with Back and Front, inc one st at each end of next row, then at each end every 3rd row until there are 48(50,54,58) sts. Continuing in stripe pat as for Back, work even until total length is 12(13,15,16)″ from beg. Bind off all sts.

POCKET (Make 2): With A, cast on 14(14,16,16) sts. Working in garter st, make 6(8,10,10) rows A; 4 rows B; 6(8,10,12) rows A. Bind off.

FINISHING: Pin each piece to measurements on a padded surface; cover with a damp cloth and allow to dry; do not press. Starting at side edges, sew 3(3,3½,3¾)″ shoulder seams, leaving center portion of top edge open for neck. Leaving top 5¾(6,6½,7)″ open for armholes, sew side seams, matching stripes. Sew sleeve seams, matching stripes. With center of top edge of sleeves at shoulder seams, sew sleeves into armholes. Sew pockets to lower portion of front, approximately 1(1,2,2)″ in from side seams, matching cast on edges and stripes. Fold cuffs to right side at lower edge of sleeves.

RAINBOW OVERALLS

(page 68)

MATERIALS: See pattern backviews, page 27, for Simplicity #7815. Scraps of primary-colored cotton fabrics for appliqués; white piqué for clouds; ¼ yd. 18″-wide fusible webbing; thread to match fabrics.

DIRECTIONS: Cut out overalls according to pattern instructions. Following directions on page 83, enlarge pattern for rainbow appliqué. Cut rainbow and hill appliqué pieces from bright cotton scraps; cut clouds from white piqué. Cut fusible webbing to

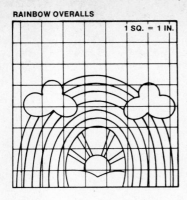

1 SQ. = 1 IN.

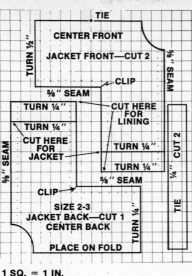

TIE

TURN ½"

CENTER FRONT

JACKET FRONT—CUT 2

⅝" SEAM

CLIP

⅝" SEAM

TURN ¼"

TURN ¼"

CUT HERE FOR LINING

CUT HERE FOR JACKET

TURN ¼"

CUT 2

¼"

TURN ¼"

⅝" SEAM

⅝" SEAM

CLIP

SIZE 2-3
JACKET BACK—CUT 1
CENTER BACK

TIE

TURN ¼"

PLACE ON FOLD

1 SQ. = 1 IN.

match appliqué pieces. Position appliqué pieces on bib as shown in photo, page 76, with fusible webbing underneath. Fuse, following manufacturer's instructions. Using a machine zig-zag stitch, satin-stitch around appliqué pieces in thread to match appliqué fabrics. Satin-stitch four sunbeams. Finish assembling overalls according to pat instructions.

CRAFT HINT: A new product has just come out on the market which would provide an alternative to these fabric appliqués. It's an iron-on color paper called "Fab-U-Print"™. To use, just trace appliqué shapes on paper, position on fabric, and iron on. Complete directions and project ideas are in the kit. "Fab-U-Print" is available in fabric and craft stores, or write to "Fab-U-Print" (see Buyer's Guide.)

ANIMAL CRACKERS JACKET AND PANTS

(page 68)

Jacket is toddler Size 2-3.

MATERIALS: See pattern backviews, page 27, for Simplicity #7629 (pants). ½ yd. 45"-wide fabric for jacket; ½ yd. bright cotton fabric for jacket lining; ¼ yd. green cotton fabric for "grass"; scraps of assorted bright cottons and white piqué 1 yd. 18"-wide fusible webbing.

DIRECTIONS: Following directions on page 83, enlarge patterns for jacket and appliqués. Cut out pants according to pattern instructions. Cut out jacket and lining from your enlarged pattern. From bright cotton fabric, cut strips for jacket ties 2" x 14½". From green fabric, cut pieces for grass, one piece 3" wide and length of bottom edge of jacket, two pieces 4" wide and length around bottom of pants leg. Cut animal appliqués from bright cottons (you'll need 7 animals for the jacket, 8 for the pants). Cut clouds from white piqué. Cut fusible webbing to match.

To Sew Jacket: With ⅝" seam allowance, join jacket fronts to jacket back at shoulders. Press seams open. Topstitch ⅛" from seams with zig-zag stitch. Press sleeve edges under ¼"; topstitch with zig-zag. Stitch underarm side seams, right sides together.

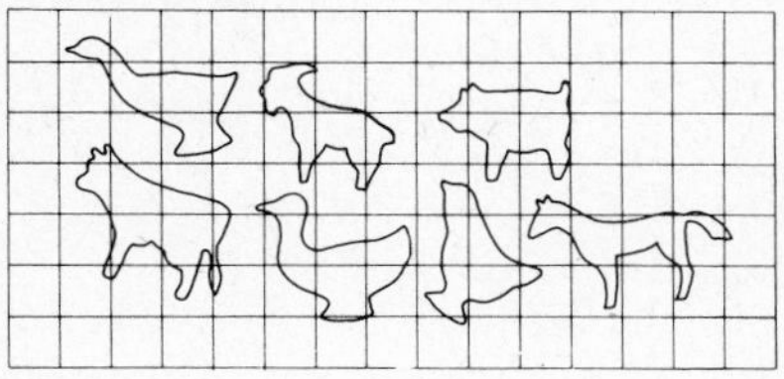

Clip seam allowance to corner at underarm. Sew lining pieces together in same way. For the grass on jacket, use 3"-wide strip of green fabric. Press under ¼" on top edge of grass. Pin strip onto jacket, matching the front edges and bottom edge. Edgestitch at top and bottom; baste front edges together. Position appliqué pieces on front and back as shown in photo (page 76) with fusible webbing underneath. Fuse, following manufacturer's instructions. Using a machine zig-zag stitch, satin stitch around appliqués with matching thread. Press under ½" at jacket hem; topstitch with zig-zag stitch. Repeat for jacket lining. Pin the right side of jacket lining to right side of jacket along front and neck edges. Stitch, using ½" seam allowance. Trim seams; clip curves. Turn jacket right side out; press. Turn jacket lining up over sleeve to form a cuff. Fold tie fabric in half lengthwise, right sides together, and stitch ¼" from edge, leaving one end open. Turn right side out and press. Repeat for other tie. Turn selvage edge of tie under ¼" and pin to center of jacket. Satin stitch turned edge to attach tie to jacket. Repeat for other tie.

To Sew Pants: For grass, use 4"-wide strips of green fabric. Press under ¼" on top edge of strip. Pin strip to bottom of pants leg piece, edge-stitch at top and bottom. Position appliqué pieces as shown in photo, with fusible webbing underneath.

Fuse, following manufacturer's instructions. Using machine zig-zag stitch, satin stitch around appliqué in matching thread. Finish pants according to pattern instructions.

CHILD'S BOAT NECK SWEATER

(page 69)

Directions are given for Size 4. Changes for Sizes 6, 8 and 10 are in parentheses.

MATERIALS: Columbia - Minerva Nantuk Knitting Worsted Weight Yarn (2 oz. balls): 5(6,7,8) balls of Natural or desired color; knitting needles, 1 pair No. 8 OR ANY SIZE NEEDLES WHICH WILL OBTAIN THE STITCH GAUGE BELOW; crochet hook, Size G.

GAUGE: 9 sts = 2"; 8 rows (4 ridges) = 1".

MEASUREMENTS:

Sizes:	4	6	8	10
Chest:	24"	25"	27"	29"
Width across back or front at underarms	12"	12½"	13½"	14½"
Width across sleeve at upper arm:	9½"	10"	10½"	11"

DIRECTIONS—BACK: Starting at lower edge, cast on 54(56,62,66) sts. Work in k 1, p 1 ribbing for 2½(2½,3,3)". Now work in garter st (k each row) until length is approximately 15½(16½, 18, 19)" from beg or desired length to shoulder. Bind off all sts.

FRONT: Work same as Back.

SLEEVES: Starting at lower edge, cast on 40(42,44,46) sts. Work in k 1, p 1 ribbing for 2½(2½,3,3)", inc 2(2,4,4) sts evenly spaced in last row. Work in garter st (k each row) over 42(44,48,50) sts until length is 11½(12½,14,16)" from beg or desired length to underarm. Bind off all sts.

POUCH POCKET: Starting at one side edge, cast on 20(22,24,26) sts. Work in k 1, p 1 ribbing for 1½(1½,2,2)". Work in garter st until piece measures 7(7½,8,9)" from beg. Work in k 1, p 1 ribbing for 1½(1½,2,2)". Bind off in ribbing.

FINISHING: Pin each piece to measurements on a padded surface; cover with a damp cloth and allow to dry; do not press. Starting at side edges, sew approximately 1½(2,2½,3)" shoulder seams across top edge, leaving center section open for neck. Baste pouch pocket over center of front, with lower edge of pocket approximately 3½(3½,4,4½)" up from bottom edge of front. With crochet hook, holding yarn on wrong side of front and working through both thicknesses, crochet 1 row of sl sts across top and bottom edges (long edges) of pocket, then sl st up center for separation. Place a marker 4¾(5,5¼,5½)" from shoulder seams on both back and front side edges for armholes. Fold sleeves in half lengthwise to find center of top edge of each sleeve; match center of sleeves with shoulder seams and sew top edges of sleeves to armhole sections of back and front (between markers). Sew side and sleeve seams. With crochet hook, holding yarn on wrong side, from right side work 1 row or sl sts evenly over each seam, being careful to keep work flat.

CHILD'S STRIPED PATCHED SWEATER

(page 70)

Directions are given for Size 4. Changes for Sizes 6, 8 and 10 are in parentheses.

MATERIALS: Lion Brand Knitting Worsted 4 Ply (4 oz. skeins): 1(1,1,2) skeins of # 114 Cardinal (A), 1 skein each of # 113 Scarlet (B), # 133 Tile (C), # 141 Dusty Rose (D), # 145 Orchid (E), # 130 Emerald (F), # 148 Turquoise (G); knitting needles, 1 pair No. 8 OR ANY SIZE NEEDLES WHICH WILL OBTAIN THE STITCH GAUGE BELOW; crochet hook, Size G.

GAUGE: 9 sts = 2″; 8 rows (4 ridges) = 1″.

MEASUREMENTS:

Sizes:	4	6	8	10
Chest:	24″	25″	27½″	29″
Width across back or front at underarms:	12″	12½″	13¾″	14½″
Width across sleeve at upper arm:	9½″	10″	10½″	11″

DIRECTIONS—(**Note:** The stripe patches for Back and Front are made in 3 strips, then strips are joined together. Work in garter st (k each row) throughout.)

BACK—FIRST STRIP: Starting at lower edge with B, cast on 18(19,21,22) sts. **Rows 1 through 4:** With B, work 4 rows in garter st (k each row). Mark Row 1 for right side. Drop B; pick up A. **Rows 5 through 8:** With A, k 4 rows. Drop A; pick up B. Rpt last 8 rows (Rows 1 through 8) 3(3,4,4) more times. Cut A and B; attach E and F. **Next 8 Rows:** Working in garter st, make 4 rows F and 4 rows E. Rpt last 8 rows 3(3,4,4) more times. Cut E and F; attach C and D. **Following 8 Rows:** Working in garter st, make 4 rows D and 4 rows C. Rpt last 8 rows 3 (3,4,4) more times. Bind off. Cut D and C. Cut and attach colors as needed.

SECOND STRIP: Starting at lower edge with E, cast on 18(19,21,22) sts. **Rows 1 through 8:** Working in garter st, make 4 rows E and 4 Rows G. Mark Row 1 for right side. Rpt last 8 rows 3(3,4,4) more times. **Next 8 Rows:** Work 4 rows C and 4 rows A. Rpt last 8 rows 3(3,4,4) more times. **Following 8 Rows:** Work 4 rows F and 4 rows G. Rpt last 8 rows 3(3,4,4) more times. Bind off. Cut F and G. **THIRD STRIP:** Starting at lower edge with D, cast on 18(19,21,23) sts. **Rows 1 through 8:** Work 4 rows D and 4 rows A. Rpt last 8 rows 3(3,4,4) more times. **Next 8 Rows:** Work 4

rows E and 4 rows F. Rpt last 8 rows 3(3,4,4) more times. **Following 8 Rows:** Work 4 rows A and 4 rows B. Rpt last 8 rows 3(3,4,4) more times. Bind off. Cut A and B. Darn in all loose ends on wrong side. Using a darning needle, sew strips together, matching rows.

Ribbing: With right side facing, working along lower edge of joined strips, with A, pick up and k 54(56,62,66) sts evenly along lower edge. Work in k 1, p 1 ribbing for 3(3½,3½,4)″. Bind off loosely in ribbing.

FRONT: Work same as Back.

RIGHT SLEEVE: Starting at lower edge with A, cast on 40(42,44,46) sts. Work in k 1, p 1 ribbing for 2½(2½,3,3)″, inc 2(2,4,4) sts evenly spaced in last row—42(44,48,50) sts. **Rows 1 through 8:** Working in garter st (k each row), make 4 rows A and 4 rows C. Rpt last 8 rows for stripe pat until the total length is 11½(12½,14,16)″ ending with a complete stripe. Bind off all sts.

LEFT SLEEVE: Work same as Right Sleeve until ribbing has been completed—42(44,48,50) sts. Drop A; attach D. **Rows 1 through 8:** Working in garter st, make 4 rows D and 4 rows A. Rpt last 8 rows until same length as Right Sleeve. Bind off all sts.

FINISHING: Pin each piece to measurements on a padded surface; cover with a damp cloth and allow to dry; do not press. Starting at side edges, sew approximately 1½(2,2½,3)″ shoulder seams across top edge, leaving center section open for neck. With center of top edges of sleeves at shoulder seams, sew top edges of sleeves along 4¾(5,5¼,5½)″ of back and front side edges. Sew sleeve and side seams, matching stripes. With crochet hook, holding yarn on wrong side, from right side work 1 row of sl sts evenly over each seam, being careful to keep work flat.

NEEDLEPOINT PICTURE MATS

(page 62-63)

These mats are designed to be used with inexpensive plastic box frames, available in all dime stores. Our mats will accommodate standard size photographic prints; to vary them to fit other sizes, see directions on the next page.

Pastel mat - measures 8″x10″—inside opening is 4″x6″. **Plaid mat** - measures 8″x10″—inside opening is 3¾″x5¾″. **Blue/white lace-trimmed mat** - measures 5″x7″—inside opening is 2″x2¾″. **Heart mat** - measures 5″x7″—inside opening is 1½″x2″.

MATERIALS: Columbia-Minerva Needlepoint FashionEase canvas (one sheet will be enough for one 8″x10″ mat and one smaller mat); Columbia-Minerva Nantuk 4-ply yarn, or any leftover 4-ply yarn in

colors of your choice; single-edged razor blade; one 3-yd. package Wright's polyester lace, #191-2930 (for blue/white lace-trimmed mat).

DIRECTIONS: Using charts above as guides, mark outer and inner borders of mats on canvas with permanent marking pen. (Note that all inside openings of mat are centered on canvas except opening in rainbow mat, which is 1½″ from top, 2¾″ from bottom.) Use canvas count, *not measurements,* for accuracy. Carefully cut on markings with razor blade. Trim inside opening to get a smooth edge. Work needlepoint as indicated in charts in continental stitch, with details in French knots and straight stitches. Also, narrow lace can be glued over needlepoint strips as shown on blue and white mat. Since canvas is plastic, finished mats will not need blocking.

To adjust mats to fit other size pictures: Select the picture and mat design you plan to use. Mark outer border as above. Center your picture within outer border; trace around picture. Draw inner border two threads in from tracing marks. Cut on inner and outer borders. For larger picture, eliminate as many rows of design as necessary. For smaller picture, add extra rows of needlepoint.

RAINBOW JUMPER AND JACKET

(page 69)

Directions are given for Size 2. Changes for Sizes 4, 6 and 8 are in parentheses.

MATERIALS: Coats & Clark's Knitting Worsted, 4 Ply (4 oz. skeins): *For Each Article:* 1(1,2,2) skein of Navy (A), 1 oz. each of Red (B), Orange (C), Dark Yellow (D), Yellow (E), Green (F), Dark Green (G), Blue (H), Purple (I); crochet hook, Size G OR ANY SIZE HOOK WHICH WILL OBTAIN THE STITCH GAUGE BELOW; 3 buttons for dress, ½″ in diameter; 3(3,4,4) buttons for sweater, ¾″ in diameter.

GAUGE: 7 dc = 2″; 2 dc rows = 1″.

MEASUREMENTS:

Sizes:	2	4	6	8
JUMPER:				
Chest:	21″	23″	24″	26″
Width across base of Rainbow motif:	9″	9½″	10″	10½″
JACKET:				
Chest:	23″	25″	26″	29″
Width across back at underarms:	12″	13″	13″	15″
Width across each front at underarm:	5½″	6″	6½″	7″
Width across sleeve at upperarm:	9″	10″	11″	11½″

DIRECTIONS—JUMPER: Rainbow Motif: Starting at center of base with B, ch 4. Join with sl st to form ring. **Row 1:** Ch 3, 8 dc in ring. Ch 3, turn. **Row 2:** Dc in first dc, make (dc in next dc, 2 dc in next dc) 3 times; dc in next

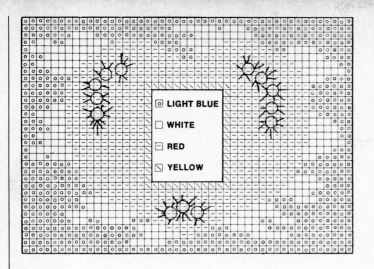

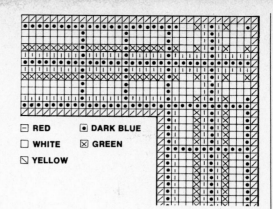

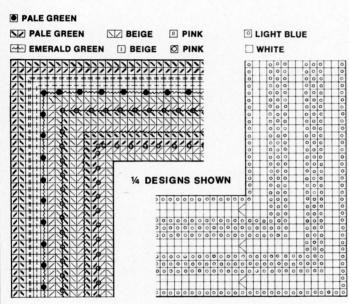

¼ DESIGNS SHOWN

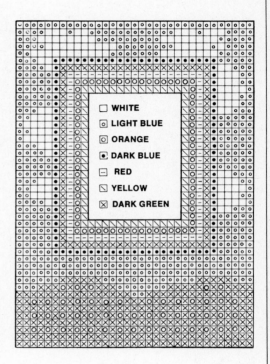

dc, 2 dc in top of ch-3—14 dc, counting ch-3 as 1 dc. Cut B; attach C to end of row. With C, ch 3, turn. **Row 3:** *Dc in first dc*—**inc made at beg of row;** make (dc in each of next 2 dc, 2 dc in next dc) 4 times; dc in top of ch-3—5 incs made. Cut C; attach D. (**Note:** Cut and attach colors as needed.) With D, ch 3, turn. **Row 4:** Dc in first dc, (dc in each of next 3 dc, 2 dc in next dc) 4 times; dc in next dc, dc in top of ch-3—24 dc. With E, ch 3, turn. **Row 5:** Increasing 5 dc evenly spaced across, dc in each dc and in top of ch-3—29 dc. With F, ch 3, turn. **Row 6:** With F, work same as for Row 5. With G, ch 1, turn. **Row 7:** With G, sc in each of first 7 dc, (2 dc in next dc, 1 dc in each of next 3 dc) 5 times; sc in each of rem 7 sts—39 sts. With H, ch 1, turn. **Row 8:** With H, sc in each sc to within next dc, sc in next dc; increasing 5 dc evenly spaced, dc in each dc to within last dc before sc group, sc in next dc, sc in each sc to end of row—44 sts. With I, ch 1, turn. **Row 9:** With I, work same as for Row 8—49 sts. With I, rpt last row 0(1,2,3) more times—49(54, 59,64) sts. Cut yarn and fasten.

Back Section—Row 1: Attach A to first sc on last row, ch 1, sc in same sc, sc in each of next 8(9,11,12) sts; do not work over rem sts. Ch 3, turn. **Row 2:** Sk first sc, dc in each rem sc. Ch 3, turn. **Row 3:** Sk first dc, dc in each dc across, dc in top of ch-3—9(10,12,13) dc, counting ch-3 as 1 dc. Ch 3, turn. Rpt last row until back section measures (slightly stretched) 11½(13,13½,15)″. Cut yarn, fasten.

Skirt—Rnd 1: Working along lower edge of back section and Rainbow motif, attach A to end st of last row of motif, placing sts along ends of rows, make 75(80,85,90) sc evenly along entire lower edge of motif and back section. Join with sl st to first sc of this rnd. **Rnd 2:** Ch 3, dc in each of next 3 sc, * 2 dc in next sc, dc in each of next 4 sc; rpt from * around, ending with 2 dc in last sc. Join with sl st to top of ch-3—90(96,102,108) dc. Always count ch-3 as 1 dc. **Rnd 3:** Ch 3, sk joining, * dc in each of next 16(18,19,20) dc, 2 dc in next dc; rpt from * 4 more times; dc in each rem dc. Join with sl st to top of ch-3. **Rnd 4:** Ch 3, sk joining, increasing 5 dc evenly spaced around, dc in each dc

around. Join to top of ch-3—100(106,112,118) dc. **Rnd 5:** Ch 3, sk joining, dc in each dc around. Join to top of ch-3. Rpt Rnd 4 until there are 125(136,142,153) dc. Now rpt Rnd 5 until length from first rnd of skirt is 6(8,11,13)″. Cut A; attach I.

Border—Rnd 1: With I, ch 1, sc in same st as joining sc in each st around. Join with sl st to first sc. Cut I; attach H.

Next 7 Rnds: Working same as for Rnd 1, make 1 rnd of each color in the following order: H,G,F,E,D,C and B. At end of last rnd, cut yarn and fasten.

Strap (Make 2): Starting at back end with A, ch 7. **Row 1:** Sc in 2nd ch from hook, sc in each of next 5 ch. Ch 1, turn. **Row 2:** Sc in each of 6 sc. Ch 1, turn. Rpt last row until total length is 7(7½,8,8½)″. Ch 1, turn. **Buttonhole Row:** Sc in each of first 2 sc, ch 2, sk next 2 sc for buttonhole, sc in each of last 2 sc. Ch 1, turn. **Next Row:** Sc in each sc and in each ch across. Ch 1, turn. Rpt Row 2, 4 times; then rpt Buttonhole Row and following row. Work 1 more row even. Break off and fasten.

FINISHING: Pin dress to measurements on a padded surface; cover with a damp cloth and allow to dry; do not press. **Button Loop:** Sk end 8(9,11,12) sts on last row of Rainbow motif at free side edge of motif; attach I to next st, ch 5 for button loop, sl st in same st where yarn was attached. Cut yarn and fasten. Sew one ½" button to upper corner at side edge of back sections. Sew starting chains of straps to center of top edge of back section, 1(1½,2,2)" apart. Sew two ½" buttons to top of motif 3(3½,4,4)" apart.

JACKET—Back—Rainbow Motif: Work same as for Dress.

Top Shaping—Row 1 (right side): With right side of last row facing, sk first 8(9,11,12) sts on last row of motif, attach A in next st, ch 3, 1 dc in each of next 3(4,4,5) sts, sc in each st to within last 12(14,16,18) sts, dc in each of next 4(5,5,6) sts; do not work over rem sts. Ch 3, turn. **Row 2:** Sk first dc, dc in next 2(3,3,4) dc, sc in each st to within last 3(4,4,5) sts, dc in each of last 3(4,4,5) sts. Ch 3, turn. **Row 3:** Sk first dc, dc in next 1(2,2,3) dc, sc in each st to within last 2(3,3,4) sts, dc in each of rem sts. **For Size 8 Only:** Ch 3, turn. **Row 4:** Sk first dc, dc in next st, hdc in next st, sl st in each st to last 3 sts, hdc in next st, dc in last 2 sts. **For all sizes:** Cut yarn and fasten. **Lower Section—Row 1:** Working along ends of rows at base of Rainbow motif, attach A to end of last row of motif, make 30(32,34,36) sc evenly across lower edge of motif. Ch 3, turn. **Row 2:** Sk first sc, dc in each sc across. Ch 3, turn. **Row 3:** Sk first dc, dc in each dc across, dc in top of ch-3. Ch 3, turn. Rpt last row until total length from top edge of motif is 10 (11½,13,14)". Do not cut yarn. Do not turn. **Side Section—Row 1:** Ch 3, working along ends of rows, make 2 dc over end of each row along side edge of lower section; dc in each free st on motif, 2 dc over end of each row along top shaping. **For Size 8 Only:** Rpt Row 3 of Lower Section 2 times. **For All Sizes:** Cut yarn and fasten. Turn. **Armhole Shaping:** For armhole, sk first 12(13,14,15) sts on last row, attach A in next dc, ch 3, dc in each rem dc and in top of ch-3. Ch 3, turn. Work even in dc's over these sts for 3(5,5,5) more rows, ending at armhole edge. At end of last row, ch 14(15,16,17) for front edge of armhole. **Right Front—Row 1:** Dc in 4th ch from hook, dc in each ch and in each st across last row. Ch 3, turn. Work even in dc's over these sts for 2(2,4,4) more rows, ending at lower edge. Ch 3, turn. **Neck Shaping—Row 1:** Sk first dc, dc in each dc to within last 4 sts; do not work over rem sts. Ch 3, turn. **Row 2:** Sk first dc, *holding back on hook last loop of each dc, make dc in each of next 2 dc, yarn over hook,*

draw through all 3 loops on hook—Dec made at neck edge; dc in each rem st to end of row. Ch 3, turn. **Row 3:** Sk first dc, dc in each dc to within last 2 sts, dec over last 2 sts. Continuing to dec one st at neck edge every row, make 3 more rows. Cut yarn and fasten. Work other Side Section, Armhole Shaping and Left Front to correspond with opposite side. Sew front shoulders to corresponding top edges of back.

SLEEVES: With right side facing, attach A in center of underarm, ch 3; along armhole make 2 dc over end of each row at underarm, dc in each ch and in each st around. Join with sl st to top of ch-3—32(36,38,40) dc. **Rnd 2:** Ch 3, sk joining, dc in each dc around. Join. Rpt last rnd 4(5,6,7) more times. Cut A; attach I. Working same as last rnd, work 1 rnd of each color in the following order: I,H, G,F,E,D,C, and B. Cut yarn and fasten. Work other sleeve in same manner.

Neck Ruffle—Row 1: With right side facing, starting ½" in from front edge, with A, sc evenly along neck edge to within ½" from front edge, easing in neck to desired fit. Ch 3, turn. **Row 2:** Dc in first sc, * dc in next sc, 2 dc in next sc; rpt from * across, ending with dc in last sc. Ch 3, turn. **Row 3:** Rpt last row. Cut yarn and fasten. **Edging and Button Loops:** With pins, mark the position of 3(3,4,4) button loops evenly spaced along right front edge, placing first pin ½" below neck edge and last pin 1½(1½,2,2½)" above lower edge. **Row 1:** Attach A to upper left front corner at neck; making 3 sc in same st at each lower corner, sc evenly along left front edge and across lower edge, * along right front edge sc in each st to next pin, ch 4 for button loop; rpt from * 2(2,3,3) more times; sc in each st to next corner. Ch 1, turn. **Row 2:** (Sc in each sc to next loop, 6 sc in ch-4 loop) 3(3,4,4) times; sc in each sc across last row. Cut yarn and fasten. **FINISHING:** Block same as for Dress. Sew buttons opposite loops.

CHILD'S HOODED JACKET

(page 71)

Directions are given for Size 4. Changes for Sizes 6, 8 and 10 are in parentheses.

MATERIALS: Coats & Clark's Red Heart Knitting Worsted 4 Ply (4 oz skeins): 3(4,4,5) skeins #858 Navy (A), 1 skein each of #909 Scarlet (B),#253 Tangerine (C),#230 Yellow (D), #676 Emerald Green (E),#848 Skipper Blue (F),#588 Amethyst (G) for each size; knitting needles, 1 pair No. 10½ OR ANY SIZE NEEDLES WHICH WILL OBTAIN THE STITCH GAUGE BELOW; crochet hook, Size J.

GAUGE: 3 sts = 1"; 6 rows (3 ridges) = 1".
(Note: Two strands of yarn held together are used throughout; color A, together with another color, is used throughout as directed, except for edging. Entire jacket is worked in garter st.)

MEASUREMENTS:

Sizes	4	6	8	10
Chest:	26"	28"	30"	32"
Width across back at underarms:	13"	14"	15"	16"
Width across each front at underarm:	6½"	7"	7½"	8"
Width across sleeve at upper arm:	10"	10½"	11¼"	12"

DIRECTIONS—BACK: Starting at lower edge with one strand each of A and B held together, cast on 39(42,45,48) sts. **Rows 1 and 2:** With A and B, k 2 rows. Cut B; pick up C. **Rows 3 and 4:** With A and C, k 2 rows. Cut C; pick up D. **Rows 5 and 6:** With A and D, k 2 rows. Cut D; pick up E. **Rows 7 and 8:** With A and E, k 2 rows. Cut E; pick up F. **Rows 9 and 10:** With A and F, k 2 rows. Cut F; pick up G. **Rows 11 and 12:** With A and G, k 2 rows. Cut G; pick up B. Rpt these 12 rows (Rows 1 through 12) for pat until total length is 10(11,12½,14)" from beg. **Armhole Shaping:** Continuing in pat throughout, bind off 3(3,4,4) sts at beg of next 2 rows. Dec one st at each end every other row 2 times—29(32,33,36) sts. Work even in pat until length from first row of armhole shaping is 4½(5,5½,6)". **Shoulder Shaping:** Continuing in pat, bind off 4(5,5,6) sts at beg of next 2 rows. Bind off 4 sts at beg of following 2 rows. Bind off rem 13(14,15,16) sts for back of neck.

LEFT FRONT: Starting at lower edge with A and B held together, cast on 19(21,23,25) sts. Work same as for Back to underarm. **Armhole Shaping:** Continuing in pat throughout, bind off 3(3,4,4) sts at beg of next row. Dec one st at same edge every other row 2 times—14(16,17,19) sts. Work even in pat until length from first row of armhole shaping is 3(3,3½,4)", ending at front edge. **Neck Shaping:** Continuing in pat, from front edge bind off 4(5,5,6) sts in next row. Dec one st at neck edge every other row 2(2,3,3) times. Work even over rem 8(9,9,10) sts until length of armhole is same as on Back, ending at armhole edge. **Shoulder Shaping:** From armhole edge, bind off 4(5,5,6) sts at beg of next row. Work 1 row even. Bind off rem 4 sts.

RIGHT FRONT: Work to correspond with Left Front, reversing shaping.

SLEEVES: Starting at lower edge with A and B held together, cast on 18(18,20,22) sts. Work same as for

Back until 6(6,8,10) rows have been completed. Continuing in pat same as for Back, inc one st at each end of next row, then every 6th row 6(7,7,7) times in all—30(32,34,36) sts. Work even in pat until total length of sleeve is 10(11,13,15)″ or desired length to underarm.

Top Shaping: Continuing in pat, bind off 3(3,4,4) sts at beg of each of next 2 rows. Dec one st at each end every 2nd (2nd,3rd,3rd) row until 10 (10,12,12) sts rem. Bind off 2 sts at beg of next 2 rows. Bind off rem sts.

HOOD: Starting at front edge with A and B held together, cast on 54(54,56,58) sts. Work in pat same as for Back until length is 5½(5½,6,6)″ from beg. Continuing in pat throughout, bind off 18(18,19,20) sts at beg of each of next 2 rows. Continue in pat over rem 18 sts for back section for 6(6,6¼,6½)″. Bind off all sts.

FINISHING: Pin each piece to measurements on a padded surface; cover with a damp cloth and allow to dry; do not press. Darn in all loose ends on wrong side. Sew shoulder, side and sleeve seams. Sew in sleeves. Sew side edges of back portion of hood to back bound-off edges of front section of hood. Starting and ending approximately 1(1,1½,1½)″ in from front edges, sew lower edge of hood to neck edge, adjusting to fit. **Edging:** With 2 strands of E held together and crochet hook, starting at lower end of a side seam, sc evenly along entire outer edge of jacket and hood, making 3 sc in same st at each corner and being careful to keep work flat. Join with sl st to first sc. Cut yarn and fasten.

CHILD'S PULLOVER WITH EMBROIDERY

(page 71)

Directions are given for Size 4. Changes for Sizes 6, 8 and 10 are in parentheses.

MATERIALS: Coats and Clark's Red Heart Knitting Worsted 4 ply (4 oz. skeins): 2 (2,3,4) ozs. Skipper Blue (A), 1(1,2,2) oz. each of Emerald Green (B), Red (C), Mid Orange (D), Yellow (E), Deep Purple (F), or any other 6 colors; knitting needles, 1 pair No. 7 OR ANY SIZE NEEDLES WHICH WILL OBTAIN THE STITCH GAUGE BELOW; tapestry needle.

GAUGE: Stockinette St—9 sts = 2″; 6 rows = 1″.

MEASUREMENTS:

Sizes:	4	6	8	10
Chest:	24″	26″	28″	30″
Width across back or front at underarms:	12″	13″	14″	15″
Width across sleeve at upper arm:	9½″	10″	11″	11½″

DIRECTIONS—BACK: Starting at lower edge with B, cast on 55(59,64,68) sts. Work in garter st (k each row) for 6(8,10,12) rows, form-

ing 3(4,5,6) ridges. At end of last row, cut B, attach A. Now work Stripe pat as follows: With A, work 8(8,10,10) rows in st st (k 1 row, p 1 row). Cut A; attach C. With C, work 8(8,10,10) rows in st st. (**Note:** Cut and attach colors as needed. Continuing in st st work: 8(8,10,10) rows D, 8(8,10,10) rows E, 8(8,10,10) Rows F, 8(8,10,10) rows B. Change to A. With A, work 2(2,2,8) rows garter st. **Armhole Shaping:** Continuing with A and in garter st (k each row), bind off 4(4,5,5) sts at beg of next 2 rows. Continuing in garter st throughout, dec one st at each end every other row 3(4,4,4) times—41(43,46,50) sts. Work even in garter st until length is 5(5½,6,6½)″ from first row of armhole shaping. **Shoulder Shaping:** Continuing in garter st, bind off 5(5,6,7) sts at beg of next 2 rows; bind off 6 sts at beg of following 2 rows. Place rem 19(21,22,24) sts on a st holder for neckband.

FRONT: Work same as Back until length from first row of armhole shaping is 3(3½,4,4½)″. **Neck Shaping—Row 1:** K 15 (16,17,18); place rem 26(27,29,32) sts on a separate st holder. Working in garter st over sts on needle only, dec one st at neck edge every other row 4(5,5,5) times. Work even over rem 11(11,12,13) sts until length of armhole is same as on back end at armhole edge. **Shoulder Shaping:** From armhole edge, bind of 5(5,6,7) sts at beg of next row. K 1 row even. Bind off rem 6 sts. Leaving center 11(11,12,14) sts on front holder, slip rem 15(16,17,18) sts onto a needle, attach A to neck edge and work to correspond with opposite side, reversing shaping.

SLEEVES: Starting at outer edge of cuff with B, cast on 29(31,31,33) sts. Work in garter st (k each row) for 12(16,20,24) rows, forming 6(8,10,12) ridges for cuff. At end of last row, cut B; attach A. Working in st st in the same stripe pat as for Back, inc one st at each end of first row, then every 6th row until there are 43(45,49,51) sts. Work even continuing stripe pat same as for Back up to underarms, including last 2(2,2,8) A garter st rows. **Top Shaping:** Continuing with A in garter st, bind off 4(4,5,5) sts at beg of next 2 rows. Dec one st at each end every other row until 15 sts rem. Bind off 2 sts at beg of next 4 rows. Bind off rem sts.

FINISHING: Pin each section to measurements on a padded surface, cover with a damp cloth and allow to dry; do not press. Sew left shoulder seam.

Neckband: With right side facing, using B, k sts from back holder, pick up and k 13 sts along left side edge of neck to front holder, k sts from front holder, pick up and k 13 sts along right side edge of neck— 56(58,60,64) sts. Work in garter st

over these sts for 10(10,12,14) rows. Bind off loosely. Sew right shoulder seam, including neckband. Sew side and sleeve seams, matching stripes. Sew in sleeves. Fold neckband in half to wrong side and stitch loosely in place. Fold cuffs in half to right side.

Embroidery: Using a contrasting color and tapestry needle, work rounds of embroidery between stripes, making a different stitch for each round on Body as follows: 1 round Feather Stitch, 1 round Cross Stitch, 1 round Closed Buttonhole Stitch, 1 round Chain Stitch and 1 round Fly Stitch. Embroider Sleeves to match Body.

TURKEY JUMPER

(page 71)

MATERIALS: See pattern back-views, page 27, for Butterick #4930. Scraps of assorted print cottons for appliqué (we recommend a small-scale rust calico for turkey body, bright prints for feathers); ½ yd. 18″-wide fusible webbing.

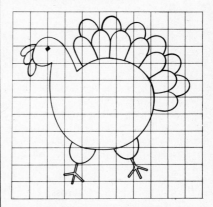

DIRECTIONS: Following directions on page 83, enlarge appliqué pieces. Cut out jumper as directed in pattern. Cut appliqué pieces from printed fabrics. Cut fusible webbing to match appliqué pieces. Position turkey body and feathers on jumper front, as shown in photo. Fuse, following manufacturer's instructions for fusible webbing. Using machine zig-zag stitch, satin-stitch around edges of turkey and feathers, using thread to match appliqué fabrics. Satin-stitch combs and eye onto turkey head. Satin-stitch feet. Finish assembling jumper according to pattern.

VEGETABLE GARDEN JUMPER

(page 71)

MATERIALS: See pattern back-views, page 27, for McCalls #5668. ¼ yd. brown print cotton for earth; assorted solid and print cottons in bright colors for appliqués (see photo for suggestions); ½ yd. 18″-wide fusible webbing.

DIRECTIONS: Cut out jumper ac-cording to pattern instructions. Fol-

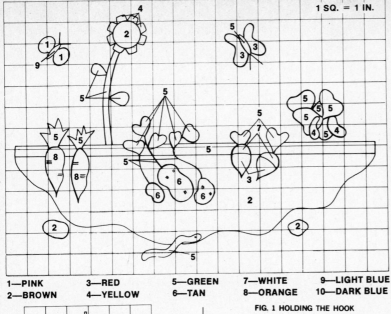

1 SQ. = 1 IN.

| 1—PINK | 3—RED | 5—GREEN | 7—WHITE | 9—LIGHT BLUE |
| 2—BROWN | 4—YELLOW | 6—TAN | 8—ORANGE | 10—DARK BLUE |

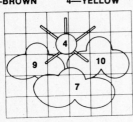

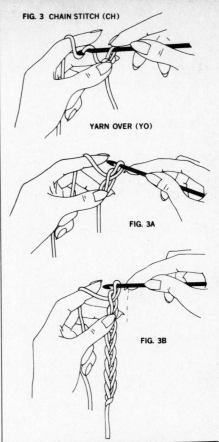

FIG. 3 CHAIN STITCH (CH)

YARN OVER (YO)

FIG. 3A

FIG. 3B

FIG. 1 HOLDING THE HOOK

knot (*see* FIG. 2) and base chain (*see* FIG. 3).

For Left-handed Crocheters
FIGS. 1 to 3 for right-handed crocheters and are repeated in FIGS. 1 Left to 3 Left for left-handed crocheters.

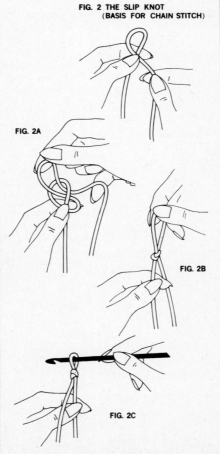

FIG. 2 THE SLIP KNOT
(BASIS FOR CHAIN STITCH)

FIG. 2A

FIG. 2B

FIG. 2C

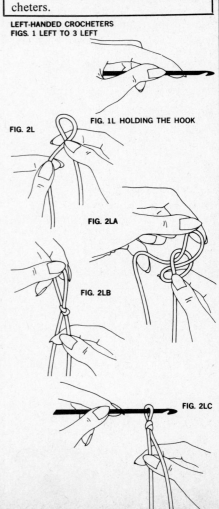

LEFT-HANDED CROCHETERS
FIGS. 1 LEFT TO 3 LEFT

FIG. 1L HOLDING THE HOOK

FIG. 2L

FIG. 2LA

FIG. 2LB

FIG. 2LC

lowing directions on page 83, enlarge appliqué pieces for sun with clouds and vegetable garden. Cut out appliqué pieces from scraps of assorted fabrics. Cut fusible webbing to match appliqué pieces. Position appliqué pieces on jumper bib and skirt as shown in photo, with fusible webbing under each appliqué. Fuse, following manufacturer's instructions. Using a machine zig-zag stitch, satin stitch around appliqué shapes, using thread to match appliqué fabrics. Satin stitch vines, butterfly antennae, and "eyes" on potatoes and carrots. Finish assembling jumper according to pattern instructions.

HOW TO CROCHET

Directions for right-handed and left-handed crocheters
Most crochet stitches are started from a base of chain stitches. However, our stitches are started from a row of single crochet stitches which gives body to the sample swatches and makes practice work easier to handle. When making a specific item, follow the stitch directions as given.

Holding the crochet hook properly (*see* FIG. 1), start by practicing the slip

BIAS STRIPE SWEATER AND SCARF

(page 72)

Directions are given for size Small (8-10). Changes for size Medium (12-14) are in parentheses.

MATERIALS: Berga Ullman Yarn (3½ oz. skns): 4(5) skns of Tan (A), 2(3) skns Lt. Red (B), 1 skn each of Dk. Red (C), Green (D) and White (E); knitting needles, No. 10 OR ANY SIZE NEEDLES WHICH WILL OBTAIN THE STITCH GAUGE BELOW.

GAUGE: 3 sts = 1″.

MEASUREMENTS:

Sizes:	Small (8-10)	Medium (12-14)
Bust:	34″	36″
Width across back or front at underarms:	17″	18″
Width across sleeve at upper arm:	13″	14″

Scarf measures 6½″ X 70″.

DIRECTIONS — SWEATER —

BACK: Start at lower left corner with A, cast on 3 sts. **Row 1 (wrong side):** P across. **Row 2:** *Cast on 2 sts — lower edge,* k across to last 2 sts, *inc in next st, k 1 — inc made at side edge.* **Row 3:** P across. **Rows 4 through 11:** Rpt Rows 2 and 3 — 18 sts. **Row 12:** With A cast on 2 sts; break off A; attach B, k to last 2 sts, inc in next st, k 1. **Row 13:** P across — 21 sts. **Row 14:** With B cast on 2 sts, break off B; attach C and work as Row 12. Break off C; attach B. **Row 15:** With B, p across. **Note:** Break off and attach colors as needed. **Row 16:** With B cast on 2 sts; with A work as Row 12. **Row 17:** P across. **Rows 18 and 19:** With A, rpt Rows 2 and 3 — 30 sts. **Rows 20 through 23:** Continuing to work as for Rows 2 and 3, make 1 row B, 1 row A, 1 row B and 1 row C — 36 sts. **Rows 24 and 25:** With C work as for Rows 2 and 3. **Note:** When 2 colors are being used in same row, when changing color always twist color not in use around the other once to prevent making holes in work. Carry color not in use loosely along wrong side of work. **Row 26:** With C cast on 2 sts, * with B k 3, with C k 1; rpt from * across to last 2 sts, inc in next st, k 1. **Row 27:** With C p across — 42 sts. **Row 28:** With C cast on 2 sts, * with C k 3, with B k 1; rpt from * across to last 2 sts, inc in next st, k 1. **Row 29:** With C p across — 45 sts. **Rows 30 through 35:** Continuing to work as Rows 2 and 3, make 2 rows C, 1 row B, 3 rows C — 54 sts. **Row 36:** With C cast on 2 sts, k 4, * with E k 1, with C k 3; rpt from * to last 2 sts, inc in next st, k 1. **Row 37:** With C p across — 57 sts. **Row 38:** With C cast on 2 sts, k 2, * with E k 1, with C k 3; rpt from * across to last 2 sts, inc as before. **Row 39:** With E p across — 60 sts. **Row 40:** With E cast on 2 sts, k 2, * with C k 1, with E k 3; rpt from * across to last 2 sts, inc as before. **Row 41:** With E p across — 63 sts. **Row 42:** With E cast on 2 sts, k 2, * with A k 1, with E k 3; rpt from * across to last 2 sts, inc as before. **Row 43:** With A p across — 66 sts. With A, rpt Rows 2 and 3, 0(2) times — 66(72) sts. This completes incs at lower edge.

Side Shaping — Row 1: With A, k 1, k 2 tog, k across to last 2 sts, inc in next st, k 1 — 66(72) sts. **Row 2:** With A p across. Continue to work shaping same as for last 2 rows throughout, maintaining same number of sts in every row, and working in st st (k 1 row, p 1 row), work Stripe pat as follows: **Rows 3 and 4;** 2 rows A. **Row 5:** With A k 1, k 2 tog, k 1, * with E k 1, with A k 3; rpt from * across, inc at end of row as before. **Row 6:** With A p across. **Row 7:** With A k 1, k 2 tog, k 1, * with D k 1, with A k 3; rpt from * across, inc at end of row. **Row 8:** With D p across. **Rows 9 and 10:** 2 rows D. **Row 11:** With D k 1, k 2 tog, k 2, * with A k 1, with D k 3; rpt from * across, inc at end of row. **Row 12:** With D rpt Row 2. **Rows 13 through 30:** Working as for Rows 1 and 2, work 2 rows D, 1 row A, 1 row B, 1 row A, 3 rows D, 1 row E, 1 row D, 2 rows E, 1 row B, 1 row C, 1 row B, 3 rows C. **Row 31:** With C k 1, with B k 2 tog, * with C k 1, with B k 1, rpt from * across, inc at end of row. **Row 32:** Working B sts with C and C sts with B, p across. **Row 33:** With C k 1, k 2 tog, * with B k 1, with C k 1; rpt from * across, inc at end of row. **Row 34:** Rpt Row 32. **Rows 35 through 40:** Working as for Rows 1 and 2, work 2 rows B, 2 rows D, 1 row A, 1 row B. **Row 41:** With B k 1, k 2 tog, k 1, * with A k 1, with B k 3; rpt from * across, inc at end of row. **Row 42:** With A p across. **Row 43:** With A k 1, k 2 tog, k 2, * with B k 1, with A k 3; rpt from * across, inc at end of row. **Row 44:** With A p across. **Rows 45 and 46:** With A work 2 rows. **Row 47:** With A k 1, k 2 tog, k 2, * with D k 1, with A k 3; rpt from * across, inc at end of row. **Row 48:** With A p across. **Row 49:** With A k 1, with D k 2 tog, * with A k 3, with D k 1; rpt from * across, inc at end of row. **Row 50:** With A p across. **Top Shaping — Row 1:** With A only, k 1, k 2 tog, k across to end of row (do not inc). **Row 2:** Bind off 2 sts, p across. Rpt last 2 rows until 3 sts rem. K 1, k 2 tog. Bind off rem 2 sts. This completes the 17(18)″ wide rectangle for Back.

FRONT: Starting at lower left corner, with A cast on 3 sts. **Row 1:** P across. **Row 2 (right side):** K 1, inc in next st — side edge; k 1, cast on 2 sts at end of row — lower edge. **Row 3:** P across. **Row 4:** K 1, inc in next st, k to end of row, cast on 2 sts. **Row 5:** P across. **Rows 6 through 11:** Rpt Rows 2 and 3 — 18 sts. Work to correspond with Back, reversing all shaping as established.

FIRST SLEEVE: Start at left top corner with A, cast on 3 sts. **Row 1 (wrong side):** P across. **Row 2:** K 1, inc in next st, k 1; cast on 2 sts at end of row. Mark this end for armhole edge. **Row 3:** P across. **Row 4:** K 1, inc in next st, k rem sts, cast on 2 sts. Rpt Rows 3 and 4 until there are 57(63) sts on needle, end with p row. This completes armholes shaping. Now work side shaping as follows: **Row 1:** K 1, inc in next st, k across to within last 3 sts, k 2 tog, k 1. **Row 2:** P across. **Rows 3 through 14:** Rpt last 2 rows 6 times — 57(63) sts. Break off A; attach B. Continuing to work same as for Rows 1 and 2 of side shaping, work Stripe pat as follows: 2 rows B, 2 rows A, 14 rows B, 2 rows C, 2 rows B, 8 rows C, end with p row.

Lower Edge Shaping — Row 1: With C, bind off 2 sts, k across to last 3 sts, k 2 tog, k 1. **Row 2:** P across. Rpt last 2 rows until 3 sts rem. Bind off.

SECOND SLEEVE: With A cast on 3 sts. **Row 1:** P across. **Row 2:** Cast on 2 sts, k across to last 2 sts, inc in next st, k 1. **Row 3:** P across. Rpt Rows 2 and 3 until there are 57(63) sts. Work to correspond with First Sleeve, reversing shaping (as established).

FINISHING: Pin each rectangle piece to measurements on a padded surface; cover with a damp cloth and allow to dry; do not press. Leaving center 9½″ open for neck, sew shoulder seams. Leaving top 6½(7)″ open for armholes, sew side seams. Sew sleeve seams. Sew top edges of sleeves into armholes. Turn 2½″ cuffs to right side at lower edges of sleeves.

SCARF: With A, cast on 3 sts. **Row 1 (wrong side):** P across. **Row 2:** Cast on 2 sts — lower edge, k across to last 2 sts, inc in next st, k 1. **Row 3:** P across. **Rows 4 through 19:** Rpt Rows 2 and 3 — 30 sts. **Row 20:** Cast on 2 sts, break off A; attach B and k across to last 2 sts, inc in next st, k 1. **Note:** Break off and attach colors as needed. **Row 21:** With B p across. **Rows 22 through 35:** Continuing to work same as for Rows 2 and 3 throughout, work 1 more row B, 1 row C, 1 row B and 11 rows A — 54 sts. This completes lower edge shaping. Now work side shaping as follows: **Row 1:** With A k 1, k 2 tog, k across to last 2 sts, inc in next st, k 1. **Row 2:** P across. **Rows 3 through 10:** Working shaping same as for Rows 1 and 2 of side shaping, make 4 more rows A, 1 row B, 1 row A, 1 row B, 1 row C, 2 rows B — 54 sts. **Row 11:** With B k 1, k 2 tog, k 1, * with C k 1, with B k 3; rpt from * across to last 2 sts, continuing in same pat inc in next st, k 1. **Row 12:** With C, p across. **Row 13:** With C k 1, k 2 tog, k 2, * with B k 1, with C k 3; rpt from * across, inc at end of row. **Row 14:** With

C p across. Working in st st (k 1 row, p 1 row), continue side shaping as for Rows 1 and 2 throughout, maintaining same number of sts in every row. **Rows 15 through 22:** Work 4 rows C, 1 row B, 3 rows C. **Row 23:** With C k 1, with E k 2 tog, * with C k 3, with E k 1; rpt from * across, inc at end of row. **Row 24:** With C p across. **Row 25:** With C k 1, k 2 tog, k 1, * with E k 1, with C k 3; rpt from * across, inc at end of row. **Row 26:** With E p across. **Row 27:** With E k 1, k 2 tog, * with E k 3, with C k 1; rpt from * across, inc at end of row. **Row 28:** Rpt Row 26. **Rows 29 and 30:** With E, rpt Rows 1 and 2. **Row 31:** With E k 1, k 2 tog, * with E k 3, with A k 1; rpt from * across, inc at end of row. **Row 32:** With A p across. **Rows 33 and 34:** With A rpt Rows 1 and 2. **Rows 35 through 62:** Work same as Rows 7 through 34 of Back of Sweater Side Shaping. **Rows 63 through 74:** Work 6 rows B, 1 row A, 1 row D, 1 row A, 3 rows B. **Row 75:** With B k 1, k 2 tog, * with B k 3, with A k 1; rpt from * across, inc at end of row. **Rows 76,77 and 78:** Work 3 rows A. **Row 79:** With A k 1, with B k 2 tog, * with A k 3, with B k 1; rpt from * across inc at end of row. **Rows 80 through 88:** 9 rows A. **Row 89:** With A k 1, with D k 2 tog, work one st A and one st D across row, inc at end of row. **Row 90:** Working A sts with D and D sts with A, p across. **Row 91:** With A k 1, k 2 tog, work one st D and one st A across row, inc at end of row. **Row 92:** Rpt Row 90. **Row 93:** With D k 1, k 2 tog, work one st A and one st D across row, inc at end of row. **Rows 94, 95 and 96:** 3 rows D. **Rows 97,98 and 99:** Using E in place of A, work same as for Rows 89,90 and 91. **Rows 92 through 130:** Continuing side shaping, work 2 rows E, 1 row A, 1 row E, 13 rows A, 1 row E, 1 row A, 1 row E, 15 rows A, 1 row E, 1 row A, 2 rows E. **Rows 131,132 and 133:** Rpt Rows 97,98 and 99. **Rows 134,135 and 136:** 3 rows D. **Rows 137 through 141:** Rpt Rows 89 through 93. **Rows 142 through 150:** 9 rows A. **Row 151:** Rpt Row 79. **Rows 152,153 and 154:** 3 rows A. **Row 155:** Rpt Row 75. **Rows 156 through 166:** Work 3 rows B, 1 row A, 1 row D, 1 row A, 5 rows B. **Rows 167 through 170:** Rpt Rows 31 through 34 of Back Side Shaping. **Rows 171 through 190:** Work 3 rows C, 1 row B, 2 rows C, 2 rows E, 3 rows D, 1 row E, 2 rows D, 1 row A, 1 row B, 1 row A, 3 rows D. **Row 191:** With D k 1, k 2 tog, k 2. * With A k 1, with D k 3; rpt from * across, inc at end of row. **Rows 192,193 and 194:** 3 rows D. **Row 195:** Rpt Row 191. **Rows 196,197 and 198:** 3 rows A. **Row 199:** With A k 1, k 2 tog, k 2, * with E k 1, with A k 3; rpt from * across, inc at end of row. **Rows 200,201 and 202:** 3 rows A. Last row is a p row.
Shaping for Other End — Row 1: With

A k 1, k 2 tog, k to end of row; do not inc. **Row 2:** Bind off 2 sts, p across. Rpt last 2 rows 2 more times. With B, continue to rpt same 2 rows until 30 sts rem, end with p row. With C, continue to rpt same 2 rows until 3 sts rem. Bind off.
FINISHING: Pin scarf flat on a padded surface to measure 13″ X 70″. Cover with a damp cloth and allow to dry; do not press. Fold sides over center with edges meeting at center. Sew edges together for center seam. Steam folds lightly.

TWEED JACKET WITH SCARF AND HAT

(page 23)

MATERIALS: Reynolds Icelandic Tweed: 10 (11,12,13) skns; knitting needles, 1 pair each No.9 and No.10½ OR ANY SIZE NEEDLES WHICH WILL OBTAIN THE STITCH GAUGE BELOW; crochet hook, Size G; separating jacket zipper with ring, 26(28,28,30)″ length; two 5″ zippers with ring for pockets; 1 button, ¾″ in diameter.
GAUGE: On No.10½ needles — 9 sts = 4″; 3 rows = 1″.
MEASUREMENTS:

Sizes:	Small	Medium	Large	Ex. Lge.
To fit bust or chest size:	34-36″	38-40″	42-44″	46-48″
Width across back at underarms:	19″	20¾″	22½″	24½″
Width across each front at underarm:	10¼″	11″	12″	12¾″
Width across sleeve at upper arm:	12¾″	13¾″	14½″	15½″

Scarf measures 5½″ x 64.″
JACKET — BACK: Start at lower edge with No. 10½ needles, cast on 43(47,51,55) sts. K 1 row for foundation. **Row 1 (right side):** P 1, * k next st in row below, p 1; rpt from * across. **Row 2:** P 1, * p 1, k next st in row below as before; rpt from * across — 43(47,51,55) sts. Rpt Rows 1 and 2 alternately for pat. Work in pat until length is 16(17,17,18)″ from beg or desired length to underarm. Mark each end of last row for underarms. Continue to work in pat until 8(8½,9,9½)″ from markers.
Shoulder Shaping: Keeping in pat, dec one st at each end every row 4 times. Bind off 2 sts at beg of next 2 rows; bind off 3(4,4,5) sts at beg of next 4 rows; then 3(3,4,4) sts at beg of following 2 rows. Place rem 13(13,15,15) sts on a st holder.

Pocket Lining (Make 2): With No. 10½ needles cast on 12 sts. Work in st st (k 1 row, p 1 row) for 7″. Bind off.
LEFT FRONT: With No.10½ needles, cast on 23(25,27,29) sts. Work same as for Back until length is 2″, end with a right-side row.
Pocket Opening—Next Row: From front edge, work in pat over first 14(15,16,17) sts; attach another skn of yarn, with second strand, inc in next st, work in pat over rem 8(9,10,11) sts. Using 2 strands of yarn, work both sides at same time in pat for 5″, end at front edge with a right-side row. **Next Row:** Keeping in pat and working with 1 skn of yarn only, work 14(15,16,17) sts to opening, cut off second strand, work next 2 sts tog and continue across rem sts. Work in pat over 23(25,27,29) sts until same length as Back to underarm. Mark side edge of last row for underarm. Continue in pat until about 5½(5½,6,6½)″ above underarm marker, end at front edge.
Neck Shaping: Work 3(3,4,4) sts from front edge and place these sts just worked on a safety pin, *work next 2 sts tog—dec made at neck edge*; complete row in pat. Keeping in pat, dec one st at neck edge every other row 4 more times, **at the same time,** when length at side edge is same as on Back to shoulder, at side edge dec one st every row 4 times; at same edge bind off 2 sts once, then 3(4,4,5) sts every other row twice; from side edge, bind off rem 3(3,4,4) sts.
RIGHT FRONT: Work to correspond with Left Front, reversing shaping.
SLEEVES: With No.9 needles, cast on 21(23,25,27) sts. Work in pat as for Back for 8 rows. Change to No.10½ needles and continue even until length is 3″ from beg. Keeping continuity of pat throughout, inc one st at each end of next row, then every 3″, 3 more times—29(31,33,35) sts. Work even until 16½(17,17½,18)″ from beg or desired length to underarm.
Top Shaping: Keeping in pat, bind off 2 sts at beg of next 2 rows. Dec one st at each end every other row 7(8,9,10) times. Bind off rem 11 sts.
FINISHING: Pin pieces to measurements on a padded surface; cover with a damp cloth and allow to dry; do not press. Sew side seams up to markers, sew shoulder and sleeve seams. Sew in sleeves. **Collar:** With right side facing, using No. 10½ needles, k the 3(3,4,4) sts from right front safety pin, pick up and k 8(8,8,9) sts along side edge of neck, k 13(13,15,15) sts from back holder, pick up and k 8(8,8,9) sts along other side edge of neck, k 3(3,4,4) sts from left front safety pin—35(35,39, 41) sts. Work even in pat for 5½″. Bind off loosely in pat.

Crochet Trim: With right side facing, using crochet hook, attach yarn to lower end of right side seam, working from left to right, work 1 row of reverse sc evenly along lower edge, 3 sc in corner st, continue up left front, along collar, down right front edge and rem lower edge, making 3 sc in same st at each corner. Join with sl st to first sc. Break off and fasten.

Sew in front zipper, reversing tape of zipper for collar so that when collar rolls down, zipper will not show. Sew zipper in each pocket opening. Sew pocket linings in place to inside of jacket.

SCARF: With No. 10½ needles, cast on 145 sts. Work in pat as for Back of Jacket for 5½". Bind off loosely in pat.

HAT: With No.10½ needles, cast on 25(27,29) sts. Work in pat for 15(16, 17)". Bind off loosely in pat. Fold in half, matching short edges and sew back seam, easing in edges slightly. With right side facing, working from left to right, work 1 row of reverse sc along front edge. Starting at corner, work 1 row of regular sc along lower edge, easing in edge to desired fit. Do not turn; ch 1, sc in last sc made, working from left to right, work 1 reverse sc in each sc across to corner. Make a chain 4" long. Sc in 2nd st from hook, ch 2, sk next 2 sts for buttonhole, sc in each rem st of chain, sl st in next sc at corner. Break off and fasten. Sew button to opposite corner.

LEG WARMERS AND HAT

(page 22)

Directions are given for articles to fit all sizes.

MATERIALS: Coats & Clark's Red Heart "Fabulend" Knitting Worsted type Yarn, 4 Ply (4 oz. skns): 2 skns #903 Devil Red (A); 1 skn each of #848 Skipper Blue (B), #676 Emerald Green (C), #515 Dk. Turquoise (D), #588 Amethyst (E), #602 Dk. Gold (F); a few yards of #737 Pink (G) and #111 Eggshell (H); crochet hook, Size H OR ANY SIZE HOOK WHICH WILL OBTAIN THE STITCH GAUGE BELOW.

GAUGE: 4 sts = 1".

MEASUREMENT: Approximate length of Leg Warmer: 19".

DIRECTIONS — LEG WARMER (Make 2): Start at top edge with A, ch 64 loosely to measure 17". Being careful not to twist chain, join with sl st to first st to form a circle. **Rnd 1:** With A, ch 3, sk joining, dc in each ch st around. Join with sl st to top of ch-3 — 64 dc, counting ch-3 as 1 dc. Always count ch-3 as 1 dc. Break off and fasten; attach B to same st as joining. **Rnd 2:** With B, sc in same st as joining, sc in each st around. Join with sl st to first sc — 64 sc. Break off and fasten; attach C to joining. **Note:** Break off and attach colors

as needed. **Rnd 3:** With C ch 3, place strand of G along top of last rnd, with C, working over G, sk joining, dc in each of next 2 sts, *holding back on hook last loop of dc, dc in next st, drop C, pick up G and draw a loop through the 2 loops on hook — color change made;* * with G, working over C, dc in each of next 3 dc, *holding back on hook last loop of dc, dc in next st, drop G, pick up C and draw a loop through the 2 loops on hook — another color change made;* with C, working over G, dc in each of next 4 sts, changing to G in last dc; rpt from * around, end with G dc in last 4 sts; do not change color. Join with sl st to top of ch-3. **Note:** Hereafter when 2 colors are being used in same rnd, always carry color not in use inside sts, change color in last st of each color group. **Rnd 4:** With G, working over E, sk joining, dc in next 3 dc, changing to E in last dc, * with E dc in next 4 dc, changing to G in last dc, with G dc in next 4 dc, changing to E in last dc; rpt from * around, end with E dc in last 4 dc; do not change color. Join. Break off and fasten E; attach C. **Rnd 5:** Rpt Rnd 3. **Rnd 6:** Rpt Rnd 2. **Rnd 7:** With A only, ch 3, sk joining, dc in each of next 13 sts, *holding back on hook last loop of each dc, dc in each of next 2 sts, yarn over hook, draw through all 3 loops on hook — dec made;* * dc in each of next 14 sts, dec over next 2 sts; rpt from * 2 more times — 60 dc. Join. **Rnds 8 and 9:** With A ch 3, sk joining, dc in each st around. Join. **Rnd 10:** With C, work same as Rnd 2. Attach E to joining. **Rnd 11:** With E ch 3, working over F, dc in next sc, changing to F, work F dc in next 2 sc and E dc in next 2 sc around, end with 2 dc F. Join. **Rnd 12:** With C, work same as Rnd 2. **Rnd 13:** With A, rpt rnd 8. **Rnd 14:** With B ch 3, dc in each st around, dec 2 sts evenly spaced around. Join — 58 dc. **Rnd 15:** With B ch 3, sk joining, dc in each st around. Join. **Rnd 16:** With C, draw up a loop in same st as joining, drop C, draw a H loop through the 2 loops on hook, * with H, working over C, *draw up a loop in next st, drop H, draw a C loop through 2 loops on hook — color change made in sc;* with C, sc in next st, changing to H; rpt from * around, end with H sc. Join. **Rnd 17:** Rnd 15. **Rnd 18:** With G work same as Rnd 15. **Rnd 19:** With D ch 3, dc in each st around, dec 2 sts evenly spaced around. Join — 56 dc. **Rnd 20:** With D, working over A, ch 3, dc in next dc, changing to A, work 2 dc A and 2 dc D around, end 2 dc A. Join. **Rnd 21:** Rpt last rnd. **Rnds 22 and 23:** With A ch 3, sk joining, dc in each st around. Join. **Rnd 24:** With B, sc in each st around, dec 2 sc evenly spaced around — 54 sc. **Rnd 25:** With E ch 3, working over C, dc in next 2 sts, changing to C, * with C dc in next st, changing to E, with E dc in next 5 sts, changing to C; rpt from * around, end last rpt with E dc in last 2 sts. Join. **Rnd 26:** With E ch

3, dc in next dc, changing to C, work 3 dc C and 3 dc E around, end with 1 dc E. Join. **Rnd 27:** With E ch 3, * with C dc in 5 dc, with E dc in next dc; rpt from * around, end with C dc in 5 dc, with E join. **Rnd 28:** Rpt Rnd 2. **Rnd 29:** With A ch 3, dc in each st around, dec 2 sts evenly spaced around — 52 dc. **Rnds 30 and 31:** Rpt Rnds 22 and 23. **Rnd 32:** With E, sc in each st around. Join. **Rnd 33:** With H ch 3, working over C, dc in next st changing to H, work 2 dc H and 2 dc C around, end 2 dc C. Join. **Rnd 34:** Rpt Rnd 32. **Rnd 35:** Rpt Rnd 22. **Rnd 36:** With D sc in each st around. Join. **Rnd 37:** With B ch 3, work 1 dc F, 1 dc B around, end 1 dc F. Join. **Rnd 38:** Rpt Rnd 37. **Rnd 39:** With B ch 3, dc in each st around. Join — 52 sts. **Rnd 40:** Rpt Rnd 36. **Rnd 41:** Rpt Rnd 22. **Rnd 42:** With B ch 3, dc in each st around. Join. **Rnd 43:** With D ch 3, dc in next dc, changing to E, work 2 dc E and 2 dc D around, end 2 dc E. Join. **Rnd 44:** Rpt Rnd 22. **Rnd 45:** Work 1 sc C and 1 sc H around. Join. Break off both colors and fasten. Working along opposite side of starting chain, rpt Rnd 45 along top edge.

HAT: Start at center top with A, ch 4. Join with sl st to form ring. **Rnd 1:** Ch 1, 10 sc in ring. Join with sl st to first sc. **Rnd 2:** Ch 3, dc in same sc as joining, 2 dc in each sc around. Join with sl st to top of ch-3 — 20 dc, counting ch-3 as 1 dc. Always count ch-3 as 1 dc. **Rnd 3:** Ch 3, * 2 dc in next dc, dc in next dc; rpt from * around, end 2 dc in last dc. Join to top of ch-3 — 30 dc. Break off and fasten; attach B to same st as joining. **Rnd 4:** With B ch 3, dc in next dc, * 2 dc in next dc, dc in each of next 2 dc; rpt from * around, end 2 dc in last dc. Join to top of ch-3 — 40 dc. **Rnd 5:** Ch 3, dc in each of next 2 dc, * 2 dc in next dc, dc in each of next 3 dc; rpt from * around, end 2 dc in last dc. Join — 50 dc. Break off and fasten; attach C. **Rnd 6:** Work same as Rnd 16 of Leg Warmer. **Note:** Break off and attach colors as needed. Change colors same as for Leg Warmer. **Rnd 7:** With B, ch 3, dc in each of next 3 sc, * 2 dc in next sc, dc in each of next 4 sc; rpt from * around, end 2 dc in last sc. Join to top of ch-3 — 10 incs made. **Rnd 8:** With A ch 3, making 10 incs evenly spaced around, dc in each dc around. Join — 70 dc. **Rnd 9:** With B, making 2 incs evenly spaced around, sc in each st around. Join to first sc — 72 sc. **Rnd 10:** Work same as Rnd 11 of Leg Warmer. **Rnd 11:** With C, sc in each st around. Join. **Rnd 12:** With A ch 3, dc in each sc around. Join to top of ch-3 — 72 dc. **Rnd 13:** With B sc in each st around. Join. **Rnds 14 through 17:** Rpt Rnds 25 through 28 of Leg Warmer. **Rnd 18:** With A ch 3, dc in each st around. Join. Break off and fasten.

Earflaps: Sk first 11 dc in last rnd, attach B to next dc, ch 9. **Row 1:** With B dc in 5th ch from hook, dc in each of next

4 ch sts, sk next dc on last rnd, sl st in next dc. Break off and fasten. Sk next dc in last rnd, attach D to next st, turn. **Row 2:** With D, working over A, dc in each of first 2 dc of last row, changing to A in last dc, with A, working over D, dc in next 2 dc, changing to D in last dc, with D dc in next dc, in chain loop at end of row make 1 dc D, 2 A, 3 D, 2 A and 1 D; working along opposite side of ch-9, make D dc in next ch st, changing to A, A dc in each of next 2 sts, D dc in next 2 sts, sk next dc on last rnd of hat, sl st in next dc. Break off and fasten. For corner, sk next st on last rnd, attach G to next st and turn. Make 3 G dc in same st as next sl st; sk 1 dc on last row, sl st in next dc. Break off and fasten. Work other corner at opposite side of earflap to correspond. With wrong side facing, sk next 21 free dc on last rnd of hat for back edge, attach B to next dc, ch 9, turn; work other earflap in same way.

Edging: With right side facing, attach C to joining of last rnd of hat, working over H, sc in same st, changing to H, work 1 sc H and 1 sc C evenly along entire outer edge, including earflaps, being careful to keep edge flat. Join to first sc. Break off and fasten.

Tassel (Make 2): Hold one strand of each color tog, wind strands twice around a 5½″ square of cardboard. Tie at one end, cut at opposite end. Starting ½″ below tied end, wind separate strand of A tightly around strands, covering about ¾″ of tassel, tie ends of this strand tog. Trim tassel evenly. Tack tassel to end of each earflap.

ARAN ZIPPERED SWEATER, HAT AND SCARF

(page 23)

Directions for sweater are given for size Small (8-10). Changes for sizes Medium (12-14) and Large (16-18) are in parentheses. Hat will fit all sizes.

MATERIALS: Bucilla Knitting Worsted (4 oz. balls): 7(8,9) balls of Winter White; knitting needles, 1 pair each Nos. 5, 6 and 8 OR ANY SIZE NEEDLES WHICH WILL OBTAIN THE STITCH GAUGE BELOW; 1 double-pointed needle, No. 8. 1 separating jacket zipper, 18(18,20)″ length.

GAUGE: Pat Stitches on No. 8 needles — 4 sts = 1″. Pat Stitches on No. 5 needles — 5 sts = 1″.

MEASUREMENTS:

Sizes:	Small (8-10)	Medium (12-14)	Large (16-18)
Width across back at underarms:	17″	18″	20″
Width across each front at underarm:	9″	9½″	10½″
Width across sleeve at upper arm:	13″	14″	15″

Scarf measures 5″ X 58″.

PATTERN STITCHES—PAT A: Moss stitch, worked over an even number of sts. **Rows 1 and 2:** * K 1, p 1; rpt from * across. **Rows 3 and 4:** * P 1, k 1; rpt from * across. Rpt these 4 rows for Pat A.

PAT B: Baby cable, worked over 2 sts. **Row 1:** Sk first st, from back of work k in back of 2nd st, k skipped st and drop both sts off left-hand needle. **Row 2:** P 2. Rpt these 2 rows for Pat B.

PAT C: Cable panel worked over 10 sts. **Row 1:** P 2, k 6, p 2. **Row 2:** K 2, p 6, k 2. **Rows 3 and 4:** Rpt Rows 1 and 2. **Row 5:** P 2, sl next 3 sts onto d p needle and hold in front, k next 3 sts, k 3 sts from d p needle, p 2. **Row 6:** Rpt Row 2. **Rows 7 through 10:** Rpt Rows 1 and 2 twice. Rpt these 10 rows (Rows 1 through 10) for Pat C.

PAT D: Ribbed block with popcorn, worked over 11 sts. **Row 1:** P 2, k 7, p 2. **Row 2:** K 11. **Rows 3 through 6:** Rpt Rows 1 and 2. **Row 7:** P 2, (k next st in row below, p 1) 3 times; k next st in row below, p 2. **Row 8:** K 2, (p 1, k next st in row below) 3 times; p 1, k 2. **Rows 9 through 12:** Rpt Rows 7 and 8 twice. **Row 13:** P 2, k next st in row below, p 1, k next st in row below, in next st (k and p) twice for popcorn, turn, k 4, turn, p 4 tog; holding popcorn forward, k next st in row below, p 1, k next st in row below, p 2. **Row 14:** K 2, p 1, k next st in row below, p 1, k 1, p 1, k next st in row below, p 1, k 2. **Rows 15 through 20:** Rpt Rows 7 and 8 3 times. Rpt these 20 rows (Rows 1 through 20) for Pat D.

PAT E: Double baby cable panel, worked over 6 sts. **Row 1:** *Sk first st, from back of work k 2nd st, k skipped st and drop both sts off left-hand needle — baby cable made;* p 2, make baby cable over next 2 sts. **Row 2:** K 2, p 2, k 2. Rpt these 2 rows for Pat E.

DIRECTIONS — SWEATER —

BACK: Start at lower edge with No. 6 needles, cast on 68(72,80) sts. Work in k 2, p 2 ribbing for 2½″. Change to No. 8 needles and establish pats as follows: **Row 1 (right side):** Following Row 1 of each pat, work 4(6,10) sts in pat A, p 2, work 2 sts pat B, 10 sts pat C, 2 sts pat B, 11 sts pat D, 6 sts pat E, 11 sts pat D, 2 sts pat B, 10 sts pat C, 2 sts pat B, p 2, 4(6,10) sts pat A. Working in pats as established and having 2 sts between pats A and B at each end in reverse st st (k on wrong side, p on right side), work even until length is 14(14,15)″ from beg, end with a wrong-side row.

Raglan Armhole Shaping: Keeping continuity of pats throughout, bind off 2(2,4) sts at beg of next 2 rows. Dec one st at each end every other row 2(4,6) times, end on wrong side. **Next Row:** P 2, work 2 sts pat B, k 2 tog; keeping in pats work across to within last 6 sts, sl 1, k 1, p s s o, work 2 sts pat B, p 2 — dec made at each end inside pat B. **Next Row:** K 2, p 2; work in pats to within last 4 sts,

p 2, k 2. Rpt last 2 rows alternately until 20 sts rem. Bind off rem sts in pat.

LEFT FRONT: Start at lower edge with No. 6 needles, cast on 36(38,42) sts. **Row 1:** * K 2, p 2; rpt from * across, end k 0(2,2). Work in ribbing as established for 2½″. Change to No. 8 needles and establish pats as follows: **Row 1 (right side):** Following Row 1 of each pat, work 4(6,10) sts in pat A, p 2, work 2 sts pat B, 10 sts pat C, 2 sts pat B, 11 sts pat D, 2 sts pat B, *k 3 — front band.* Working pats as established, and having 2 sts between pats A and B at side edge in reverse st st as for Back and 3 sts at front edge in garter st (k each row), work even until same length as Back to underarm, end at side edge.

Raglan Armhole Shaping: Keeping continuity of pats throughout, bind off 2(2,4) sts at beg of next row. Dec one st at armhole edge every other row .2(4,6) times, end at armhole edge. **Next Row:** P 2, work 2 sts pat B, k 2 tog; complete row in pats as established. **Next Row:** Work even in pats. Rpt last 2 rows alternately until 22 sts rem, end at front edge.

Neck Shaping: Continue to dec at armhole edge inside B pat every other row as before, **AT THE SAME TIME,** from front edge, bind off 4 sts at beg of next row, then dec one st at neck edge over last 2 sts every other row 6 times, end at armhole edge. Now, dec one st at neck edge only every other row until 2 sts rem. Bind off.

RIGHT FRONT: Work to correspond with Left Front, reversing shaping.

SLEEVES: Start at lower edge with No. 6 needles, cast on 36(40,40) sts. Work in k 2, p 2 ribbing for 3″, inc 3 sts at center of last row — 39(43,43) sts. Change to No. 8 needles and establish pats as follows: **Row 1 (right side):** Following Row 1 of each pat, p 0(2,2), work 2 sts pat B, 10 sts pat C, 2 sts pat B, 11 sts pat D, 2 sts pat B, 10 sts pat C, 2 sts pat B, p 0(2,2). Working pats as established and having 0(2,2) sts in reverse st st at each end, work even until length is 4″ from beg. Working inc sts in reverse st st, inc one st at each end of next row; then every 1″ until there are 47 sts on needle, end with a wrong-side row. **Next Row:** Work 2 sts pat A, p 2; work pats across as established to within last 4 sts, p 2, work 2 sts pat A. Now, working inc sts in pat A, and keeping continuity of other pats as established, continue to inc one st at each end every 1″ until there are 51(55,59) sts. Work even until length is about 17″ from beg, end with same pat C row as on Back to underarm.

Raglan Top Shaping: Keeping in pats, bind off 2(2,4) sts at beg of next 2 rows. Dec one st at each end every other row 2(4,4) times. Work 0(0,4) rows even. Now, dec one st inside pat B at each end of every other row, same as for Back Raglan Armhole Shaping until 9 sts rem, end with a wrong-side row. **Next Row:** P 2, k 2 tog, p 1, sl 1, k 1, p s s o, p 2. **Next Row:** K 2, p 3, k 2. **Next Row:** P 2, k 2 tog, k 1, p 2. **Next Row:** K 2, p 2, k 2. Bind off.

Collar: Start at neck edge with No.6 needles, cast on 68(68,72) sts. **Row 1:** K 3, * p 2, k 2; rpt from * across to last st, k 1. **Row 2:** K 1, p 2, * k 2, p 2; rpt from * across to last st, k 1. Rpt these 2 rows alternately until 1½" from beg. Change to No.8 needles and continue in same way until length is 3½" from beg. Bind off loosely in ribbing.

FINISHING: Pin pieces to measurements on a padded surface, cover with a damp cloth and allow to dry; do not press. Sew side and sleeve seams. Sew raglan seams. Sew collar to neck edge, adjusting to fit. Sew in zipper.

HAT: Start at outer edge of cuff with No.5 needles, cast on 98 sts. Work in k 1, p 1 ribbing for 2½", inc one st in last row — 99 sts. Continue with No.5 needles and establish pats as follows. **Row 1:** * Work 11 sts pat D, 6 sts pat E, 10 sts pat C, 6 sts pat E; rpt from * 2 more times. Working in pats as established, work even until length above ribbing is 6½", end with a wrong-side row.

Top Shaping — Row 1: * P 2 tog, k 1; rpt from * across. **Rows 2,3 and 4:** * P 1, k 1; rpt from * across. **Row 5:** * K 2 tog, p 1, p 2 tog, k 1; rpt from * across. **Rows 6,7 and 8:** Work in p 1, k 1 ribbing. **Row 9:** * P 2 tog, k 2 tog; rpt from * across. Leaving a 20" length, break off yarn. Thread end of yarn into a darning needle and draw through rem sts. Pull sts together, fasten securely; then sew center back seam. Turn cuff to right side.

SCARF: With No.8 needles, cast on 18 sts. Work in k 1, p 1 ribbing for 58" or desired length. Bind off loosely in ribbing.

CHILD'S DRESS AND CAP

Directions are given for Size 4. Changes for Sizes 6, 8 and 10 are in parentheses. Hat will fit all sizes.
MATERIALS: Bernat Knitting Worsted (4 oz. skns): For Dress: 3(4,4,5) skns of Natural. For Hat: 1 skn of same color. Knitting needles, 1 pair each Nos. 6 and 8 OR ANY SIZE NEEDLES WHICH WILL OBTAIN THE STITCH GAUGE BELOW; double-pointed needles, 1 set each Nos. 6 and 8; crochet hook, Size G.
GAUGE: Pats — 11 sts = 2".
MEASUREMENTS:

Sizes:	4	6	8	10
Width across back or front at underarms:	12"	13"	14"	15"
Width across sleeve at upperarm:	9½"	10"	10¾"	11½"

PATTERN STITCHES

PATTERN 1: Worked over 12 sts. **Row 1:** P 3, *place next 3 sts on a d p needle and hold in front of work, k next 3 sts, k 3 sts from d p needle — front cable made;* p 3. **Row 2:** K 3, p 6, k 3. **Row 3:** P 3, k 6, p 3. **Rows 4 through 7;** Rpt Rows 2 and 3 alternately twice. **Row 8:** Rpt Row 2. Rpt these 8 rows for Pat 1.
PATTERN 2: Worked over 7 sts. **Row 1:** K 1, p 2, *in next st k 1, p 1 and k 1 — 3 sts made in one st;* p 2, k 1. **Row 2:** P 1, k 2, p 3, k 2, p 1. **Row 3:** K 1, p 2, k 3, p 2, k 1. **Row 4:** P 1, k 2, p 3 tog, k 2, p 1. Rpt all 4 rows for Pat 2.
PATTERN 3: Worked over 5 sts. **Row 1:** P 5, **Row 2:** K 5. **Rows 3 and 4:** Rpt Rows 1 and 2. **Row 5:** P 2, *in next st (k 1, p 1) twice; then k 1 — 5 sts made in one st;* p 2. **Row 6:** K 2, p 5, k 2. **Row 7:** P 2, k 5, p 2. **Rows 8 through 11:** Rpt Rows 6 and 7 alternately twice. **Row 12:** K 2, p 5 tog, k 2. **Row 13:** P 5. **Row 14:** K 5. Rpt these 14 rows for Pat 3.
PATTERN 4: Worked over 21 sts. **Row 1:** P 3, *place next 3 sts on a d p needle and hold in back of work, k next 3 sts, k 3 sts from d p needle — back cable;* p 3, *place next 3 sts on d p needle and hole in front of work, k next 3 sts, k 3 sts from d p needle — front cable;* p 3. **Row 2:** (K 3, p 6) twice; k 3. **Row 3:** (P 3, k 6) twice; p 3. **Rows 4 through 7:** Rpt Rows 2 and 3 alternately twice. **Row 8:** Rpt Row 2. **Row 9:** P 3, work front cable over next 6 sts, p 3, back cable over next 6 sts, p 3. **Rows 10 through 16:** Rpt Rows 2 through 8. Rpt these 16 rows for Pat 4.
DRESS — BACK: Start at lower edge, with No.8 long needles, cast on 85(89,95,101) sts. P 1 row. Now establish pats as follows: **Row 1 (right side):** K 1 (3,6,9), following Row 1 of each pat, work pat 1 over next 12 sts, pat 2 over 7 sts, pat 3 over 5 sts, pat 2 over 7 sts, pat 4 over center 21 sts, pat 2 over 7 sts, pat 3 over 5 sts, pat 2 over 7 sts, pat 1 over 12 sts, k 1(3,6,9) sts. **Row 2:** P 1(3,6,9), work Row 2 of each pat as established to last 1(3,6,9) sts, p rem sts.

Working 1(3,6,9) sts at each end of each row in st st (k 1 row, p 1 row), work other sts in pats as established until 1(2,3,5)" from beg, end with a wrongside row. **Note:** While shaping, if not enough sts rem at each end to complete cable pat, work rem sts of panel in reverse st st (p on right side, k on wrong side). Keeping continuity of pats as established, dec one st at each end of next row and every 2" 2 more times; then every 1½" 2(4,6,6) times. Dec one st at each end every 1" 4(2,0,0) times — 67(71,77,83) sts. Keeping in pats, work even until length is 13(15,17,19)" from beg, end with a wrong-side row.
Armhole Shaping: Keeping continuity of pats throughout, bind off 4(5,5,6) sts at beg of next 2 rows. Dec one st at each end every other row 3(3,4,4) times —

53(55,59,63) sts. Work even until length from first row of armhole shaping is 4½(5,5½,6)".
Shoulder Shaping: Bind off 8(8,9,9) sts at beg of next 4 rows. Place rem 21(23,23,27) sts on a st holder for back of neck.
FRONT: Work same as for Back until length above first row of armhole shaping is 2½(3,3½,3½)", end on wrong-side — 53(55,59,63) sts.
Neck Shaping: Work in pat over first 20(21,23,24) sts. Place rem sts on a st holder. Working in pat over sts on needle only, dec one st at neck edge every other row 4(5,5,6) times. If necessary, work even until length of armhole is same as on Back, end at armhole edge.
Shoulder Shaping: At armhole edge, bind off 8(8,9,9) sts at beg of next row. Work 1 row even. Bind off rem 8(8,9,9) sts. Leaving center 13(13,13,15) sts on front holder, sl rem 20(21,23,24) sts onto No.8 needle; attach yarn and work to correspond with opposite side, reversing shaping.

SLEEVES: With No.6 long needles, cast on 37(37,39,41) sts. **Row 1:** K 1, * p 1, k 1; rpt from * across. **Row 2:** P 1, * k 1, p 1; rpt from * across. Rpt these 2 rows of ribbing for 1½(1½,2,2)". Change to No.8 needles and p 1 row. Establish pats as follows: **Row 1(right side):** K 1(1,2,3); following Row 1 of each pat, work pat 2 over next 7 sts, pat 4 over center 21 sts, pat 2 over next 7 sts, k 1(1,2,3). **Row 2:** P 1(1,2,3), work Row 2 of pat 2 over 7 sts, pat 4 over 21 sts, pat 2 over 7 sts, p 1(1,2,3). Working 1(1,2,3) sts at each end in st st and all other sts in pats as established throughout, work 2 more rows. Working inc sts in st st, inc one st at each end of next row and every 5th(5th,6th,6th) row thereafter 8(9,10,11) times in all — 53(55,59,63) sts. Work even until length is 10(11½,13,14½)" from beg, end with a wrong-side row.
Top Shaping: Keeping in pats, bind off 4(5,5,6) sts at beg of next 2 rows. Dec one st at each end every other row 4(5,6,7) times; then at each end every row 4 times. Bind off 2 sts at beg of next 4 rows. Bind off rem sts.

FINISHING: Pin pieces to measurements on a padded surface, cover with a damp cloth and allow to dry; do not press. Sew left shoulder seam. **Neckband:** With right side facing and No.6 needles, pick up and k 74(78,80,84) sts along entire neck edge, including sts on holders. Work in k 1, p 1 ribbing for 11(11,13,13) rows. Bind off loosely in ribbing. Fold neckband in half to wrong side and stitch loosely in place. Sew right shoulder seam, including neckband. Sew side and sleeve seams. Sew in sleeves. With right side facing, starting at lower end of a side seam, sc evenly along lower edge, being careful to keep work flat. Join with sl st to first sc. Break off and fasten.

BERET: Start at lower edge with No.6 d p needles, cast on loosely 108 sts. Divide sts evenly on 3 needles. Being careful not to twist sts, join. Mark end of each rnd. Work in rnds of k 1, p 1 ribbing for 6 rnds, increasing 6 sts evenly spaced on last rnd. Change to No.8 d p needles, work in pat over 114 sts as follows: **Rnd 1:** * P 6, k 6, p 6, k 1; rpt from * around. **Rnd 2:** P 6, sl next 3 sts on a No.6 d p needle and hold in front of work, k next 3 sts, k 3 sts from No.6 needle — front cable; p 6, k 1; rpt from * around. **Rnd 3:** Rpt Rnd 1. **Rnd 4:** P 6, k in bar between last st used and next st — inc made; k 6, k in bar between sts, p 6, k 1; rpt from * around — 12 sts increased. **Rnd 5:** * P 7, k 6, p 7, k 1, rpt from * around — 126 sts. **Rnd 6:** Rpt Rnd 5. **Rnd 7:** * P 7, inc one st as before, k 6, inc one st, p 7, k 1; rpt from * around — 138 sts. **Rnds 8 and 9:** * P 8, k 6, p 8, k 1; rpt from * around. **Rnd 10:** * P 8, front cable over next 6 sts, p 8, k 1; rpt from * around. **Rnds 11 through 17:** Rpt Rnd 8. Rpt last 8 rnds (Rnds 10 through 17) 2 more times. **Next Rnd:** Rpt Rnd 10. **Next 2 Rnds:** Rpt Rnd 8.
Top Shaping — Rnd 1: * P 6, p 2 tog, k 6, p 2 tog, p 6, k 1; rpt from * around — 12 sts decreased. **Rnd 2:** * P to within cable panel, k 6, p to next k-1 ridge, k 1; rpt from * around. **Rnd 3:** P to within 2 sts before cable panel, p 2 tog, k 6, p 2 tog, p to k-1 ridge, k 1; rpt from * around. Making front cables in 8th row from last cable rnd, continue to dec before and after each cable panel every other rnd as before until 54 sts rem on needles. **Next Rnd:** P 1, (k 6, p 3 tog) 5 times; k 6, p 2 tog — 43 sts. Leaving a 10″ length, break off. Using a darning needle, draw end of yarn through rem sts, pull sts tog and fasten off securely.
Pompon: Cut 2 cardboard circles, each 2″ in diameter. Cut a hole 1½″ in diameter at center of each circle. Cut 4 strands of yarn, each 9 yds long. Place cardboard circles tog and wind yarn around the double circle, drawing yarn through center opening and over edge until center hole is filled. Cut yarn around outer edge between circles. Double ½-yd length of yarn and slip between the 2 cardboard circles, tie securely around strands of pompon. Remove cardboard and trim evenly. Tack to center top of beret.

CHILD'S MIDDY SWEATER

Directions are given for size 4. Changes for sizes 6, 8 and 10 are in parentheses. Cap will fit all sizes.
MATERIALS: Spinnerin "Wintuk" Sport (2 oz. ball): For Blouse: 3(4,4,5) balls of Navy (A), 1 ball White (B) and a few yards Scarlet (C). For Cap: 1 ball A; a few yards of B and C. Knitting needles, 1 pair each of Nos. 4 and 5 OR ANY SIZE NEEDLES WHICH WILL OBTAIN THE STITCH GAUGE BELOW; crochet hook, Size G for cap; 2 small red stars and a sleeve ornament; if desired.
GAUGE: Blouse — 6 sts = 1″. Cap — 11 sc = 2″.
MEASUREMENTS:

Sizes:	4	6	8	10
Width across back or front at underarms:	12″	13″	14″	15″
Width across sleeve at upper arm:	9″	9¾″	10¼″	11¼″

DIRECTIONS — SWEATER — BACK: Start at lower edge with No.4 needles and A, cast on 72(78,84,90) sts. Work in st st (k 1 row, p 1 row) for 5 rows for hem, ending with a k row. Knit next row for hemline. Change to No.5 needles and starting with a k row, work in st st until length is 9(9½,10,10½)″ from hemline.
Armhole Shaping: Continuing in st st throughout, bind off 4(5,5,6) sts at beg of next 2 rows. Dec one st at each end every other row 2(3,4,4) times — 60(62,66,70) sts. Work even until length from first row of armhole is 4½(5,5½,6)″.
Shoulder Shaping: Bind off 8(8,9,9) sts at beg of next 4 rows. Bind off rem 28(30,30,34) sts.
FRONT: Work same as for Back until length from hemline is 8½(9,9½,10)″, end with a p row.
Armhole and Neck Shaping — Row 1: Continuing in st st throughout, k 36(39,42,45); place rem sts on a st holder. Work over sts on one needle only. **Row 2:** P across. **Row 3:** At side edge, bind off 4(5,5,6) sts; complete row, decreasing one st at end of row — neck edge. Dec one st at each end every other row 2(3,4,4) times. Keeping armhole edge straight, continue to dec one st at neck edge every other row until 18(18,20,20) sts rem; then every 4th row until 16(16,18,18) sts rem. If necessary, work even until length of armhole is same as on Back, end at armhole edge.
Shoulder Shaping — Row 1: At armhole edge, bind off 8(8,9,9) sts; complete row. **Row 2:** Work across. Bind off rem sts. Place sts from holder on a No.5 needle; attach A at neck edge and work to correspond with opposite side, reversing shaping.
SLEEVES: With No.4 needles and A, cast on 38(40,42,44) sts. Work 5 rows in st st for hem. K next row for hemline. Change to No.5 needles. Starting with a k row, work in st st, increasing one st at each end every 1″, 8(9,10,12) times — 54(58,62,68) sts. Work even in st st until length from hemline is 11(12,13½,15½)″, end with a p row.
Top Shaping: Continuing in st st, bind off 4(5,5,6) st at beg of next 2 rows. Dec one st at each end every other row 8(9,11,13) times; then at each end of every row 5 times. Bind off 2 sts at beg of next 4 rows. Bind off rem 12 sts.
Collar: With No.4 needles and B, cast on 61(61,65,65) sts. **Row 1:** K 1, * p 1, k 1; rpt from * across. **Next 3 Rows:** Work in k 1, p 1 ribbing as established. **Next Row:** Work in ribbing over first 5 sts for side border; place these 5 sts on a safety pin; break off B; attach A and change to No.5 needles; with A, cast on one st, k across to within last 5 sts, cast on one st; place rem 5 sts on another safety pin — 53(53,57,57) sts on needle. P across sts on needle. Work in st st until A portion measures 4½(4½,5,5)″, end with a p row.
Neck Shaping — Row 1: K 13(13,15,15); place these sts just worked on a separate safety pin; bind off center 27 sts; complete row. **Row 2:** P across 13(13,15,15) sts on needle. **Row 3:** Inc in first st — inc made at neck edge; k across. Working in st st, inc one st at neck edge every 6th row 2 more times — 16(16,18,18) sts. P next row. Now shape both edges as follows: Continuing to inc one st at neck edge every 6th row as before 3 more times at the same time, dec one st at outer edge of collar on next row and every other row thereafter 13(13,15,15) times in all — 6 sts. Dec one st at outer edge on every row until 2 sts rem. Bind off. Sl the 13(13,15,15) A sts from safety pin onto a No.5 needle, attach A and work to correspond with opposite side, reversing shaping. Sl the 5 B border sts from first safety pin onto a No.4 needle; attach B and cast on one st at inner edge. Work in k 1, p 1 ribbing as established over these 6 sts until strip fits (slightly stretched) along entire side edge of collar. Bind off in ribbing. Work other side rib border in same way. Sew B borders along side edges of collar.
Tie: With No.4 needles and B, cast on 15 sts. Work in k 1, p 1 ribbing same as for beg of collar, for 8 rows; mark first row for right side; break off B; attach C. With C k 1 row; then work in ribbing as established for 5 rows. Break off C; attach B. With B, k 1 row, then work in ribbing until length is 25(26,26½,27)″ from beg, end on wrong side. Break off B; attach C. With C, k 1 row, then work in ribbing for 5 rows. Break off C. With B, k 1 row, work in ribbing for 7 rows. Bind off in ribbing.
Tie Loop: With A, cast on 3 sts. **Row 1:** K 1, p 1, k 1. Work in ribbing as established for 3″. Bind off.
FINISHING: Pin pieces to measurements on a padded surface; cover with a damp cloth and allow to dry; do not press. Sew side, shoulder and sleeve seams. Sew in sleeves. Turn hems to wrong side at hemlines and stitch in place. Sew collar to neck edge, adjusting to fit. Sew tie loop to center front, ½″ below neck edge. Place tie around neck, under collar and draw ends through loop. Sew ornament to center of upper section of left sleeve; sew a star to each corner of collar.

GUATEMALAN VEST

CHART NO. 1

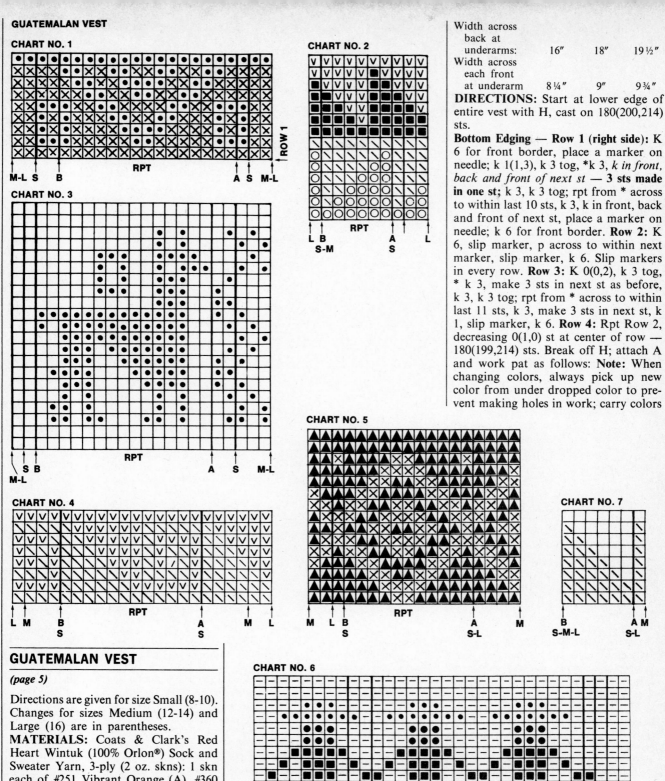

M-L S B   RPT   A S M-L

CHART NO. 3

S B   RPT   A S M-L
M-L

CHART NO. 4

L M   B   RPT   A   M L
S   S

CHART NO. 2

L B   RPT   A   L
S-M   S

CHART NO. 5

M L B   RPT   A   M
S   S-L

CHART NO. 7

B   A M
S-M-L   S-L

CHART NO. 6

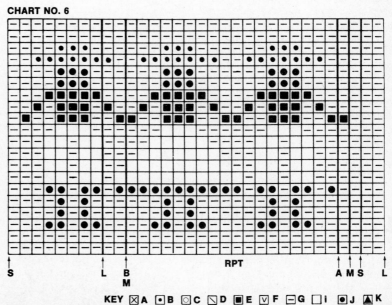

S   L B   RPT   A M S L
M

KEY ⊠A ⊡B ◉C ⊠D ▣E ⊽F ⊟G □I ◉J ▲K

| Width across back at underarms: | 16″ | 18″ | 19½″ |
| Width across each front at underarm | 8¼″ | 9″ | 9¾″ |

DIRECTIONS: Start at lower edge of entire vest with H, cast on 180(200,214) sts.

Bottom Edging — Row 1 (right side): K 6 for front border, place a marker on needle; k 1(1,3), k 3 tog, *k 3, *k in front, back and front of next st* — **3 sts made in one st;** k 3, k 3 tog; rpt from * across to within last 10 sts, k 3, k in front, back and front of next st, place a marker on needle; k 6 for front border. **Row 2:** K 6, slip marker, p across to within next marker, slip marker, k 6. Slip markers in every row. **Row 3:** K 0(0,2), k 3 tog, * k 3, make 3 sts in next st as before, k 3, k 3 tog; rpt from * across to within last 11 sts, k 3, make 3 sts in next st, k 1, slip marker, k 6. **Row 4:** Rpt Row 2, decreasing 0(1,0) st at center of row — 180(199,214) sts. Break off H; attach A and work pat as follows: **Note:** When changing colors, always pick up new color from under dropped color to prevent making holes in work; carry colors

GUATEMALAN VEST

(page 5)

Directions are given for size Small (8-10). Changes for sizes Medium (12-14) and Large (16) are in parentheses.

MATERIALS: Coats & Clark's Red Heart Wintuk (100% Orlon®) Sock and Sweater Yarn, 3-ply (2 oz. skns): 1 skn each of #251 Vibrant Orange (A), #360 Wood Brown (B), #686 Paddy Green (C), #740 Atomic Pink (D), #515 Dk. Turquoise (E), #224 Baby Yellow (F), #905 Red (G), #814 Robin Blue (H), #648 Apple Green (I), #1 White (J), #858 Navy (K); knitting needles, No.5 OR ANY SIZE NEEDLES WHICH WILL OBTAIN THE STITCH GAUGE BELOW; crochet hook, Size F.

GAUGE: 11 sts = 2″; 6 rows = 1″.

MEASUREMENTS:

Sizes:	Small (8-10)	Medium (12-14)	Large (16)
Bust:	32½″	36″	39″

not in use loosely along wrong side. Break off and attach colors as needed. Front and armhole borders are worked in garter st (k each row) throughout. Patterns are worked between borders in st st (k 1 row, p 1 row). Border sts are not shown on Charts. To follow Charts, for **each right-side row,** start at line on right side edge indicating size being made and follow Chart across to B, rpt A to B across; then work to line indicating size being made. For **each wrong-side row,** start at left side edge and repeating B to A across, follow Chart from left to right between lines indicating size being made. Always follow Charts over sts between front borders. **Rows 1 through 9:** Using A for garter st front borders, follow Chart 1 as directed over sts between borders from Row 1 to end of top row. **Rows 10 through 23:** Making borders with C for first 7 rows and with E for following 7 rows, follow Chart 2. **Row 24:** With G k 6 for border, p across to within next marker, k 6. **Row 25:** With G k 6, *with H k 2, with G k 2; rpt from * across to next marker, end with H k 2, with G k 2(1,0); with G k 6. **Row 26:** Working colors as established on last row, k 6,p across to next marker, k 6. **Row 27:** With G, k across. **Rows 28 through 48:** Using I for borders, follow Chart 3. **Rows 49 through 56:** Using D for borders, follow Chart 4.

To Divide Stitches for Armholes — Row 1: From right side, with K, k 38(42,45); place these sts just worked on a stitch holder for upper right front; bind off next 13(15,17) sts for underarm, k until there are on right-hand needle 78(85,90) sts for upper back; place rem sts on another stitch holder.

Upper Back — Row 2: With K, k 6 for armhole border, place a marker on needle, p across to within last 6 sts, place a marker on needle; k 6 for armhole border. **Rows 3 through 17:** Continuing to use K for armhole borders, follow Chart 5. **Rows 18 through 37:** Using G for borders, follow Chart 6. **Rows 38 through 45:** Using D for borders, follow Chart 7. With I only, continuing garter st borders, work 1(3,6) more rows. Bind off.

Upper Left Front — Row 1: Sl sts front 2nd holder onto a needle; attach K, with right side facing bind off 13(15,17) sts for underarm, k until there are 6 sts on right-hand needle, place a marker on needle, k across — 38(42,45) sts. **Row 2:** K 6, p to next marker, k 6. **Rows 3 through 17:** Using K for borders, work rpt only on Chart 5, 2(2,3) times across center 22(22,33) sts, working any rem sts between borders in st st with K. **Neck Shaping — Row 18:** Using G, k 6 for border, p to last 6 sts, k 6. **Row 19:** K 6 for border, follow rpt only on Row 3 of Chart 6 once over next 18 sts; with G, k to within 2 sts before next marker, *k 2 tog* — **dec made inside border at neck**

BUYER'S GUIDE

YARN
Belding Lily Co.
P.O. Box 88
Shelby, North Carolina 28150
Berga/Ullman, Inc.
P.O. Box 98
59 Demond Avenue
North Adams, Mass. 02147
Emile Bernat & Sons Co.
Depot & Mendon Sts.
Uxbridge, Mass. 01569
Brunswick
230 Fifth Avenue
New York, N.Y. 10001
Bucilla
30-20 Thomson Avenue
Long Island City, N.Y. 11101
Coats & Clark
75 Rockefeller Plaza
New York, N.Y. 10022
Columbia-Minerva Corp.
295 Fifth Avenue
New York, N.Y. 10016
D.M.C.
107 Trumbull Street
Elizabeth, New Jersey 07206
Forklorico Yarn Co.
522 Ramona Street
Palo Alto, California 94310
Lion Brand Yarn Co.
1270 Broadway
New York, N.Y. 10001
Paternayan Bros., Inc.
312 East 95th Street
New York, N.Y. 10028
Plymouth Yarn Co.
Bristol,
Pa. 19007
Reynolds Yarn Co.
15 Oser Avenue
Hauppague, L.I., N.Y. 11787
Spinnerin Yarn
230 Fifth Avenue
New York, N.Y. 10001

FABRIC AND TRIM COMPANIES
Bates/Dayton
1412 Broadway
New York, N.Y. 10018
Cohama Fabrics
1407 Broadway
New York, N.Y. 10018
Concord Fabrics
1411 Broadway
New York, N.Y. 10018
Dan River
111 West 40th Street
New York, N.Y. 10018
Franetta Fabrics, Inc.
110 West 40th Street
New York, N.Y. 10018
Icelandic Fashions Corp.
1441 Broadway
New York, N.Y. 10018
Liberty of London
108 West 39th Street
New York, N.Y. 10018
M&M Marketing, Inc. (Fab-U-Print)
951 N.E. 167th St.
North Miami Beach, Florida 33162
Pendleton Woolen Mills
489 Fifth Avenue
New York, N.Y. 10017
Sheru Beads
49 West 38th Street
New York, N.Y. 10018
Stacy Fabrics (Stitch Witchery)
469 Seventh Ave.
New York, N.Y. 10018
Stylecrest Fabrics, Ltd.
214 West 39th Street
New York, N.Y. 10018
Waldon Textiles (Rubber Slicker)
566 Seventh Avenue
New York, N.Y. 10018
Wrights
West Warren,
Mass. 01092

edge; k 6 for border. **Rows 20 through 37:** Working borders with G, continue to work rpt on Chart 6 over the 18 sts immediately next to armhole border as established, **at the same time,** dec one st at neck edge inside front border as before every other row until 17(21,24) sts rem between borders. **Rows 38 through 45:** Using D for borders, follow rpt on Chart 7, 2(3,3) times over sts next to armhole border, using D for all other sts and decreasing one st inside front border 4 more times. With I only, continuing decs at neck edge, work 1(3,6) rows. Bind off rem 24(27,29) sts for shoulder.

Upper Right Front: Sl sts from first holder onto a needle and work to correspond with Upper Left Front, reversing shaping

and position of pats.
FINISHING: To block, pin vest to measurements on a padded surface, cover with a damp cloth and allow to dry; do not press. Fold fronts over back and sew front shoulders to corresponding sts of back. With right side facing, using crochet hook and H, sc evenly along right front edge, back of neck and left front edges. Break off and fasten. **Ties:** With 1 strand each of H and D held tog, using crochet hook attach yarn to right front edge in line with beg of neck shaping; make a chain desired length. Break off and fasten. Make 3 more ties along right front edge at 3½" intervals. Make ties along left front edge to correspond with opposite edge.